Choices and Constraints
in Family Life

Maureen Baker

OXFORD
UNIVERSITY PRESS

OXFORD
UNIVERSITY PRESS

70 Wynford Drive, Don Mills, Ontario M3C 1J9
www.oup.com/ca

Oxford University Press is a department of the University of Oxford.
It furthers the University's objective of excellence in research, scholarship,
and education by publishing worldwide in

Oxford   New York

Auckland   Cape Town   Dar es Salaam   Hong Kong   Karachi
Kuala Lumpur   Madrid   Melbourne   Mexico City   Nairobi
New Delhi   Shanghai   Taipei   Toronto

With offices in

Argentina   Austria   Brazil   Chile   Czech Republic   France   Greece
Guatemala   Hungary   Italy   Japan   Poland   Portugal   Singapore
South Korea   Switzerland   Thailand   Turkey   Ukraine   Vietnam

Oxford is a trade mark of Oxford University Press
in the UK and in certain other countries

Published in Canada
by Oxford University Press

Copyright © Oxford University Press Canada 2007

The moral rights of the author have been asserted

Database right Oxford University Press (maker)

Library and Archives Canada Cataloguing in Publication Data

Baker, Maureen
Choices and constraints in family life / Maureen Baker.

Includes bibliographical references and index.
ISBN-13: 978-0-19-542105-7
ISBN-10: 0-19-542105-1

1. Family—Textbooks I. Title.

HQ519.B34 2007   306.85   C2006-906113-0

Cover Image: Fancy Photography / ©Veer
Cover Design: Sonya Thursby / Opus House

1 2 3 4 – 10 09 08 07

This book is printed on permanent (acid-free) paper ∞.

Printed in Canada

Contents

4 Child-bearing, Child-rearing, and Childhood   70

5 Family Work and Family Money   93

Preface and Acknowledgements

Many young students seem to believe that they can create their own 'personal biographies' or freely develop their own individual lifestyle and domestic relationships. Although I agree that more personal choices are now available, I argue in this book that many of the old constraints on relationships continue and some new ones have been added. Current knowledge and controversies about intimacy and families are examined, as well as the results of earlier studies from sociology, psychology, anthropology, and social history about the nature of marriage and family life.

Over the past few decades, the study of family life has changed in terms of the basic assumptions behind the field, the issues being researched, and the practical relevance of the research. In my view, new life has been breathed into the subdiscipline by paying greater attention to gender relations and domestic work as well as issues relating to cohabitation, same-sex relationships, the creation of personal identity, new reproductive technologies, fathering, and public discourse about parenting and family responsibilities. I show that while innovative family patterns have developed in recent years, some of these 'new' patterns are really variations on older themes. In addition, a number of battles fought in the 1960s and 1970s relating to gender equity and work/family balance continue unresolved into the twenty-first century.

A number of friends and colleagues have assisted with the preparation of this book. Almost 25 years ago when I was an assistant professor, Professor Lorne Tepperman from the Sociology Department at the University of Toronto encouraged me to edit my first book about families by recommending me to a publisher. A few years ago, Lorne once again recommended me for this project with Oxford University Press. I am very grateful for both suggestions. Second, I would like to thank Lisa Meschino and Roberta Osborne from Oxford University Press, who deftly managed the process of transforming my manuscript into a book. Although I live in Auckland, New Zealand, and they operate from Toronto, Canada, the process seemed to run very smoothly with electronic mail. Third, I would like to thank my partner, David Tippin, for his continuing support for my academic projects.

Maureen Baker
University of Auckland
New Zealand
July 2006

Chapter 1

Conceptualizing Families

Learning Objectives

- To understand the various ways that families have been defined, conceptualized, and studied.
- To relate the conceptualization of families to theoretical frameworks used in sociology and the social sciences, as well as to social policy objectives.
- To explore how family and marriage systems vary by culture and family experiences vary by gender.

CHAPTER OUTLINE

This chapter defines 'families' and discusses the many cultural variations in the meaning of marriage and in family experiences. The chapter also examines three major ways that academics have conceptualized family life and offers some insights into the advantages and problems of each theoretical framework, as well as various research methodologies.

INTRODUCTION

Compared to a few generations ago, family life has changed considerably, along with many aspects of the larger society. For one thing, our intimate relationships now involve more personal choices about our partners and sexual behaviour. In the twenty-first century, more of us believe that we have the right to choose our partners without interference from relatives or officials, and that we should not be forced to remain with that partner if our relationship proves unsatisfactory. In addition, more people feel that whether or not they legally marry and produce children should be their own decision rather than something they might be pressured to do by family members, religious leaders, or politicians.

In this book, I argue that relationships and marriage are certainly influenced by our personal choices, but that these are shaped by our family circumstances and events in the wider society, such as changes in educational opportunities, employment trends, social policies, technological innovations, media representations, and new ideas about human rights or personal entitlements. Consequently, patterns are noticeable in family life, including rising rates of cohabitation among both heterosexual and same-sex couples, fewer births of which more occur outside marriage, and higher rates of separation, re-partnering, and stepfamilies. In fact, similar trends are apparent in most Western industrialized countries (Lewis, 2003; OECD, 2005b).

Although more of us insist on making our own choices about living partners and reproduction, many people also expect government or public agencies to safeguard their human rights, to protect them from violent relationships, to help them manage problem children, or to supplement their inadequate household incomes. New public expectations have heightened controversies about who is responsible for protecting and supporting vulnerable family members and those in need. Public debates have also questioned the validity of new forms of marriage, sought solutions to declining fertility and the enforcement of financial child support after separation, and examined new ways of interacting with immigrants whose family practices diverge from the majority.

Reductions in income tax rates and social spending in countries such as Canada and the United States have also led to controversies about the role that the state should play in regulating, promoting, or assisting family life. 'Child poverty' is growing in many countries despite political promises to reduce or abolish it, and this poverty is aggravated by higher rates of marriage breakdown and labour market deregulation (UNICEF, 2005). Especially in the 'liberal' welfare states (or Canada and the English-speaking countries), policy-makers continue to search for ways to reduce this poverty. However, they are also concerned about maximizing personal responsibility for family well-being and reducing income taxes and social spending—and one set of goals seems to counteract the other. Nevertheless, controversies over relationships and family obligations permeate public policy debates as well as our personal conversations.

This book aims to understand how relationships and family practices have changed over the past decades in Western industrialized countries, and to differentiate between *actual* changes and the misconceptions voiced in political speeches or perpetuated in the media. Discussions of social research will reveal that our personal choices about intimate partners, having children, dissolving relationships, and maintaining contact with parents and siblings are influenced by our family and cultural upbringing, our socio-economic circumstances, the social policy environment, and political and economic events in the larger society. This means that the nature of family and personal life is always changing, although some aspects remain remarkably stable.

The studies and examples used to illustrate the arguments in this book are derived from several different countries but focus particularly on Canada and the English-speaking countries. These countries have been labelled **liberal welfare states** (Esping-Andersen, 1990) because they tend to expect individuals to rely on employment earnings and the assistance of their household members and voluntary organizations for well-being. Relatively ungenerous state assistance is typically made available only when people cannot cope. However, by examining relationships and families in various countries, eras, income levels, and cultural circumstances, we are better able to understand the diverse factors that influence personal choices about love, sex, and marriage.

DEFINING FAMILIES

The word 'family' is used in various ways in popular usage, referring in different contexts to our parents and siblings, our spouse and children, all the relatives sharing a household, and the larger group of relatives with whom we maintain some contact. Social scientists usually feel the need to clarify the meaning by adding qualifiers such as **nuclear family** (husband, wife, and children sharing a household with no other adults present) or **extended family** (husband, wife, and children sharing a household with other relatives such as grandparents, aunts, or uncles). Most academic and policy definitions focus on the structure of family households—whether it is nuclear or extended, and whether it contains one or two parents. They also emphasize the legality of the relationships—whether partners are married or cohabiting—rather than considering feelings of love or obligation.

Early social scientists called the family a **social institution**, emphasizing the rules and expectations that guided family interaction. They stated that the family consisted of at least two adults of the opposite sex, united by marriage, living together, pooling their resources, sharing intimacy, and producing and raising children (Murdock, 1949; Goode, 1964). Over the years, this definition has been challenged as ideological, outmoded, and overemphasizing the heterosexual nuclear family. Increasingly, academics and ordinary citizens argue that the structure of families or the legality of their relationships is less meaningful and affects lifestyle less than the services that household members provide or how they feel about each other. Consequently, both researchers and advocacy groups suggest that definitions should be broadened to encompass caring and enduring intimate relationships regardless of their legal or blood ties (Eichler, 1997; Jamieson, 1998; Smart and Neale, 1999).

Governments, however, are particularly concerned about who shares a dwelling, whether or not couples are legally married or share a 'marriage-like relationship', and the legal relationship between adults and any children living in the household. This information tells state officials who should be held accountable for financial support, care, and protection. They are particularly interested in whether households contain two adults or only one, how much income is available to support the children, and whether families require state income assistance. The state develops specific definitions of family for planning and policy purposes and is unwilling to allow people to create their own definitions, especially when making decisions about entitlement for social benefits or immigration status. However, advocacy groups persistently pressure the state to expand or clarify its definition of family. Many governments have recently responded by including same-sex couples and by acknowledging stepfamilies and the extended family arrangements of immigrants or indigenous peoples.

The fact that families are ancient institutions with many structural variations provides opportunities for sociologists, anthropologists, and historians to note patterns and trends over time and to identify factors promoting change, or at least associated with change. For example, social researchers try to understand how couple relationships and reproductive choices vary with social and economic transformations such as industrialization, urbanization, the expansion of the service sector of the economy, widespread migration, the global economy, the computer revolution, and a growing consumer-oriented society. Researchers and theorists study how these societal trends influence personal attitudes and behaviour, as well as public discourse, or the way people talk about sexuality, marriage, reproduction, parental responsibility, and divorce.

Despite evidence of diversity, 'the family' is still being discussed in some circles as though it were a single institution that means the same to all people. However, there is considerable evidence that family life has always varied—parents remarried, children lived with step-parents, and family members in the past often shared dissimilar views about the nature of their home life and personal relationships. Canadian sociologist Margrit Eichler (1988, 2005) argued that before the 1980s, both the academic and policy portrayal of North American families resembled the nuclear family (with a male breadwinner and female caregiver) rather than any other family configuration. Assumptions about family life were conservative and often based on the views of one family member, without acknowledging gender differences or variations in viewpoint between children and parents. Academics and policy-makers also normalized the experiences of young, white, middle-class families in which two heterosexual parents and their biological children shared a household without other relatives, and the parents maintained a gendered division of labour (Eichler, 1988, 2005).

Opponents of same-sex marriage still promote this nuclear family model even though most people no longer live in these kinds of households in OECD countries (Lewis, 2003). A growing percentage of the population lives alone, some people never marry or reproduce, many couples separate, parents re-partner, children live with step-siblings, and children grow up and leave their older parent(s) in childless households. Although social research now emphasizes the multi-dimensional nature of family life, this diversity is not always incorporated into public discourse or social policy debates. Table 1.1 shows that married couples living with children form only 41.4 per cent of Canadian families but does not indicate the rising percentage of couples living with stepchildren.

When using official statistics and especially when making cross-national comparisons, it is necessary to understand the definition used by the government or

Table 1.1   Percentage Distribution of Family Types in Canada, 1981 and 2001

Family Type	% of All Families in 1981	% of All Families in 2001
Legally married couples with children in the household	55.0	41.4
Legally married couples without children in the household	28.2	29.0
Lone-parent families	11.3	15.7
Common-law couples without children in the household	3.7	7.5
Common-law couples with children in the household	1.9	6.3

Source: Vanier Institute of the Family (2004: 40), adapted from 'Family and Household Living Arrangements, 2001 Census', Statistics Canada, *2001 Census of Population*, Catalogue no. 97F0005XCB01001, available at http://www12.statcan.ca/english/census01/products/highlight/PrivateHouseholds/index.cfm?Lang=E.

organization generating or collating the statistics. In most government analyses, a 'family with children' refers to a heterosexual couple or lone parent sharing a dwelling with never-married children. These children could be their biological offspring or the children of their partner or adopted children. A lone-parent or sole-parent family usually refers to one parent who shares a dwelling with her (occasionally, his) never-married children, without another adult present in the household. Although governments call these units 'lone-parent families', in fact they are often 'lone-parent households', because the father usually maintains some contact with his children even when he lives apart. Consequently, some researchers use the concept of the 'post-divorce family' to encompass both the non-resident father and the mother-led household containing their children. More descriptive terms, such as same-sex families, blended families, or stepfamilies, can help to clarify vague definitions.

The most prevalent definition used in policy research is the **census family**. There are cross-national variations of this term but Statistics Canada, for example, has recently redefined this unit as:

> a married couple and the children, if any, of either or both spouses; a couple living common law and the children, if any, of either or both partners; or, a lone parent of any marital status with at least one child living in the same dwelling and that child or those children. All members of a particular census family live in the same dwelling. A couple may be of opposite or same sex. Children may be children by birth, marriage or adoption regardless of their age or marital status as long as they live in the dwelling and do not have their own spouse or child living in the dwelling. Grandchildren living with their grandparent(s) but with no parents present also constitute a census family. (Statistics Canada website, 2006)

Until 2006, Statistics Canada defined the census family as a married couple with or without never-married children, or a single parent living together with never-married children. Cohabiting couples living together for longer than one year were considered to be married although separate statistics are kept for legally married and cohabiting couples. Historically, only heterosexual couples could legally marry in all parts of Canada. Since 2003, British Columbia, Ontario, and Quebec have passed legislation to permit gay and lesbian couples to legalize their relationships, following the example of several European countries such as the Netherlands and Belgium (Moore, 2003; Luxton, 2005). Federal legislation was changed in 2005 that required the Canadian government to alter the definition of family for census purposes.

Despite the focus on nuclear families, some cultural groups prefer to live in extended family households consisting of their parents and/or siblings, as well as their spouse and children. These groups argue that the 'census family' is only one family structure (essentially the nuclear family or a one-parent household) and that to assume this is the normal arrangement misrepresents sources of caring and social support in their lives. This definition also creates problems when they want to sponsor their family members as immigrants, especially their unmarried adult daughters or married siblings. Using a nuclear family definition could also create a problem if a large group of extended family wanted to visit a sick household member in hospital but were denied access because they were not 'close family'. Assuming that the normal family is nuclear also implies that the family relationships of same-sex couples are different and less valid, and deprives them of certain social benefits such as the right to be considered 'next of kin' in medical emergencies. Issues of entitlement are always contentious, but a clear definition of 'family' is essential in establishing eligibility for social benefits or for designing the government census or a research project.

Here, as in my previous publications, I continue to use the plural term 'families' to reinforce the idea that variations have always been apparent and that families were never as uniform as some people have implied. Generally, my definition of families includes lone parents and their dependent children, both legally married and long-term cohabiting couples living together with or without children, and stepfamilies. Gay/lesbian couples sharing a residence are also included, as well as couples and their children sharing a household with their adult siblings or parents (or 'extended' families). However, I acknowledge that definitions need to be more specific for some purposes, especially those relating to social policy and eligibility for social benefits, and I often use adjectives with 'family' to specify meaning (such as 'census family').

Box 1.1 What Is a Family?

The Vanier Institute of the Family takes a broad view of families. It defines a family as:

> any combination of two or more persons who are bound together by ties of mutual consent, birth, and/or adoption or placement and who, together, assume responsibilities for variant combinations of some of the following:
>
> • Physical maintenance and care of group members
> • Addition of new members through procreation or adoption
> • Socialization of children
> • Production, consumption, distribution of goods and services, and
> • Affective nurturance—love.

This definition directs attention towards the work and accomplishments of people who commit themselves to one another over time—to what people do as distinct from where they live and how they are related to each other. It is a definition that acknowledges and respects heterosexual and same-sex couples, lone-parent families, extended patterns of kinship, stepfamilies and blended families, couples with children and those without, the commitments of siblings to one another, and the obligations and affection that unite the young and the old as their lives weave together. People in families provide for and care for one another, they teach and discipline, they are financially, economically, and psychologically dependent on one another, and they love one another. Within families, we encounter the opportunity and responsibility to act not just as isolated individuals, but as spouses and lovers, mothers and fathers, brothers and sisters, sons and daughters and friends.

Source: Vanier Institute of the Family (2004: xii). Reprinted by permission of the publisher.

In this book, I also discuss various 'family policies' or official decisions to implement state-sponsored social programs, services, regulations, and laws that specifically affect families with children. These policies might relate to reproductive health, family well-being, or the maintenance of family income. They could also enforce financial or caring obligations among family members, protect vulnerable family members from harm or neglect, or enable the integration of employment and caring work. Family programs do not have to be delivered directly by the state but they must be mandated or regulated by the state to be included in my definition. Therefore, programs contracted out to voluntary agencies or subsidized by public money could be included, such as child welfare services contracted to the Children's Aid Society or to a First Nations or indigenous tribal group. Employer-sponsored programs for maternity leave or for family responsibilities also are included in the definition of **family policy** because governments often require employers to provide these benefits or their provision is required by international agreements among countries (Baker, 2006).

For over a hundred years, academic researchers have studied family life in different cultures, investigating the connections among family structure, patterns of authority, marriage systems, descent and residence rules, and how cross-cultural variations relate to systems of economic production, religious beliefs, and other cultural patterns. Academics have also questioned whether or not the nuclear family is a universal institution, whether men are always family 'heads', and what difference it makes when the marriage system permits more than one spouse at a time. One of the central debates has been whether or not the nuclear family is a product of industrialization, urbanization, and westernization. If so, will families begin to look more similar around the world if westernization and global culture expand? In the next section, some of these issues will be outlined as I discuss cultural variations in family patterns.

CULTURAL VARIATIONS IN FAMILIES

Family Structure: Nuclear and Extended Families

When people in Western industrialized countries live in family households, they usually form nuclear families consisting of husband, wife, and their children sharing a dwelling without other relatives present. Some academics assume that, in the past, most households in both Western and non-Western societies consisted of extended families in which several generations shared a residence. They believe that more people came to live in nuclear families with the pressures of **industrialization** and urban migration between the seventeenth and the nineteenth centuries.

In France, Frédéric Le Play (1806–82) studied changes in the rural European 'stem family', an extended family consisting of parents and one married son who would eventually inherit the family property. He lamented the rise of the 'unstable' nuclear family and the demise of patriarchal authority caused by industrialization and modernization. Friedrich Engels (1972 [1884]) also saw the nuclear family as the product of industrialization, theorizing about the ways that society and family structure were transformed from the times when people lived in large hunting-and-gathering clans or kin groups through to private nuclear families in the industrial cities of England. American sociologists Parsons and Bales (1955) were also concerned about the loss of the extended family, which they felt provided more effective authority, household labour, child care, companionship, and economic security than the nuclear family.

Social historians have demonstrated, however, that nuclear family households were always the most typical living arrangements both in Europe and among the European settlers to the colonies (Laslett, 1971; Goldthorpe, 1987). One reason that living arrangement persisted is that life expectancies were much shorter than today and many parents died before their children married. In the colonies, extended family households were even less common among Europeans because many of these settlers had left their parents and older relatives behind when they migrated. Canadian sociologist Emily Nett (1981) contended that it had never been a widespread practice for married couples to live with their parents at any time in the Canadian history of European settlement. However, indigenous tribes, such as the Huron and Iroquois, often lived in extended family households (Baker, 2001b). In addition, lower-income families with British backgrounds were more likely than richer settlers to share accommodation with parents and children, especially in times of financial need, separation, or widowhood.

Despite the prevalence of nuclear families in North America, extended families continue to serve as living arrangements and support groups in parts of Africa, South Asia, and the Middle East. Extended families continue to be more prevalent among many of the indigenous peoples of the Americas, Australia, and New Zealand (ibid.). They have become slightly more prevalent in high-immigration countries such as Canada and the United States as they accept more immigrants from countries with extended-family systems. In Canada, the percentage of three-generation households increased by 39 per cent from 1986 to 1996, mainly as a result of increased Asian immigration. However, only 3 per cent of households in Canada included three generations in 1996 (Che-Alford and Hamm, 1999). Statistics Canada data also showed that 13 per cent of Canadian-born people lived with relatives in 1996 compared to 26 per cent of a sample of immigrants who came to Canada in 1985 (Thomas, 2001: 18).

Practical constraints as well as cultural traditions influence family structure and living arrangements. Immigrants with few economic resources and limited skills in the host country's official language are more likely to share accommodation than wealthier immigrants who can afford separate housing, those who can communicate more effectively, and those able to find employment (ibid.). Furthermore, living with relatives is not necessarily permanent but could involve sharing accommodation with adult siblings until separate housing can be located or financed. Living with relatives is more prevalent among female immigrants, those with lower education and incomes, and recent arrivals (ibid., 21).

This suggests that gender, social class, and culture (as well as personal choice) influence whether immigrants continue to live in extended families. Immigrants often attempt to integrate into the culture of the new country by giving up some aspects of their cultural practices, which means that the family demography of the second generation tends to look more like that of others born in that country

(Albanese, 2005). In other countries, especially in rural areas or those with few Western influences, cultural traditions strongly influence marriage and family patterns, and the decisions of elders might override the personal choices of youth.

Authority and Lineage

Most family systems around the world designate a 'head' to make family decisions and represent the group to the larger community and to state authorities. In both Western and non-Western societies, the oldest male typically is the family head, and this system, called **patriarchy**, has a long tradition that permeates laws and practices around the world. In the liberal welfare states, families were legally patriarchal in the past, but these countries have reformed their laws and practices and no longer assume that men officially lead the family (Kamerman and Kahn, 1997). In fact, most Western states have been pressured to eliminate most remnants of patriarchy and to create legal equality between men and women, both within the household and in the larger society. However, vestiges of patriarchy are still apparent, such as the practice of fathers 'giving away' their daughters to the groom during some traditional marriage ceremonies.

Matriarchy is an authority system in which women are granted more authority than men, but such systems are rare throughout the world. At the time of European contact, the Iroquois tribes of North America were described as matriarchal because women's power in the economy, politics, religious ceremonies, and family life exceeded that of women in French and English cultures, as well as women in other Native tribes (Brown, 1988). In the 1930s, the American anthropologist Margaret Mead referred to the Tchambuli people of New Guinea as matriarchal because women seemed to run the economy and make most practical decisions while men were engaged in cultural pursuits (Mead, 1935). Working-class black families in the Caribbean and the United States have been called matriarchal, or at least **matrifocal**, because so many of these households are led by lone mothers while the fathers live elsewhere, or the mother/wife is the pivotal figure in many of these two-parent families (Queen et al., 1985; Smith, 1996). For a family to be considered matriarchal, women must hold considerable control over resources or family money, as well as decision-making.

Some sociologists and anthropologists have argued that laws, unwritten rules, and social expectations guide behaviour within and between families in all societies. Family law designates certain categories of people as 'out of bounds' for sex and marriage but less formalized rules or cultural traditions also govern family behaviour. For example, patterns of descent may determine where newly married couples live, how they address family members, what surname their children will receive, and from whom they inherit. When people marry, they may also be encouraged to grant more importance to their relationships with one set of parents or siblings, as we will see in the next section.

Marriage Systems

Marriages are arranged in many cultures, as we will discuss in more detail in Chapter 3. In these arrangements, close intimate relationships between the couple are not priorities because marriage represents a union between extended families rather than between individuals. Young people are encouraged to want to marry in order to acquire adult status, to augment their position in the community through parenthood, to gain satisfaction from watching their children mature, to continue the family name, and eventually to become respected elders within their family and community. In cultures where the inheritance of wealth and the continuity of kin lines and family name are important, arranged marriages or partially arranged marriages remain widespread. Young people sometimes appreciate family assistance with the difficult task of finding a compatible life partner who meets their relatives' expectations. They may justify parental assistance by the high divorce rate among Western or free-choice marriages, which suggests that young people who make their own decisions often make ill-informed ones that they later regret. Furthermore, many immigrants and indigenous people guard their family practices as part of their cultural identity that they are unwilling to shed.

It is still legal in many parts of the world for a man to marry more than one wife at a time if he has the resources to support them. In 1949, the American anthropologist George Murdock studied 554 different societies around the world and concluded that only about 20 per cent were strictly monogamous. About three-quarters permitted **polygyny**, or marrying more than one wife at a time, even though not all men would choose to take on a second or third wife. Instead, these societies were characterized by a mixture of polygyny and monogamy (Murdock, 1949).

In the 1990s, three-quarters of the world's societies still preferred polygyny (Saxton, 1993) although the percentage actually living in these unions was lower. Polygyny continues to be practised in some African countries as well as some in Southern and Western Asia, especially those using Islamic law. In sub-Saharan Africa throughout the 1990s, about half of married women aged 15–49 were in polygynous unions in Benin, Burkino Faso, and Guinea, and over 40 per cent in Mali, Senegal, and Togo (UN, 2000: 28). Wealthy men are more likely than those with fewer resources to take on more than one legal wife (Broude, 1994).

Polygynous unions tend to be associated with patriarchal authority and wider age gaps between husbands and wives. They are more common among rural and less-educated women, as well as those who do not formally work for pay outside the household (UN, 2000: 28). Multiple wives, who are sometimes sisters, may resent their husband taking a new partner, but they may also welcome her assistance with household work, child care, and horticulture, and may value her companionship in a society where marriage partners are seldom close friends. Furthermore, the husband's second marriage typically elevates the rank of the first wife, who then becomes the supervisor of the younger wife's household work.

Polygamy refers to the practice of having more than one spouse at a time, but polygyny is much more prevalent than **polyandry**, which is marriage between one woman and several husbands. When polyandry does occur, the husbands are often brothers (fraternal polyandry) and the practice may relate to the need to keep land in one parcel (Ihinger-Tallman and Levinson, 2003). However, most societies prefer polygyny because more children can be born into marriages with multiple wives and this could be important if children are the main source of labour for the family or community. Also, the identification of the father is particularly important in **patri-lineal** societies because children receive their father's surname, belong to his kin group, and inherit from him, and married men are responsible for supporting their children. Knowing who the father is would be difficult with multiple husbands, so this is not usually an acceptable form of marriage in patrilineal systems. Most societies have been patriarchal and men more often have the power to ensure that the marriage system suits their own interests.

All westernized countries have prohibited polygamy. Judeo-Christian beliefs promote sexual exclusivity. Some explain these doctrines on the assumption that men would experience difficulty providing adequate financial and emotional support for more than one wife. However, some groups have practised polygamy in nineteenth- and twentieth-century North America, including some Mormons in Utah and British Columbia, but the general population strongly objected and insisted that the authorities put a stop to this practice. In New Zealand, some Maori tribes practised polygyny at the time of European contact, but the Christian missionaries and British settlers opposed the practice as 'uncivilized' and ensured that it did not continue (Baker, 2001b).

Although polygamy is now against the law in all the liberal welfare states, it may continue to exist clandestinely in some communities where a man has one legal wife but also cohabits with other women. Neighbours or state officials might not interfere because they assume that these other women are close relatives or boarders rather than sexual partners or wives. In addition, some men who travel for a living have maintained female partners who are unknown to each other. However, this is neither legal nor socially acceptable in Christian countries.

Some new immigrants come from countries accepting polygamous marriage. This could lead to problems for immigration departments of receiving countries unless they develop clear policies about how polygamous marriage should be treated in terms of legal recognition, support obligations, and inheritance rights. The receiving country can refuse to permit new polygamous arrangements. If it accepts immigrants in these circumstances and refuses to recognize their previous legal obligations, official wives and legitimate children could be left destitute when their husbands emigrate (Beeby, 2006).

Group marriage continues to exist but in Western industrialized countries it is illegal and socially unacceptable. Historically, it was practised in utopian communities, such as the Oneida Community in nineteenth-century New York state or more recent communal experiments in the 1960s. In these marriages, more than one couple consider themselves married to one another, and share resources, meals, child-rearing, and sexual access. However, these arrangements tend to last only a few years, partly due to opposition from the authorities, but also as an outcome of interpersonal conflicts (Ihinger-Tallman and Levinson, 2003).

People in westernized countries are permitted to marry only one partner at a time, although an increasing percentage of the population divorces and remarries, or cohabits without any social or legal ceremony. However, even when couples initially live together without a wedding, many legally marry when they make a long-term commitment to each other or when they decide to have children. Among these, many participate in formal wedding ceremonies and celebrations with the traditional cultural symbols of virginity, fertility, and patriarchy.

At the time of marriage, most family systems require the exchange of gifts. Time-consuming negotiations as well as traditional practices may guide families when they select these gifts, which may be distributed or consumed in formal ceremonies. Some cultures require families to provide dowries as part of the marriage settlement, which I discuss in more detail in Chapter 3, but these practices are most often retained in rural areas where wives lack formal education or do not work for pay. When women acquire Western education and become self-supporting, they or their families are less likely to participate in arranged marriages, dowry negotiations, or polygamous marriages.

Multiculturalism and Cultural Clashes

With high immigration rates in countries such as Canada and the United States, more people become aware of variations in family patterns although they may not accept them as normal, acceptable, or fair. A number of contentious practices relate to the status of girls and women. Female circumcision, for example, is practised in some cultures to discourage non-marital sexual activity among women. However, the United Nations, many Western governments, and women's groups have viewed this practice as unacceptable, a violation of human rights, and a risk to women's health and well-being.

Prenatal screening is routinely done for pregnant women in most countries but in some cultural communities it has included the selective abortion of female fetuses. Males are still preferred in some cultures because they are granted higher status, continue the family lineage, financially support the extended family, and bring wealth in the form of wedding gifts or marriage settlements. Selective abortions are prohibited in Western countries but they continue to occur because abortions can sometimes be performed in private clinics or with less official scrutiny. The United Nations and state authorities have also attempted to reduce the preference for male babies by eliminating all forms of discrimination against girls and women, including making the dowry system illegal in some countries.

Another controversial issue has been the veiling of Muslim women, a religious practice that requires women to cover their hair with a scarf when in the presence of unrelated males. Women's arms and legs are also covered with long sleeves and long dresses or trousers, and sometimes their entire bodies, including their faces, are enrobed beneath a 'burqa'. France recently outlawed the wearing of religious symbols in state schools, angering the Muslim community by requiring their schoolgirls to remove their headscarves during lessons.

In 2004, two Muslim refugee women living in New Zealand were asked to serve as Crown witnesses in an insurance fraud trial (Devereux, 2004). The women wanted to remain veiled during their court appearance, but the lawyer for the accused man successfully argued against their request. He stated that the court and his client are entitled to see the faces of witnesses in order to help verify their verbal statements by observing their demeanour or body language. The women refused to remove their burqas in court and one claimed that she would rather kill herself than show her face in public. Religious leaders were consulted, who stated that the burqa was not required by the Koran but was simply a religious custom exemplifying female modesty in the company of unrelated males. The New Zealand authorities subsequently asked these women to remove their veils but permitted them to give evidence behind a screen so that the male public could not observe them during the trial.

These examples, as well as the discussion about structural variations in family systems, shed some light on the cultural relativity of personal beliefs and family practices. They also suggest a close association between family practices and religion, educational attainment, urban/rural residence, patterns of authority, and factors relating to work and economic production in the larger society. The above section has also underlined the importance of different and sometimes contradictory explanations for the existence and maintenance of family patterns, which I address below.

CONCEPTUALIZING FAMILY PATTERNS

A social scientific approach to family studies is based on the assumption that intimate relationships and family practices do not occur in random ways and do not result merely from personal choices. Instead, attitudes, desires, and behaviours are influenced by family experiences, gender, culture, religion, and socio-economic circumstances in ways that create noticeable patterns. Three different conceptual approaches are used here to analyze and explain family patterns in the social sciences. The first approach argues that social structure, including rules and cultural expectations, influences and constrains family life, and that socio-economic and cultural changes continue to alter our relationships. The second argues that psychosexual development and interpersonal interaction shape personal identity and future family relationships. The third approach emphasizes the importance of prevailing ideas and images in creating desires and moulding attitudes and behaviour.

Structural Explanations of Family Change

Researchers and theorists have argued since the nineteenth century that transformations in the larger society alter family life. We already mentioned the research studies of the rural European family by Frédéric Le Play, who was considered to be the pioneer of empirical sociology. Le Play argued that socio-economic changes such as urbanization and industrialization led to the rise of the nuclear family (which he called the 'unstable family') and to the demise of patriarchal authority and family hierarchy. Despite the conservative biases in his analysis, Le Play helped legitimize the study of family structure and social history (Gilding, 1997: 46).

Friedrich Engels (1884) also studied the impact of transformations such as urbanization and industrialization in the economy on family structure and authority patterns in England. He noted that changes in the political and economic basis of society from feudalism to capitalism altered family life by moving production outside households and into factories. These changes in production promoted a patriarchal family structure in which men became the intermediaries between their families and the larger community, because they were household wage earners, while their wives were expected to care for the children and home. As wives played a reduced role in economic production, Engels noted that their status and authority declined because society increasingly measured personal worth by earning capacity. Family research using this 'political economy' perspective has continued until the present, emphasizing the ways that labour market restructuring and the development of the global economy alter family income and living arrangements.

Political economists also argue that people's access to wealth, production, and power influences their desires, values, and behaviour. In this approach, interpersonal relations, community stability, and social cohesion are de-emphasized. The focus, instead, remains on the impact of historical trends in paid and unpaid work on family structure, different life chances based on social class, and political influences on personal life. Historically, political economists often attributed greater importance to **social class** than to gender, sexual orientation, age, ethnicity, or race. In recent years, however, more political economists have acknowledged the importance of gender and race to the kinds of work people are forced to accept and to their earning capacity.

Another structural approach, **structural functionalism**, argues that 'the family' is the basic 'social institution' of society, containing rules, expected forms of behaviour, and hierarchical relationships. The family influences social stability because it ideally offers emotional support, companionship, sexual expression, reproduction, and the socialization of children. This institution also provides important functions for the larger society by maintaining social order and control through the disciplining of children and other family members. Especially the extended family offers protection from outsiders, while individuals often relate to the outside world through their family head. Families usually co-operate financially and help each other through hard times by sharing resources. Finally, people acquire money and property through inheritance from family members, which suggests that social status and wealth are largely established and perpetuated through families.

European anthropologists, such as Bronislaw Malinowski (1884–1942) and Alfred Radcliffe-Brown (1881–1955), used a structural functional approach to compare culture and family life in various parts of the world, including the South Pacific and Australia. They studied how family systems were integrated into the entire culture. Later the American, Margaret Mead (1901–78), became one of the first female anthropologists to carry out field research among South Pacific cultures and focused primarily on how cultural expectations and practices influenced girls as they matured into women. The ideas of these researchers were very influential and widely debated among academics and educated citizens at the time.

Throughout the 1950s and 1960s, the American sociologist Talcott Parsons (1902–79) and his collaborator Robert Bales researched and theorized about family life from a structural functionalist perspective. Focusing on the American family, they concluded that industrialization and urbanization produces a smaller and relatively isolated nuclear family that specializes in the socialization of children and in meeting the personal needs of family members (Thorne, 1982: 7). They assumed that the family as an institution has two basic structures: a hierarchy of generations in which children are expected to obey their parents, and a differentiation of adults into instrumental and expressive **roles**. Parsons and Bales made the debatable argument that the wife necessarily takes the expressive role or maintains social relations and cares for others, while the husband assumes the instrumental role or earns the money for the family and deals with the outside world (ibid.).

Present-day structural functionalists now acknowledge that gender roles have changed within many families and in the larger society. However, some continue to imply that a certain type of family structure (male breadwinner/female homemaker) was maintained throughout history because it was 'functional for society' when it may have been functional mainly for heterosexual men (ibid.). Functionalists still talk about 'the family' as though there is one acceptable family form rather than many variations. They also believe that behaviour is largely determined by social expectations, rules, and family upbringing and therefore not easily altered through personal choice. Change is sometimes considered to be disruptive rather than normal or progressive, and individual opposition to social pressure has been viewed as 'deviance'. Consequently, the structural functionalists do not deal with social change and conflict as well as the political economists, and neither focuses on the dynamic nature of interpersonal relations or sees the individual as the agent of social change.

A variation of structural functionalism is **systems theory**. In this perspective, the family is viewed as a social system because its members are interdependent and any change in the behaviour of one member affects the behaviour of others. Furthermore, the family is seen as a task-performing unit that is expected to meet the requirements of both the larger society and its own internal needs (Hill, 1971: 12). The family is also a relatively closed boundary-maintaining unit that closes ranks against outside interference and criticism, as well as being an adaptive organization that incorporates new forms of behaviour and attitudes from the outside world.

Family systems theory has enjoyed influence in several disciplines such as psychiatry and family therapy because it focuses attention on interrelationships within families. This has enabled therapists and counsellors to assist clients to co-operate in order to enhance couple communication and to work towards positive change (Cheal, 1991: 66–7). Critics of family systems theory point out that emphasizing social interaction leaves no way of explaining why some clients exhibit certain kinds of problems more than others (ibid., 82). Furthermore, the analysis is generally ahistorical, limited to one culture, and often focuses on one family. Viewing the family as an open system takes into consideration the external influences on family interaction but the systems approach does not focus on the social, economic, or political context within which families live.

Structural approaches may emphasize change and conflict (as does the political economy approach) or focus on consensus and cohesion (structural functionalism). However, both versions suggest that personal choices about relationships and family practices are limited by societal constraints such as access to money and power, the enforcement of regulations and rules, and social expectations about behaviour. Structuralists emphasize that we are all born into families that are part of a larger culture with existing social traditions, legal and educational systems, and expected patterns of behaviour. We cannot choose our parents or family circumstances. Some children are privileged from the beginning while others must struggle to grow up and fend for themselves under difficult circumstances. Although structuralists acknowledge that life involves personal choices, they argue that 'life chances' as well as attitudes and patterns of behaviour are shaped by forces beyond the individual.

Personal Development and Social Interaction Shape Family Life

In contrast to the structural approaches, other social scientists have focused on early family experiences that influence our personal identity, our attachments to parents and siblings, and intimate relationships throughout life. For example, Sigmund Freud (1856–1939) believed that the first few years of a child's life are critical for the development of sexual identity, personality, and the ability to form lasting relationships. He argued that children are influenced by reactions to their physiology and to early interaction with parents, including the ways they are held, fed, toilet trained, talked to, listened to, and disciplined. The Western process of socialization involves teaching children to control their selfish urges, but much of their personality development is influenced also by unconscious motives and repressed emotions. Freud also observed that children learn partly by identifying with their same-sex parent (Baker, 2001b).

Freud's research has been criticized because it was based almost exclusively on a sample of upper-class female patients in nineteenth-century Vienna, and because he refused to believe the accounts of sexual abuse these women reported to him and instead concocted theories that 'explained' their 'fantasies' by portraying women as 'defective men' who subconsciously envy men's power, symbolized by their penises. Freud also assumed that socialization takes place only in early childhood. Later, social scientists concluded that socialization continues throughout life. Freud made a major impact on Western thought and despite his blunders is credited with useful insights into personality development that stimulated further research and theorizing.

Although psychoanalysis was initially rejected by early feminists such as Kate Millet (1970), it was modified and developed by Juliet Mitchell (1974) and Nancy Chodorow (1978, 1989), who used Freudian theory to analyze patriarchal society (Humm, 1995: 102). More recent theorizing about gender and sexuality has also relied heavily on psychoanalysis (Butler, 1997).

Another developmental approach was initiated in the 1920s and 1930s by the Swiss psychologist Jean Piaget, who studied systematic patterns of change occurring in children's thought processes as they mature. Like psychoanalytic theorists, Piaget suggested that all children pass through similar stages of cognitive development, but he concluded that they could not learn particular tasks or concepts until they had reached a certain level in their development. He further theorized that children's experiences and interpretations of the physical and social world modify the timing of these stages, as children actively participate in their own socialization (Baker, 2001b). In the 1960s, Erik Erikson (1963, 1968) argued that children pass through stages of development or preoccupation in which they must resolve certain crucial life issues in order to reach maturity. These include developing a capacity for trust, autonomy from parents, initiative, industry, identity, and intimacy.

Psychoanalytic theory and **developmental theory** remain influential but learning theory became a popular way of explaining child development from the 1920s to the 1980s, especially in the United States. Learning theory emphasized the importance of 'nurture' in debate as to whether inherited characteristics ('nature') or social learning ('nurture') plays a more important role in personality and social development. According to learning theory, parents and care providers retain almost infinite potential to shape infants' attitudes and behaviour and to socialize children through rewards or punishments. Children also learn from observing and imitating adults, especially their parents and siblings. These above approaches, which tend to be psychological rather than sociological, downplay the political and socio-economic context of family life. They also suggest that adult behaviour is difficult to understand and modify without some knowledge of the early interaction experiences with parents, siblings, and other family members.

Social interaction is also the focus of the social construction or **symbolic interaction perspective**. This approach assumes that social life is determined neither by social structure nor early psychological experiences but is constructed by individual 'actors' who create their own reality through their interactions with others in families, schools, and workplaces (Berger and Luckmann, 1967). This theoretical perspective originated with the work of Americans Charles H. Cooley (1864–1929) and George Herbert Mead (1863–1931), who separately studied childhood socialization, how children develop an identity, and the importance of family interaction in this process. They noted that, early in life, parents communicate with their children through words but also through gestures, facial expressions, and tones of voice. Symbolic communication alters behaviour as individuals interpret these messages about themselves and their world. Within this perspective, the ways that children and young people interpret non-verbal communication from 'significant others' are more important than parental rules or social expectations for the development of personal identity and future relationships.

How people treat us and react to us can be influenced by the image we project, including our demeanour, dress, posture, and speech, which sociologist Erving Goffman (1959) called the 'presentation of self'. **Social constructionism** argues that the interpretation of reactions to us is critical in shaping our personalities, as a strong association exists between the development of self and what we believe others think of us (Cooley, 1902; Mead, 1934). In addition, part of growing up and becoming a social being requires developing the ability to look at the world through the eyes of others and to anticipate a particular role before taking it (anticipatory socialization). According to this theory, socialization takes place throughout the life cycle rather than only in early childhood.

Social constructionist research is often centred on interpersonal communication processes during everyday experiences. However, researchers using this perspective argue that it is not enough to observe people's behaviour; we also must understand why they behave that way, how they interpret their own actions, how they *feel* about what they do, and why they feel this way (Scanzoni and Scanzoni, 1988: 10). In other words, perceptions and 'definitions of the situation' influence actions or behaviour, a perspective that could be seen as the precursor of post-structuralist theory, which is discussed later in this chapter.

Social exchange theory, which uses economic analogies from cost-benefit analysis to explain human behaviour, is also derived from symbolic interactionism. The German sociologist Georg Simmel (1858–1918) argued that all human interactions involve some form of social exchange even when they appear to be altruistic, and he emphasized the importance of reciprocity in everyday life. His work was translated into English during the 1950s and became influential in American sociological theory. In 1961, the American sociologist George Homans (1910–89) argued that values and norms govern behaviour but that people also attempt to minimize costs and maximize benefits when interacting with others.

Within social exchange theory, the anticipation of a 'reward', such as social approval or emotional security, motivates social behaviour. All interpersonal behaviour, including deciding on a dating or marriage partner or accepting a household division of labour, is assumed to involve a process of negotiation and bargaining (Scanzoni, 1982). Social exchange theory has been used to explain why some relationships break up and others last. When one partner feels that he or she contributes more time or emotional energy to a relationship, feelings of resentment may develop and he or she may start looking elsewhere for gratification. Huber and Spitze (1980) found that among a variety of subject groups in an American study, married women who worked for pay and whose husbands did not share the housework were most likely to consider divorce. These women tended to feel dissatisfied because they believed that they were working hard for the relationship but were not receiving enough acknowledgement or assistance in return.

Theoretical approaches that focus on social interaction can provide insights into the dynamics and satisfactions of relationships but they cannot explain the historical or cultural change in family patterns. Nevertheless, these approaches have been popular since the early 1900s and still form the basis of research on topics relating to child development, the development of self-esteem, and marital satisfaction.

Ideas, Global Culture, and Public Discourse Influence Family Life

Some social theorists and researchers believe that focusing on changes in the political economy, social structure, early psychological experiences, or social interaction cannot adequately explain trends in sexuality, relationships, and family life. Instead, they emphasize the importance of ideas and, more recently, of global culture, such as advertising and media representations, when explaining personal choices and the creation of lifestyles.

Max Weber (1864–1920), one of the founders of modern sociology, wrote about how prevalent Protestant (especially Calvinist) ideas regarding individualism, hard work, rational conduct, and self-reliance actually led in the nineteenth century to the transformation of society and the development of capitalism (Abercrombie et al., 1994: 452). Since then, many theorists have focused on the influence of ideas in shaping family life, including the decline in religious observance; the growth of individualism; new ideas about gender equity, body rights, or the right to control one's fertility; and the desirability of being rich, famous, or changing one's physical appearance through hair dye, piercing, or cosmetic surgery.

Much has been written about the rise of individualism, including the widespread and growing belief that people have the right to choose their own marital partners, to be happy in marriage, and to find new partners if their relationships turn out to be unsatisfactory. Particularly the generation born after World War II has been called the 'me generation' because this cohort placed unprecedented emphasis on their own self-development, education, and personal fulfillment, shunning some of the earlier obligations voiced by their parents. The pre-war generation of women who wanted to further their education and establish careers had been admonished for being selfish and for contributing to the decline in the nuclear family, but the post-war generation was more likely to downplay or disregard these ideas and values.

Post-structuralists have argued that as Western societies grow more consumer-oriented, old expectations and divisions—including the authority of the church and state, social expectations, income differentials, and social class—become less important. Sociologists such as Anthony Giddens (1992) and Elisabeth Beck-Gernsheim (2002) have argued that intimacy has been transformed in postmodern society partly by the separation of sex from reproduction but also by new ideas about 'creating one's own biography'. Freedom from religious and family constraints has encouraged more people to live in ways that are different from their parents, including creating families of choice or groups of close associates with whom they want to spend time rather than spending time with biological relatives who oppose their values and lifestyle.

More people feel that they have the right to create households and lifestyles according to their own beliefs and desires. However, social scientists argue that beliefs and desires are not entirely invented by each individual but rather are shaped by images in the media, advertising, the Internet, films, and global culture. For example, by watching 'extreme makeover' programs on television, we are encouraged to view our wardrobe as 'un-cool', out of fashion, and in need of replacement, and to see our aging bodies as undesirable and in need of expensive repair. We are continually told that our confidence and self-esteem are derived from our personal appearance and sexiness, which encourages us to de-emphasize our personality development, social skills, intellect, occupational accomplishments, and caring responsibilities.

Post-structuralism also 'deconstructs' or questions the origins and intended meanings of certain ideas and beliefs about 'the family', arguing that prevalent images have been socially constructed. As such, they are a product of a certain historical period or organization, and may be used to advance particular political or commercial goals. In the recent past, the family was often conceptualized as a monolithic social institution instead of a range of various living patterns that have been transformed over the centuries, that vary by stage throughout the life cycle, and that represent gendered and cultural experiences. In addition, the state uses particular images of family to further its own interests. For example, recent discourses surrounding the role of non-custodial parents appeal to moral principles that do not appear to be contentious—that all parents should support their children even after separation and divorce. Yet much of the policy impetus has been driven by more pragmatic financial concerns (such as enforcing private paternal support), as governments committed to dismantling their welfare states redirect responsibility back to families (Mitchell and Goody, 1997; Dalley, 1998).

Public discourse, or the ways that people express certain ideas and the language they use, influences how others see themselves. For example, policy-makers and journalists often talk about 'workless households', 'dependants', or 'welfare moms' when they are discussing mother-led households with incomes assisted by state income support. This discourse encourages the general public to see these mothers in an unflattering light and perhaps to vote for cuts in income support that force beneficiaries into paid work (Mink, 2002). It encourages these mothers to see themselves as social failures who are making no contribution to society even though they may be doing a considerable amount of housework and raising children into healthy and productive adults.

Recent theorizing acknowledges and elaborates differences in family formation and family structure, and refutes the 'norm' of the nuclear family with father as earner and mother as care-provider. This theorizing notes that in most industrialized countries, socio-demographic trends in family life are moving in the same direction, as sexuality is becoming separated from marriage, and marriage is being reconstructed as a terminable arrangement with the greater acceptance of serial monogamy. Child-bearing and child-rearing are also becoming separated from marriage, many couples are renegotiating the division of labour based on gender, and more same-sex couples are expecting social and legal recognition of their living arrangements (Baker, 2001b). At the same time, more immigrants with different family patterns are migrating to industrialized countries and indigenous family patterns are being re-acknowledged by governments, social workers, and academics. These social and demographic trends have led to a contestation of the nuclear family as a core concept in both kinship and policy and to a theoretical reworking of what defines family in the twenty-first century.

METHODS OF FAMILY RESEARCH

We have seen that scholars searching for patterns and trends in family life tend to approach their research from a variety of theoretical perspectives, but they also use different methodologies. Most large-scale research projects involve several different methods of investigation at the same time but will always include a thorough review of previous research on the topic. Studies might also use some of the following methods of research: an examination or reanalysis of relevant background statistics from official sources; the development of special questionnaires or the reanalysis of older ones; face-to-face interviews; focus groups; personal observations to gain information about the social context; analysis of historical or policy documents.

Many researchers create their own family-related surveys and send them through the mail or by e-mail, or personally deliver them to participants. For example, a few years ago my research team in New Zealand mailed out a questionnaire to lone mothers who were receiving income support but were still expected to find paid work, asking them to rate their own health and the health of their children, their use of health services and facilities, employment-related experiences, and family circumstances. The question behind the **survey research** was whether poor people are more likely to experience poor health, since family health problems are not always considered by policy-makers developing welfare-to-work programs. Some researchers shy away from surveys that ask respondents to choose among specific answers or tick appropriate boxes; they believe that self-answered questionnaires provide superficial data even though answers may come from many participants. Also, the response rates for such surveys are often low.

Family researchers also use personal interviews that include both background contextual questions and open-ended ones where participants can talk at length about their personal circumstances and experiences with a particular family issue. These interviews are often audio-taped and transcribed in full so they can be analyzed by research assistants, often with the assistance of computer programs that electronically search for common themes in the interviews. The New Zealand study mentioned above also involved personal interviews with lone mothers. During these interviews, we investigated the details of family health issues, the mothers' employment experiences, problems with children and former partners, and their views of case management services. In the same study, we also gained research material from observations in the government office providing case management and income support, from the department's written and electronic advice to their case managers, and from focus groups with the case managers working with lone mothers.

Before sending questionnaires or talking to people, researchers in most countries must gain approval from local human subjects' ethics committees associated with universities, hospitals, or research centres to ensure that their projects have the informed consent of participants, do no harm, respect people's privacy, and keep their answers confidential and anonymous. Ethics committees, comprised of researchers and community members, are particularly vigilant when researchers want to talk to 'vulnerable subjects', such as children, beneficiaries, or prisoners. Family researchers, however, may neither talk to 'human subjects' nor send them questionnaires. Instead, they may rely on the analysis of public policy documents, personal diaries, family law reforms, court records, or documents from government departments. They may also reanalyze official statistics, using the government census, labour market statistics, or household surveys to uncover changes such as trends in maternal employment or rates of cohabitation, marriage, fertility, and divorce.

Official statistics are not available on all topics within family studies and some researchers also argue that these statistics provide less information than specialized family studies, especially those that talk at length to people in their own homes. Yet meeting ethics requirements, finding people who are willing to participate in research projects, talking to individuals in their homes, and mailing out surveys can be challenging and costly in terms of both time and money. Furthermore, researchers often have quite different opinions about which method of research is the best for their particular family project. They are sometimes asked to research a particular topic in a certain way by a government department or other research sponsor. Therefore, the method of research used in family studies, as in other subject areas, might be influenced by a number of factors, including ideas about the validity and wisdom of certain methods of research, the time and resources availability for research, requirements of the sponsors of research, or the availability of existing data. In fact, practical constraints may outweigh academic ones when researchers decide which method of research to use in their search for new knowledge about family life.

CONCLUSION

Over the past two decades, most academics have altered the ways that they conceptualize and study families. They now place more emphasis on identity formation, gendered and cultural experiences, the influence of global culture on family life, balancing caring and earning, and the analysis of political discourse. The growth of post-structural theorizing in the social sciences and humanities has influenced much of family research and theory, as more academics now acknowledge the considerable diversity in household formation, lifestyles, and identities that vary in different social settings, throughout the life course and throughout history. Although some academics adhere to one theoretical or methodological approach and view all others as mutually exclusive, most combine several approaches or borrow ideas from more than one perspective.

Many scholars now argue that family life in advanced industrial societies has become more fragmented and complex with a number of sources of differentiation, including social class, gender, sexual preference, ethnicity, and age (Abercrombie et al., 1994: 326). Furthermore, social conditions are dominated by economic markets that are internationally competitive, specialized, and non-unionized. Popular culture has become more consumer-oriented and more young people and families are falling into debt. At the same time, more governments have been attempting to dismantle aspects of the welfare state, arguing that families need to be more self-sufficient and less dependent on state income support.

These issues are acknowledged within the theoretical framework of this book, which gives priority to a **feminist political economy perspective** but also draws on post-structural research. By this I mean that analysis of gender relations is central to this book, but I also focus on the ways that family income, laws, and cultural practices influence people's intimate relationships and personal desires. At the same time, I note the areas where choices can be made (and are actually made) to create people's own biographies.

In the next chapter, I discuss social research relating to relationship formation, which includes how people find sexual partners, who they select as 'dates' and 'mates', and at what stage in their lives they seek permanent intimate relationships. The two basic questions we ask are which patterns are new and how do we explain the changes?

SUMMARY

The chapter concludes that the academic and policy definitions of family need to be sufficiently broad to encompass the variations in structure and experience, as 'family' is conceptualized differently in other cultures, in various theoretical frameworks, and by different government departments. The chapter also concludes that choice of theoretical framework shapes the focus of family investigations, the findings of research, and how findings are interpreted.

Questions for Critical Thought

1. What factors influence cross-cultural variations in family structure?
2. Is there any evidence that, with industrialization and globalization, families around the world are becoming more similar?
3. How does the theoretical perspective of family research influence methodology and data analysis?

Suggested Readings

Albanese, Patrizia. 2005. 'Ethnic Families', in M. Baker, ed., *Families: Changing Trends in Canada*, 5th edn. Toronto: McGraw-Hill Ryerson, 121–42. This chapter discusses the family patterns of various immigrant groups in Canada.

Luxton, Meg. 2005. 'Conceptualizing "Families": Theoretical Frameworks and Family Research', in M. Baker, ed., *Families: Changing Trends in Canada*, 5th edn. Toronto: McGraw-Hill Ryerson, 29–51. This chapter discusses three major sociological theories about the nature of family life.

Vanier Institute of the Family. 2004. *Profiling Canadian Families III*. Ottawa: VIF. This monograph provides numerous tables and succinct commentary about family trends in Canada.

Suggested Websites

Vanier Institute of the Family
www.vifamily.ca
This privately funded organization based in Ottawa provides educational material, news items, and research on Canadian families. The Vanier Institute also publishes a magazine called *Transition*.

Statistics Canada
www.statcan.ca.
Statistics Canada provides a wide range of statistics relating to families and households.

Chapter 2

Forming Relationships

Learning Objectives
- To relate patterns in dating and sexual behaviour to the changing social context over the decades.
- To differentiate between social attitudes and actual behaviour relating to sexuality.
- To search for social patterns in marital choices.

Chapter Outline

This chapter discusses some aspects of the social history of dating and courtship in order to understand why young people were pressured to choose a 'suitable' partner and marry according to their social position and family preferences. The chapter also examines changing patterns in partnering choices and lifestyles outside of marriage.

Introduction

Do men and women search for similar kinds of intimate partners as in the past, or do they locate partners and develop relationships differently from a few decades ago? Family researchers continue to search for new trends in dating and family formation because these can provide insights into social change in the wider society as well. In this chapter we note that ways of locating new partners and establishing relationships have changed somewhat over the years in most Western industrialized countries. Essentially, developing intimate partnerships has become easier, less formalized, less gendered, and more a matter of personal choice.

Nevertheless, traditional attitudes and practices remain, with some of the same gendered and cultural patterns underpinning personal preferences. Furthermore, current research suggests that the timing of first sexual experiences and partner choices continues to be shaped by family circumstances, social pressures from 'significant others', social class background, and cultural expectations. The state of the economy and opportunities for education and work can also influence the timing of family formation, whether or not couples become parents, and the number of children they actually have compared to the number they desire.

In Western industrialized countries, most people choose their own intimate partners, although elders in some cultural communities try to assist their young people to form viable partnerships and to prevent unsuitable liaisons. Among cultural groups that encourage arranged or partially **arranged marriage**, dating is seldom tolerated because parents expect to control their children's relationships and the timing of marriages. Potential partners are identified by elders from kin networks or from the cultural community and the young people involved do not always know each other in advance. Supervised meetings between the potential partners and negotiations between the two families determine whether or not a marriage will take place, but young people now have more say in marriage decisions, including the opportunity to veto all or some of their parents' choices. The laws of all westernized countries support free-choice marriages by requiring the written consent of both the bride and the groom. This means that, at least theoretically, no one living in these countries can be coerced into a wedding, even within cultural communities practising arranged marriages.

In free-choice relationships, individuals may spend several years attending social functions or enjoying leisure activities with several different intimate or sexual partners before making any concrete plans to cohabit or share the future with any of them. Eventually, however, most individuals develop an exclusive relationship that they would like to be ongoing or permanent. Nowadays, many people cohabit in a marriage-like relationship before making a long-term commitment, a pattern that used to be unacceptable in middle- and upper-class society. Choosing a partner is usually based on such factors as physical attraction, similar outlooks and interests, compatible personalities, desire for emotional stability and parenthood, and love. However, these characteristics may depend on the type of relationship wanted at the time. Distinctions normally are made among the attributes expected from a 'one-night stand', a suitable dating partner, a compatible cohabitation partner, and one who is potentially 'marriageable' for life. What patterns are apparent in the way individuals make these decisions?

DATING AS A RECENT SOCIAL PHENOMENON

Social history and comparative family studies reveal that current dating practices are relatively recent in westernized countries and are not as widespread as we might think in other parts of the world. The origins of romantic love in Europe date back to feudal times (Leslie and Korman, 1989). Marriages at that time were arranged—to suit family alliances, to provide heirs, and to improve or maintain family wealth—and 'love' was not considered essential to the participants in the contract. Husbands and wives were not expected to have their emotional needs satisfied in marriage, although that sometimes did happen, but sought satisfaction in their children, their work, in same-sex friendships, or in other relationships.

People of the higher classes were more likely to develop love relationships but these were often outside marriage and did not always involve sexual activity. Instead, they involved idealized (romanticized) love, public acts of gallantry, and deferential attention. Acts of chivalry, or treating noblewomen with extra respect, accorded a new kind of power to women beyond their roles as wives and chatelaines and their potential capacity to produce heirs to their estates. Women, in the courtly love relationship, were recognized as holding the power to subdue the male through innocent affection. This, along with related attitudes being developed through greater honour accorded to the Virgin Mary in the Church, advanced the dissociation of women from largely material interests. That is, the woman became less a chattel and purveyor and overseer of wealth, and more a personal influence in the male sphere. Noblewomen exerted their influence by virtue of inherited position, wealth, and personal abilities. Of course, women of other classes, like their male peers, were more nearly slaves or chattels, with the exception of those who earned status within the Church or through businesses of some sort.

From the eighteenth century, with the rise of a wealthy middle class, social power began to shift from the nobility to those who possessed economic strength. The gradual depletion of power from the aristocracy (sometimes very dramatically through revolution, as in France and the United States) granted political powers to a new class of bourgeois males through voting. Not all men, however, were immediately enfranchised; property and wealth continued to determine a man's right to vote, even though men became politically influential on a much broader scale. During the eighteenth and nineteenth centuries, partly through increasing opportunities for education, many more women moved from the impoverished to the middle classes. They had difficulty in matching the status of their male partners; their sphere of influence remained much more domestic. Furthermore, until the late nineteenth century or early twentieth century, women were not allowed to take political office, own land, or work in business or the professions, and rich women had servants to do the housework. Men's 'chivalrous' behaviour towards women became formalized and perhaps a sort of compensation—a way of keeping women happy despite their relatively low economic and legal status (ibid., 173). As society became politically more egalitarian, some of these chivalrous customs disappeared while others remained as etiquette—such as men opening doors for women, helping them on with their coats, or protecting them from rain or heavy work.

The vast majority of people in Europe and in the colonies were poor and lived in crowded and unsanitary conditions that did not permit much romance or chivalry. Survival usually meant long hours of work. Most unmarried adults lived with their parents and siblings, and were not encouraged to spend time alone with eligible partners. Although people made choices based in love as well as on economic or other factors, the leisure and privacy required to maintain romance after the wedding were difficult to find (Skolnick, 1987). Married couples shared their small living spaces with their children, who sometimes arrived within a year of the wedding, and couples occasionally shared accommodation with other relatives or boarders. Consequently, household members would not be able to disguise their sexual activity, their bodily functions, their illnesses, or other aspects of personal life from others. Nevertheless, most young people anticipated marriage and parenthood because they were synonymous with adulthood, maturity, respectability, and authority within the community. They also anticipated the sexual relationship, but that was socially approved only within matrimony. Economics played a large role in the pairing process, however; in poorer families, parents wanted their sons and daughters to marry persons wealthier, who would help them out of debt and bring productive land into the family. They wanted a child to marry a partner who was kind but also an industrious, strong, and healthy person, who would bring grandchildren and who would be able to care for them in their declining years.

Even before marriages were based on love, many children probably persuaded their parents to arrange a marriage with people they already knew and wanted to marry. Many married partners grew to love each other deeply after sharing their lives, even when their marriage was partially arranged. Despite the fact that the male head of the household had considerable authority over other family members, there were undoubtedly fathers and husbands who were sensitive to the wishes of their wives and children.

Even when chastity before marriage was considered an essential virtue, many young men frequented prostitutes or had secret sexual liaisons. Married men and, less often, married women had secret affairs, but without reliable contraception, premarital pregnancies were disguised with hasty marriages, adoptions, or back-street abortions and extramarital pregnancies were passed off as children of the existing marriage or terminated with an illegal abortion. In other words, ideal family systems in the past differed considerably from reality, as they still do today.

In the first half of the twentieth century, most unmarried young people in both urban and rural areas continued to live with their parents or relatives, and few adolescents or young adults lived with peers before marriage (Nett, 1993: 216). While living with their parents or relatives, most young people paid 'room and board' and engaged in unpaid chores to help cover household expenses. If they lived apart from their parents to attend school or earn money, they usually boarded with relatives or lived in supervised residences or boarding houses with little privacy. Working long hours without much leisure time meant that young people had few opportunities to party, to date widely, or to develop more than one intimate relationship before they married for life (Bradbury, 2005). Furthermore, social rules reinforced by the church permitted men and women little opportunity to spend time alone together in public or in private, unless they were engaged or married. Those who lived in remote areas would also have few opportunities to meet potential partners.

Securing a marriage partner was essential for young women partly because in the town they were excluded from most paid jobs and in the country they were less likely to inherit the family farm. Even if they found wage work, women earned considerably less than men and most employed women were unable to fully support themselves and/or their children. Generally, the woman needed a husband to earn sufficient money to run the household, to perform heavy chores around the house, and to provide her with sexual satisfaction and with children (who raised her status within the family and community). Similarly, few men could survive without a wife to cook, clean the home, launder the clothes, grow vegetables, provide him with sexual satisfaction, and raise the children. Housework was very time-consuming and laborious before electricity, refrigeration, and imported food. Wage labourers normally worked long hours each weekday as well as Saturday mornings, and farmers worked every day. Before the 1930s, few employees were entitled to paid holidays. The banks and food stores were closed by the time most men finished work, leaving little opportunity to run personal errands after work. Wealthy men could afford live-in servants, but most needed a wife to manage the household.

Young people met their potential spouses at school, in their neighbourhood, at their church, or through their siblings and other relatives. Sometimes they were introduced by friends or family members, and occasionally they were 'set up' by friends on 'blind dates'. They also met partners at dances, parties, and other social functions, but these were usually community activities attended by a variety of age groups, where the activities of young people were closely monitored by adult chaperones to ensure that no 'unseemly conduct' occurred. These activities were based on expectations of heterosexuality and same-sex intimate relationships were rare and not condoned.

THE SOCIAL REGULATION OF COURTSHIP

In nineteenth-century North America, courtship, love, and marriage were constrained by an intricate network of social, institutional, and familial influences (Shorter, 1975; Ward, 1990). From the eighteenth century, young men increasingly took the initiative to find their own brides but were expected to ask the father's permission to 'court' her, or gradually develop a relationship leading to marriage. This sometimes involved a formal meeting, at which the young man addressed the woman's father formally and presented his credentials, somewhat like a job interview. The father, as well as other relatives, wanted to ensure that the suitor's intentions were 'honourable', which meant that he sincerely intended to marry his daughter rather than just wanted a 'good time' that would ruin her reputation. The father also expected some assurance that the intended fiancé would become a kind, thoughtful, and faithful husband who could adequately support his daughter. The father's permission might be acquired before the 'courtship' began or at least before any formal marriage proposal was accepted by the woman (Ward, 1990).

Women were expected to encourage only one or two such courtships before marriage. When the man's proposal was accepted, the engagement (or betrothal) was publicly announced and thus became a binding agreement. However, the wedding might be delayed until the male partner more firmly established his work life or career, or until he saved money, or until he was able to persuade his employer to raise his earnings or his father to share farm earnings or even to hand over the farm. The 'banns' or the couple's intentions to marry were then read in church for three consecutive Sundays to ensure that anyone who knew of a reason why the marriage should not take place would have the opportunity to speak out. This was largely to ensure against 'bigamy' or marriage to more than one partner at a time. Later, when the state became more involved in legalizing marriage, a licence was also required to ensure that marriage partners were acceptable and appropriate from the viewpoint of community leaders and the government. However, most weddings continued to be held in places of worship until the 1960s or later.

Most young people did not develop relationships with a variety of potential partners before marriage because once a man and woman were seen together several times they became viewed by friends and relatives as a 'couple'. However, many young people voluntarily committed themselves to their teenage sweetheart through lengthy formal engagements, which then meant that no other dating partners could be accepted without violating the unspoken agreement of exclusivity. Marriage was important to the social and economic well-being of both men and women, and young women, especially, attempted to secure a partner before they became older than their marrying peers ('left on the shelf' without a partner) or found their cohort of suitable partners shrinking so that they felt forced to marry someone less desirable. Marital choices were often limited to neighbours, school or work acquaintances, and family friends because most young people attended local schools, entered the workforce at a young age, or cared for their elderly parents at home, but did not travel outside their community unless they were financially well-off.

According to public norms, sexuality was supposed to be restricted to marriage or at least to heterosexual couples who were formally engaged, although, clearly, a **double standard** existed for men and women. Premarital chastity usually was deemed more important for women, and those who proceeded to sexual intercourse were expected to marry quickly. If they did not, they could be perceived by other men as fair game for sexual advances or harassment. These women would be seen by other parents as 'damaged goods' or 'having a past', a reputation that would reduce their future chances of finding a suitable partner. However, men could use commitment, expressions of love, or formal engagement to gain sexual favours from their girlfriends and women could use the expectation of premarital chastity to pressure their boyfriends into a marriage proposal and formal engagement. If pregnancy occurred before marriage, their families and friends would pressure them to cement their relationship in legal marriage and to stay together for life. Consequently, some couples married hastily but were expected to live with the consequences.

Before the 1940s, middle-class parents seldom permitted their daughters to participate in leisure activities involving young men without the presence of chaperones, who might have been other relatives, servants, reliable neighbours, school teachers, or clergy. This was particularly the case for wealthier families, who valued female premarital chastity more than poorer families did. Rich families had more to lose in terms of lost reputation or family wealth if their daughters were forced into hasty ('shotgun') weddings with 'inappropriate' partners. Some wealthy parents engaged companions to travel with their unmarried daughters in order to protect their reputations, but middle-class parents simply restricted their daughters' activities outside the household. If there was any suspicion of sexual misconduct, and this was very broadly defined, a woman's chances of making a 'good marriage' would be reduced.

For middle-class women, a good marriage meant one to a kind and considerate man from the same religious and ethnic group who worked hard and earned a steady income that was high enough to support a wife and several children. He was also expected to come from a similar social class, preferably from a reputable family known by the woman's parents, relatives, or neighbours. A good marriage was also a gendered one, with **complementary roles** for husband and wife, who were said to be separate but equal. For middle-class men, a suitable marriage meant one to an attractive and respectable woman with social skills, a pleasant personality, good health and child-bearing potential, and valuable skills in homemaking and money management.

Education was desirable but middle-class women were expected to become home-makers and mothers after marriage rather than wage earners. A good wife also behaved in a respectable and socially appropriate manner. If she did not, she could damage her husband's career prospects, his personal reputation, and their shared social life.

Early in the twentieth century, only men were expected to propose marriage. Young men hesitated to propose or to finalize marriage arrangements until they could afford to support a wife and children because men were automatically designated as the family earner when they married. Engaged women who had paid jobs were expected to leave their employment as their wedding date approached, regardless of how interesting or lucrative their jobs were. They were expected to prepare for their wedding day and their marriage, when they would be responsible for ensuring that the home was a pleasant place and that the domestic chores were done.

Before the 1960s, the amount of housework was greater and more time-consuming than today. Physical means of birth control were also unreliable and socially unacceptable, with babies expected shortly after marriage. Reticence, sublimation of sexuality through work, and sexual self-control were widely practised as means of limiting the number of pregnancies for a couple. Couples had to save sufficient resources and the man had to acquire a steady income before they could afford to marry and establish a household separate from their parents. Without social security programs or credit cards, men often had to ask their employers for higher wages or ask their parents for a loan in order to manage their new commitments. If the boss or parents agreed, the couple could marry, but many had to postpone their marriage plans for financial reasons. In some cases, parents or other relatives also objected to the match or pressed the couple to postpone the wedding until the man completed his education or the couple saved more money.

The Great Depression of the 1930s forced many couples to delay marriage and also made people conscious of material security in a number of ways, encouraging them to focus on thrift, hard work, and self-sufficiency. In those days, few state income support programs or subsidized health-care services were available, especially in the liberal welfare states, and families needed to save money for accommodation, food, clothing, transportation, and future health-care costs, which included doctor's fees for normal childbirths but also for childbirth complications or accidents. Credit cards were not used until the 1970s and any credit given was at the personal discretion of the shopkeeper or the doctor.

Until the 1950s, rules of **endogamy** were also quite strict. For example, dating and engagements between Protestants and Catholics were frowned upon in many countries, but public opinion especially opposed interracial, intercultural, and interfaith liaisons. Most people attended regular religious services and their church leaders encouraged high moral values and family behaviour that was gendered, endogamous, and favoured reproduction. In addition, parents and schoolteachers attempted to maintain strict authority over the behaviour of children and young people. Although some children from large, poor, and rural families spent more time out of the view of their parents and teachers than they might today, young people were generally given fewer choices about any aspect of their lives, with rigid and hierarchical social rules of behaviour at home, school, and work.

World War II became a turning point for many social attitudes and behavioural patterns, including dating and sexual practices. Dating, premarital sex, and abortion rates increased sharply during the war when young people were away from parents and chaperones (Kedgley, 1996: 148; Baker, 2001b). When soldiers were on leave at home or in foreign countries, they tended to take more risks with their sexual partners, as life seemed so dangerous and short and pleasures were few. Many couples married hastily before or during the war, which enabled them to live together when the man was on leave and to have sex without social disapproval. Wartime marriages also increased the social and economic security of the brides and gave the grooms some hope of future domestic security when they returned home (if they survived combat). However, rates of separation, annulments, and divorces increased when men returned home from the war. Many relationships did not survive the long separation, which sometimes lasted for years when men were posted overseas or taken prisoner. Couples drifted apart, either the man or the woman met a new partner, and some wives could not cope with their husbands' wartime injuries, especially when they were psychological (Montgomerie, 1999).

By the late 1940s, dating without chaperones had become widespread, but this was replaced by strictly gendered etiquette rules. For example, men were permitted to invite women to attend social functions with them but women were not allowed to ask men, at least not directly. Men were expected to provide the transportation and pay for all the expenses, while women were urged to behave as congenial, attractive, and accommodating companions. Post-war affluence gave middle-class individuals more choice in clothing, food, and entertainments; couples 'dressed up' for dating (depending on the venue). They attended social events such as dances or films, or simply went for a walk in a public park or down the main street of town. As late as the 1930s, middle-class men might have dressed in a hat, jacket, and tie, and women in a dress, high-heeled shoes, hat, and gloves simply in order to go for a walk together in a public park and then return to one of their family homes for dinner. Manners and dress—including changes in 'suitable' attire—tended to ape the customs of the wealthy and/or aristocratic; Canadians looked to the British noble class for some of their guidance in such matters.

Before the 1950s, people differentiated between 'dating' and 'courtship'. Dating was defined as a short period of getting acquainted with the available partners, while courtship involved developing a serious relationship with one partner leading to lifelong marriage. Men were given the freedom to date more widely than women and were generally accorded a wider social range. A woman who invited frequent dates (flirted) and made herself to some degree sexually available to them all without distinction would be considered 'fast' or 'loose', which damaged her reputation and future chances of a good marriage. Dating activities were usually relatively public and were not supposed to include solitary or intimate activities other than handholding or chaste good-night kisses. Couple activities particularly excluded any expectation of sexual intercourse, although we know that many unmarried couples did engage in sexual activities from records of illegal abortions, illegitimate births, adoptions, hasty marriages, and 'premature' babies.

The move from dating to courtship usually involved the man proposing marriage to the woman. If she agreed, he often bought her an engagement ring made of gold or silver with a precious stone such as a diamond to represent high value and durability. This engagement ring symbolized their lifelong commitment and became a public contractual agreement to marry that could not be easily broken without mutual consent. If an engaged woman broke off the engagement, she was expected to return the ring. If he backed out after she or her family had made costly wedding preparations, she could sue him for 'breach of promise' under English common law and possibly receive a payment for 'damages' at the jury's discretion (Ward, 1990: 32). However, few jilted fiancées had the money to engage a lawyer and many knew that their former fiancé could not afford to pay even if they were successful in a civil lawsuit.

When men and women became engaged, their friends and family would allow them more privacy and intimate relations. However, if she became pregnant, parents and friends would have pressured the couple to marry quickly before the pregnancy was noticed by others. Ideas about social propriety were almost more important than the couple's feelings for each other or their future chances of marital happiness. Many couples were pressured into marriage prematurely by unintended pregnancy. If an unmarried pregnant woman was unable or unwilling to marry or to have an (illegal) abortion, she might leave her community to give birth, surrender the infant for adoption (agencies insisted on a two-parent family for adoption), and return quietly to the community. Private or church-run maternity homes assisted many unmarried mothers through childbirth and arranged for the adoption of their children. Otherwise, these women would have been subjected to disapproval or ostracism, and would have brought disrepute to themselves and their families. Early in the twentieth century, 'closed adoption' practices were widespread, which sometimes meant that birth certificates were altered and no further contact was permitted between birth mothers and their infants.

If conception occurred before the wedding date, engaged couples might simply bring forward the marriage ceremony rather than permit the child to be adopted or to be (illegally) aborted. Their earlier wedding date would ensure that the child was 'legitimate'. A legitimate child was born legally with a father and was permitted to take his surname and inherit from him, whereas an illegitimate child took the mother's surname, had no legal rights from the father, and was stigmatized socially.

This brief overview of past practices suggests that people had limited choices about sexuality and relationships because strict rules of behaviour were enforced within families, communities, and workplaces, as well as internalized. Even when individuals or couples disagreed with the rules or with their parents' wishes, few could afford, either financially or socially, to contravene them.

POST-1960s DATING AND SEXUAL PRACTICES

Since the 1960s, young people have gradually moved away from rigid and gendered expectations of dating and 'courting'. More people now attend social activities as individuals or groups rather than as couples, and others arrange to meet potential partners at social events. There is also some suggestion that Americans may be more likely than young people from countries such as Australia or New Zealand to participate in traditional dating practices that maintain some gendered expectations, but this is based largely on anecdotal evidence from university students from my years of teaching in Australia (in the 1970s) and in New Zealand (since 1998). It is possible that the fundamentalist Christian influence in parts of the United States may have prolonged the traditional dating patterns described above.

Currently, when a relationship is established, an urban couple might attend a film or concert together but would seldom 'dress up' in the way people used to in the 1930s. Of course, that is true of the society at large. (Average Canadians stopped 'dressing up' in the mid- to late 1970s.) Afterwards, they might go to a bar or café, where they might share the expenses or the better-off of the two might pay, and then they might end up at one or the other's apartment or flat to listen to music, watch a video, and/or make love. Improvements in contraception since the 1960s have enabled premarital sex without pregnancy, which has liberalized both attitudes and actual behaviour, but women still cannot have sex with multiple partners before 'eyebrows are raised'. Although the double standard of sexuality has been eroded, research (discussed below) suggests that it has not entirely disappeared. There is also evidence that desired characteristics in a dating partner still vary by gender, with more emphasis on women's youthful appearance and men's height, strength, and occupational success (McDaniel and Tepperman, 2004).

People still develop ideas about desirable and ideal partners. Often, imagined partners are sexually/physically attractive and successful, but we also expect them to be considerate of our feelings and to share similar values and interests. Although some people dismiss or flaunt prevalent expectations, researchers continue to find that most people still internalize the importance of choosing a partner from a similar social background or from the gendered hierarchy in social and physical characteristics. To women, educational and occupational success are still more important characteristics of men as potential partners, and physical attractiveness and congenial personality of women remain more important to men. Most individuals continue to search for a socially and personally desirable partner and parents still worry that their children will short-change themselves by choosing a partner who is 'not good enough' for them.

Numerous studies have concluded that men continue to search for younger women who are slim and attractive, while women still focus on a man's occupational success, as well as his maturity, athletic build, and height (Coltrane, 1998: 47). According to **exchange theory**, the closer the body approximates idealized images of youth and beauty, the higher its 'exchange value', especially for women (Featherstone, 1991). Structural theorists argue that men's preferences for younger attractive women and women's preference for taller and successful older men can lead to a 'marriage squeeze'. This means that people edged out of the **marriage market** are older and less conventionally attractive women, and younger and shorter men with low education and incomes.

Although women have become more assertive in dating practices, some traditional ideas and practices seem to persist. Mongeau and Carey (1996) found that American men are more likely than women to interpret a first date initiated by a woman as a sexual overture. Coltrane (1998) found that men see 'sexually aggressive women' as off-putting, although flirting with sexual overtones is still an integral part of dating for both men and women. In addition, heterosexual women still spend a considerable amount of time and money making themselves attractive to men and gendered patterns still exist in ideal partners (Abu-Laban and McDaniel, 1998). Introduction services and dating agencies rely on some of the same characteristics found to be important when people seek their own partners, including similar cultural, religious, and educational backgrounds—but with the man older, more educated, and taller. Introduction services also show videos to their clients of potential partners, acknowledging that many choices are based on physical appearance, first impressions, or 'chemistry'.

For decades, people have been advertising in newspapers for intimate partners. In 1982, I analyzed personal advertisements in a Canadian daily newspaper, including the ways that heterosexual men and women described themselves and what they asked for in potential partners (Baker, 1982). Men and women tended to present themselves in traditional gendered ways despite this apparently unconventional way of seeking a partner. Men more often described themselves as 'tall' and 'successful' business or professional men, gave their age, and asked for 'attractive' younger women for a lasting relationship or 'recreational sex'. In contrast, women tended to describe themselves as petite, slim, and attractive and asked for business or professional men who were the same age or older. Just as in previous decades, women focused on lasting relationships or marriage.

Similar gendered advertisements were found in Canadian newspapers from 1975 to 1988 by Sev'er (1990). In this kind of personal advertising, women (and especially older ones) tend to be disadvantaged, both as choosers and as the potentially chosen (McDaniel and Tepperman, 2000: 57). Now, more people search for partners on the Internet where they can screen candidates with preliminary questions about their habits and interests and provide detailed self-descriptions. However, creating a false identity on the Internet is easy and it can be dangerous to assume that you know someone through e-mail correspondence when you actually have never met the person.

A study by Bulbeck (cited in Connolly, 2004) revealed that Australian teenagers have retained gendered expectations about future partners. The researchers asked secondary school students from South Australia and Western Australia to imagine their future at age 70 and 80 and to reflect on the successes and failures in their lives. Despite three decades of discussion about gender equity, teenage boys wrote about a future of wealth, sex with many beautiful women, fast cars, and sport. Although 65 per cent of the girls said that they wanted a career, their stories focused on romance, meeting Mr Right, shared parenting, and relationships involving mutual understanding. A man's earning capacity is still relevant to some girls, and being rich and famous was highlighted by many of the boys. The author noted that the expectations of future fame and wealth are quite unrealistic, but also that discrepancies between the stories of men and women encouraged her to predict more divorce in the future (ibid).

In a content analysis of 1,094 personal advertisements from four British newspapers, Jagger (2005) found that 61 per cent of advertisers were men but more of the advertisers over 45 years old were women. Men were more likely to mention their age but more women qualified their age in some way that suggested it was problematic. For example, they described themselves as 'a very young 39-year-old female', '55 years young', or 'young 60-year-old widow'; or they described themselves in the language of 'positive aging', providing an optimistic, upbeat, physically active version of self. Jagger also noted the relative youthfulness of the advertisers using qualifying statements about age, with both males and females in their thirties revealing age-conscious identities ('male 37 but feels much younger'). The devaluation of age and aging has implications for advertisers when marketing the self, and advertisers seem to feel the need to reconcile the way they look with the way they feel (Turner, 1995; Jagger, 2005).

In Jagger's study, most people who stated an age preference wanted someone of a comparable age to themselves but men were more likely than women to ask for a younger partner. Among the older advertisers, men were most likely to say that they wanted a younger or much younger woman, although nearly one-fifth of older women also requested a younger man. Jagger (2005) showed that the ability to negotiate lifestyle choices from a diversity of options is shaped in complex ways by gender and age, but argued that individuals are still negotiating their identities around socially proscribed expectations that focus on the value of youth.

Box 2.1 Attitudes towards Children's Sexual Behaviour

Question (How do you feel—or did you/would you feel—about your children . . .)	Approve or Accept	Disapprove but Accept	Disapprove and Do Not Accept	Total
. . . engaging in premarital sex when they are 18 or over	53	36	11	100
. . . informing you that they are gay or lesbian	17	54	29	100
. . . engaging in homosexual acts	35	42	23	100
. . . living with a sexual partner without being married	24	31	45	100
. . . having children without being married	53	35	12	100
. . . having sexual relations with someone other than their spouse	33	50	17	100

Attitudes towards sexual activity have been changing over time.

We asked our respondents whether or not sex 'was pretty common among teenagers' in their high schools.

No less than 74 per cent of Gen-Xers said it was, compared to 41 per cent of baby boomers and 12 per cent of pre-boomers.

Source: Bibby (2004–5). Reprinted by permission of the publisher.

Despite general insistence on the importance of personal choice in locating dating and marriage partners, high rates of separation and divorce among couples suggest that decisions may not be based on qualities that lead to lasting relationships. Personal judgements based on physical appearance and sexuality are widespread in the popular media. Relationship instability is actually being encouraged by focusing on sexuality, fashionable appearance, and material success rather than shared values, companionship, or knowledge of the person's personality or background. Heavy reliance on appearance contributes to short-term relationships in cultures that already focus on individualism, self-development, and personal choice.

What has social research concluded about attractiveness and desirability in intimate partnerships? Generally, researchers have found patterns in partner choices for dating, cohabitation, and marriage but these vary substantially by gender, sexual preference, and culture, and these patterns are changing over time. Characteristics considered desirable and practices felt to be necessary by our parents may now appear old-fashioned or overly rigid and gendered. In addition, global youth culture seems to be blurring some of the international variations but accentuating generational differences. Nevertheless, partner choice is clearly influenced both by socio-economic factors and by psychological factors, as our overview of family theories suggested in Chapter 1.

WHO MARRIES WHOM?

Sociologists have relied on several theoretical approaches to explain how people choose their marital partners in free-choice systems; these are portrayed in Table 2.1. Based on a structural approach, the theory of social **homogamy** suggests that people tend to date and marry those from similar socio-economic, religious, and cultural

Table 2.1   Theories of Mate Selection or Marital Choice

Structural Theories	Psychological Theories	Social Construction Theories	Developmental Theories
• People marry those who are similar in age, socio-economic background, religion, and culture, who also happen to live nearby (social homogamy). • Patriarchal social structures expect men to be older and taller, to have more education and income, and to be the dominant decision-maker.	• People marry those they think will complement their psychological needs (complementary needs). • People marry partners who subconsciously remind them of parents, siblings, or 'significant others' from the past.	• Initial attraction is based on personal and cultural ideals about desirable mates, including those gained from popular heroes and media representations.	• Marriage decisions are influenced by emotional advances and retreats, negotiation between partners, conflict resolution skills, and chance factors, as well as social pressure from parents and friends.

Source: Derived from a variety of sources discussed in Baker (2001b).

backgrounds and those from similar age groups. These people usually live in the same neighbourhoods, attend the same schools and join the same clubs, and therefore have more opportunity to meet and socialize together. They also feel comfortable with each other because they share similar social backgrounds, lifestyles, and world views. This explanation, however, cannot say why specific individuals choose each other rather than anyone else from their community of social equals.

A variation of the structural theory argues that the ideal heterosexual partnership in a patriarchal and capitalist society requires the male to be older, taller, and more successful occupationally because he is expected to be the breadwinner, main decision-maker, and family representative in the community. The woman is expected to be smaller, attractive, and congenial, but not necessarily well-educated or a high earner because her main role is to raise children and maintain the home even if she also earns some household money. Although the laws in Western societies usually give men and women equal rights, vestiges of patriarchy continue in domestic relations. Many individuals are unaware that they are choosing partners based on these ideals because they have internalized patriarchal gender relations.

Based on the psychoanalytic approach, the theory of complementary needs argues that psychological variables are more important than structural or socioeconomic ones in determining attraction and mate selection (Winch, 1955). Rather than choosing a partner like themselves, people select someone with a different personality, who they think will complement their emotional needs, including the need for attention, care, love, deference, or social status. If two people have equally powerful personalities and are very successful occupationally, their 'egos' might clash. If one is eager to get ahead in the world while the other is more concerned about being supportive and kind, then these two people may find each other attractive and compatible marriage partners.

Another psychological theory suggests that choosing a life partner involves searching for one's ideal mate, who sometimes resembles our opposite-sex parent. Even though young people often vow that they will never marry anyone like their mother or father, they sometimes subconsciously pair up with someone remarkably similar. A more sociological variation of the ideal mate theory suggests that images of desirable partners are socially constructed, including both positive and negative characteristics of opposite-sex parents, older siblings, and experiences with previous partners. In addition, media representations, including fashion magazines and advertising, increasingly focus on sexuality, youth, and beauty, especially for women, and many people internalize these idealized images even though they are designed to increase consumption.

Developmental theories of mate selection, based on the idea that relationships are negotiated as well as socially constructed, argue that the development of 'courtship' is predetermined by neither social nor psychological variables. Instead, who one marries is the end product of a series of interpersonal interactions characterized by advances and retreats, changing definitions of the situation, negotiations, resolution of tensions, and chance encounters. People may meet unexpectedly and find each other good company, but the path to greater commitment and finally to marriage has been portrayed as similar to an escalator. Once you step on, it is difficult not to ride to the top because interpersonal and social pressure to enhance commitment comes in various forms. One partner might persuade the other that living together rather than separately would be more desirable, easier, and cheaper. Alternatively, one partner may receive a job offer in another city and request the other to follow, leading to cohabitation or legal marriage. Relatives and friends might pressure a cohabiting couple to legalize their relationship and once wedding plans are made, they are difficult to cancel even if one partner has second thoughts.

Many young people in Western countries insist that they marry for 'love' but sociologists always argue that 'love' is socially constructed, shaped by interaction and negotiation, gendered practices, socio-economic circumstances, and cultural beliefs. Usually, we 'fall in love' according to implicit gendered and class-based ideals of attractiveness and appropriate partners, as well as considering our personal values and needs. In addition, this tends to happen at a similar stage in the life cycle as our peers, such as when we finish school or find regular employment. Nevertheless, the ways that we locate our partners and our ideas about acceptable sexual behaviour before marriage have certainly changed throughout the decades. Social activities operate under less parental or community supervision as more young people seem to engage in entertainment involving music, dancing, alcohol, drugs, and sexuality that lasts well into the night. Efforts to find heterosexual and same-sex partners are now more explicit, 'recreational sex' is more open, and the search for new partners now operates in public places, newspapers, and the Internet.

Sexuality has become a marketable commodity that is romanticized in the media and sold in the consumer-oriented economy as fantasies and pleasures (McDaniel and Tepperman, 2000: 132). Increasingly, sexual expression has become separated from marriage and reproduction, which is exemplified in the growth of cohabitation, ex-nuptial births, and the legal recognition of same-sex couples. British sociologist Anthony Giddens (1992) described the new sexuality as 'plastic' because it was something to be discovered, moulded, and altered.

Using the Internet as a new way of forming relationships and meeting to have sex illustrates these points. Internet relationships transcend geographical distance and are forged on the basis of common interests rather than on common locality. They are disembodied, which provides more scope for fantasy, deception, and experimentation, making it possible to explore identities and sexualities. Men can pretend to be women and women can pretend to be men. Finally, these relationships tend to be uninhibited, which means that people can engage in more self-disclosure and riskier or harmful behaviour (Gilding, 2002). Relationships formed through cyberspace have been called 'hyperpersonal' because some people can reveal more of themselves, feel more attraction, and express more emotions on a keyboard than face-to-face. Instead of worrying about what they look like, they can concentrate on the message (Wallace, 1999).

Despite these new forms of dating and obtaining sexual pleasure, a substantial minority of young people in countries such as Canada and the United States do not engage in dating and premarital sex. In cultural communities that prefer arranged marriages, social activities continue to occur within a mixed-age community, which enables parents to monitor young people's behaviour and to prevent them from forming inappropriate couple relationships. Other cultural groups permit dating but believe that sex before marriage is risky, culturally unacceptable, or violates religious doctrine. A number of fundamentalist Christian groups, especially in the United States, have successfully encouraged substantial numbers of young people to take public vows of 'purity' and 'chastity' and to delay sexual intercourse (but not necessarily other forms of sexuality) until after marriage.

These examples show that considerable diversity remains in patterns of partnering. More individuals than formerly have intimate relationships at an early age and experience several sexual relationships before marriage, while some remain chaste until marriage or for life. More couples cohabit before legal marriage, many delay marriage until they reach 28 to 30 years of age, and more avoid legal marriage altogether compared to people in the 1960s and 1970s. A recent Australian study indicates that legal marriage remains popular among most people in that country but especially among people over 40 years old, fundamentalist Christians, other religious groups, and Asian immigrants (Dempsey and De Vaus, 2004).

Canadian statistics show that religion still matters in the choice of marriage partner. For example, in 2001 nine out of 10 grooms who were Jehovah's Witnesses married brides of the same religion, eight out of 10 non-Christians married other non-Christians, and seven out of 10 Jewish grooms married Jewish brides, as Table 2.2 indicates (VIF, 2004: 31). Sociologists continue to find patterns in 'personal choices' and these suggest that gender, age, social class, religion, and culture still influence people's choices about dating, cohabitation, and marriage. However, the very existence of greater cultural and lifestyle diversity in urban areas makes it easier for individuals to follow their own choices but those who remain living in remote

Table 2.2   Percentage of Canadian Grooms Who Married Brides of the Same Religion

Religion of Groom	Percentage Marrying within Own Religion
Jehovah's Witnesses	91
Non-Christian religions	77
Mennonite/Hutterite	76
Jewish	69
No religion	66
Pentecostal	62
Catholic	60
Eastern Orthodox	55
Baptist	44
United Church	41
Salvation Army	34
Anglican	33
Presbyterian	28
Lutheran	24

Source: VIF (2004: 32), adapted from Statistics Canada, 'Marriages', 2001, Catalogue no. 84F0212XPB.

regions simply have fewer choices and may therefore settle on a familiar neighbour rather than an 'ideal' mate. Others choose to avoid marriage altogether.

The Single Life

In recent decades, remaining single has taken on new meaning, but a smaller percentage of the population now reaches middle age without marrying compared to a century ago. Although it is difficult to find statistics that are exactly comparable, we know that 10 per cent of Canadian women in 1900 had never married by the age of 50 compared to 7 per cent of women by the ages 50 to 54 in 1996 (Dumas and Péron, 1992; Beaujot, 2000: 103). In many countries, marriage rates increased until the 1970s and then declined again as more people began to cohabit in the 1980s and 1990s. Current marriage rates remain at higher levels than in 1900 but more never-married people now live with a partner or have had sexual experience than in 1900.

Several factors lie behind the larger single and celibate population around 1900. Despite the importance of marriage for economic survival and social status, social rules discouraged people from marrying if they fell in love with someone considered to be an inappropriate marriage partner—such as a person already married or one from another religious or cultural group. Others failed to marry because they were running the family farm or caring for elderly parents and experienced few opportunities to meet potential partners. Early in the twentieth century, more people lived in remote rural areas and small communities and most did not travel as far from home for éducation or work. Consequently, many could not find a suitable partner within their home communities. Others entered religious orders that required celibacy, a choice that might have been made by some women who preferred a career over marriage and children. In addition, two world wars, by killing thousands of young men, created a shortage of eligible males, and some women could not be satisfied marrying anyone else after losing their fiancé.

Generally, marriage and child-rearing are encouraged by family, friends, and state officials because they are seen as synonymous with maturity, heterosexual identity, and social responsibility. In addition, marriage and reproduction are thought to help individuals retain permanent employment, remain law-abiding, and develop stable relationships and communities. In early settler societies such as Canada, the United States, Australia, and New Zealand, unmarried men were viewed as a threat to community life because they had higher rates than married men of heavy drinking, gambling, and other anti-social activities (Bradbury, 2005). Sexually active but unmarried women were assumed to threaten family values, although at the same time chaste women were stigmatized as virginal, unwanted, and limited in their life experiences. Ironically, single women in the nineteenth century had more legal rights and better employment opportunities than married women, even though their occupational advancement and social freedom were restricted more than men's. However, legal marriage and child-rearing continue to provide respectability and social status both to men and to women, and to encourage them to spend more time at home within their nuclear families.

Nevertheless, living alone has become easier in the twenty-first century, with urban facilities, household labour-saving devices, greater autonomy and freedom given to those living outside marriage, and more women earning their own living. Single individuals typically experience different lifestyles from married people. They are more likely to rent than to own their home, to eat out in restaurants, to travel abroad, and to seek entertainment outside the home. At the same time, unmarried men and women tend to maintain closer relationships with their parents and siblings than married people, who are often preoccupied with their spouse and children (Connidis, 1989: 40).

Single women also experience more stable career patterns and higher earnings than married women (Beaujot, 2000). This reflects the fact that single women tend to acquire more formal education and less often take employment leave, as married women more often do in order to move with a husband's job or to raise children. Nevertheless, compared to single men, unmarried women seldom achieve such high-status or well-paid positions as men, who tend to receive their education in different fields, to achieve more prestigious positions, and to receive higher pay than women. Even when they remain single, females are less likely to be encouraged by their bosses and family to excel in paid work, and employment practices often assume that men are more committed or qualified (O'Connor et al., 1999).

Although singleness among women has been associated with higher levels of education and occupational success, singleness among men has been related to lower education and lower employment rates than for married men (Glick, 1984; Scanzoni and Scanzoni, 1988: 208). This suggests that remaining single permits both men and women to follow atypical gender paths. For women, this may mean uninterrupted careers, but for men, opting out of marriage reduces their obligations to earn money to support a family. This offers men more opportunities for leisure pursuits, part-time work, career changes, retraining, or continuing education.

At all periods in time some single men and women have remained celibate, such as those who join certain religious orders or live in remote areas, but we can no longer assume that never-married people refrain from intimacy and sexual activity. Some single people engage in covert relationships, attempting to protect themselves from the risk of public disapproval because their partner is gay or lesbian or married to someone else. However, most single people introduce their sexual partners to family as well as friends, even though these people might mistakenly see these relationships as a prelude to marriage.

Some unmarried people have a series of intimate relationships throughout their lives but never settle into long-term cohabitation. This might represent an attempt to create a life free from domestic responsibilities or could indicate problems with maintaining intimate relationships. Others live in marriage-like relationships but never legally marry. Official statistics tend to blur these distinctions when they label people as 'never married', but some governments are now gathering separate statistics for cohabiting couples. This permits researchers to search for differences between singles who cohabit and those who do not, as well as between cohabiters and married people. However, it will still be difficult to distinguish between those living alone who are celibate and those with active sex lives.

In self-report studies, single people used to report lower levels of life satisfaction than married people (Glenn and Weaver, 1988), although this may be changing as the attitude towards singleness becomes more positive. In the 1970s, single women tended to rate themselves as less happy than married women, but unmarried men scored the lowest (Bernard, 1972). A recent American study indicated that unmarried men reported more health problems and lower levels of well-being, and showed that statistically these unmarried men experienced higher premature death rates than married men and than all women (Waite, 2005). These data suggest either that some unhealthy, unhappy, and anti-social men never marry or that the institution of marriage is particularly beneficial to men.

Single people who initially expected to marry usually accept their circumstances and are able to create a satisfying lifestyle outside marriage by the time they reach mid-life. Remaining single or childless is often said to bring loneliness in later life, but single people often remain socially active, retain close contact with siblings and parents, travel widely, and belong to more clubs and organizations than married people (Connidis, 1989: 40). Furthermore, single lifestyles are more socially acceptable now than they used to be, as the age of marriage has increased, marriage rates have declined, separation and divorce rates remain high, and cohabitation has become more prevalent (Sarantakos, 1996: 64–5). In addition, same-sex networks and singles organizations offer social support for those living outside family households. These factors contribute to raising the quality of life for singles and create more public acceptance of non-family lifestyles.

With age, friends and relatives usually give up trying to 'marry off' their single friends and never-married people learn how to reply to questioning remarks about their single status. Many have developed networks of friends in similar circumstances, who normalize living alone and emphasize the lifestyle advantages, such as higher disposable incomes (for men), more opportunities to travel, time to devote to career (for women), and spontaneity in leisure pursuits. Pressure to marry and bear children tends to lessen after people pass the age when their cohort has married, and especially after women reach menopause.

High levels of life satisfaction are related to perceptions of social support and maintaining intimate relationships, which are the same for everyone regardless of their sexual preference or marital status. Married people can be lonely, lack trust in their partner, have few friends, and experience little social support. Generally, single people are forced to become more gregarious than married people and many have developed a wider network of acquaintances and friends. Nevertheless, considerable social pressure is still placed on them to marry, even in later life. Well-meaning married friends and relatives sometimes treat them as less fortunate, lonely, or in need of matchmaking, and these attitudes and pressures reduce their life satisfaction.

CONCLUSION

In today's urban society, living outside marriage is increasingly feasible and desirable, although two incomes can certainly purchase a better living standard, especially when one is earned by a man. Nevertheless, remaining single has become easier with urban apartment living and household labour-saving devices. Full-time employees can now save time with 'fast food', same-day dry cleaning and laundry service, 'hire a hubby' or handyman services, housecleaning services, dishwashers, vacuum cleaners, microwave ovens, and automatic banking machines. In addition, liberal social and sexual attitudes and more effective birth control have enabled more people to enjoy a satisfying sexual life outside traditional marriage. However, less than 10 per cent of people avoid marriage altogether.

Most young people, especially those living in smaller communities and rural areas, expect to find a partner, establish a household together, and produce children; but the timing of these events still depends on their gender, their educational attainment, social class background, and culture. Women still marry at younger ages than men, to men slightly older than themselves, and this age gap grows larger with subsequent marriages. In some cultural communities, women are encouraged to marry well before the median national marriage age, especially if they are immigrants from countries that prefer arranged marriages.

Post-secondary education has become more important in finding permanent work, and those who prolong their education usually remain at home with their parents longer than early school leavers. Young people who find steady work earlier also tend to leave home, cohabit, marry, and reproduce at younger ages. However, more young people from low-income families now attend university with scholarships and loans, and more women graduate from university and move into professional or business positions. Nevertheless, educational and occupational choices are still influenced by gendered and cultural notions of appropriate work (Nelson and Robinson, 1999: 236) as well as by class-based aspirations and opportunities.

The distinction between being 'married' and 'never married' has been blurred in recent years by more liberal sexual behaviour and the practice of cohabiting without a legal ceremony. The social and legal importance of marriage will probably continue to subside as living arrangements are seen more as personal choices than as sacraments or unions regulated by religion or government. In the next chapter, we will examine more closely the differences between cohabitation and legal marriage.

SUMMARY

Over the decades, young people have been given more freedom to choose their intimate partners, although parental and social expectations persist in regard to the social and economic significance of legal marriage, who is an appropriate partner, and the importance of public commitment. The chapter also relates changes in sexual behaviour and dating practices to improvements in birth control, the changing status of women, and media representations about sexuality.

Questions for Critical Thought

1. Discuss the social regulation of courtship before World War II.
2. What influences our current choices of intimate partners? What patterns are evident in choices of whom to marry?
3. Has the single life become more socially acceptable since the 1970s? If so, why?

Suggested Readings

Jamieson, Lynn. 1998. *Intimacy: Personal Relationships in Modern Societies*. Cambridge: Polity Press. Jamieson examines the research on families to question the thesis that relationships in 'postmodern' society now involve more sharing of our innermost selves. She concludes that intimate relationships are still fundamentally shaped by power, gender, and economic considerations.

Ward, Peter. 1990. *Courtship, Love, and Marriage in Nineteenth-Century English Canada*. Montreal and Kingston: McGill-Queen's University Press. Through analysis of letters, diaries, and public records, Ward shows that courtship and marriage in nineteenth-century English Canada were influenced by social, institutional, and family constraints.

Wilson, Sue J. 2005. 'Partnering, Cohabitation and Marriage', in M. Baker, ed., *Families: Changing Trends in Canada*, 5th edn. Toronto: McGraw-Hill Ryerson, 145–62. This chapter describes the way that people develop intimate relationships, noting changes in sexual behaviour, dating patterns, and cohabitation as well as practices within legal marriage.

Suggested Website

Centre for Research on Families and Relationships
www.crfr.ac.uk
This consortium of researchers in the United Kingdom is based at the University of Edinburgh. Their website contains information about current research projects.

Chapter 3

Cohabitation and Marriage

Learning Objectives
- To understand why more people are choosing to cohabit without legal marriage.
- To trace changes in the meaning of marriage for specific categories of people.
- To explore research findings about trends in commitment, marital satisfaction, and the durability of marriage.

CHAPTER OUTLINE

This chapter discusses the rise in heterosexual cohabitation, especially among young adults, and growing acceptance of same-sex unions. It also traces changes in the meaning of legal marriage, and discusses various cultural practices in marriage as well as the 'quality' of marriage.

INTRODUCTION

In this chapter, I investigate several theoretical arguments and numerous research findings about the changing nature of cohabitation and legal marriage. We need to understand if patterns of commitment, domestic work, child-bearing, and relationship stability differ between these two types of 'marriage'. We want to know how much social change has actually occurred over past decades in both heterosexual and same-sex marriages, and whether cohabiting relationships are as gendered as legal marriage. If responsibilities and workloads differ between male and female partners, what impact does this have on the quality and stability of family relationships as well as patterns of paid work and leisure among men and women?

The British sociologist Anthony Giddens (1992) argued that intimacy in postmodern society has been transformed, partly by the separation of sexual activity from reproduction, and this transformation holds the potential for the radical democratization of heterosexual relationships. In response to this claim, numerous scholars, such as Bittman and Pixley (1997) and Jamieson (1998), have argued that more people may *want* intimate and egalitarian marriages but there is little empirical evidence that heterosexual relationships substantially differ in this respect from a few decades ago. For example, Bittman and Pixley's Australian research contended that the gap is actually growing between our expectations of intimacy and the reality of everyday family life. They argue (as I do) that we have raised our expectations but that the gendered inequalities in domestic life and labour markets often impede and frustrate people's craving for intimacy and self-fulfillment. Let us examine some of these arguments further by investigating the nature of cohabitation.

COHABITATION AMONG HETEROSEXUAL COUPLES

Cohabiting relationships or 'consensual unions' have recently become more prevalent and socially acceptable in many Western industrialized countries. Because many governments did not report them in their official statistics until the 1980s, it is difficult to measure longer-term trends. However, we know that cohabiting couples in Canada have increased from 6.3 per cent of all couples in the early 1980s to 14 per cent in 2001, but many more couples cohabit at some stage in their lives (Wu, 2000: 50; Statistics Canada, 2002a). Australian statistics indicate that cohabiting couples have increased from 4 per cent of all couples in 1982 to 12.4 per cent in 2001 and that 72 per cent of couples who married in 2001 had previously cohabited (Dempsey and De Vaus, 2004). Baxter et al. (2005) noted that the percentage of Australians cohabiting at some stage in their lives has increased from 17 per cent to 60 per cent in the last 30 years.

The increase in cohabitation rates is linked to many factors. Improvements in birth control have enabled couples to have sexual intercourse without becoming pregnant. More employment opportunities for women have reduced the importance of legal marriage for their financial security. The declining influence of organized religion and the growth of individualism have encouraged couples to follow their own choices rather than social conventions or expectations. The prevalence of consensual unions varies cross-nationally, which also suggests that these rates are influenced by laws, policies, and cultural values.

Cohabitation is more prevalent among younger people than older couples, as Table 3.1 notes, possibly suggesting some degree of generational change. Jane Lewis (2003) noted that in 1996, consensual unions formed 2 per cent of all unions in Italy and 27 per cent in Sweden, but among 16–29 year olds the rates were 9 per cent in Italy and 73 per cent in Sweden. Cohabitation rates also vary by jurisdictions within some countries. In Canada, for example, about 34 per cent of all women start their conjugal life through cohabitation but the figure reached 70 per cent within the province of Quebec (Statistics Canada, 2002b). Le Bourdais and Lapierre-Adamcyk (2004) argue that cohabitation in Quebec, as in Sweden, is nearly indistinguishable from marriage while in the rest of Canada it is still accepted predominantly as a childless phase in conjugal life, as is the case in the United States. Most Canadian cohabiters eventually marry although demographers predict that this will be less likely in the future. Three-quarters of those aged 30 to 39 in 2001 are expected to marry at some point in their lives but 90 per cent of 50- to 69-year-olds are currently

Table 3.1   Percentage of Canadian Population Aged 15 and Over Living in a
Common-Law Relationship, by Age

Age Group	% Living Common-Law
15–19	1.4
20–24	13.1
25–29	20.6
30–34	17.5
35–39	14.6
40–44	12.0
45–49	9.8
50–54	7.9
55–59	6.3
60–64	4.4
65–69	1.7
All age groups	9.5

Source: VIF (2004: 24), adapted from Statistics Canada, 'Marriage Status of Canadians, 2001 Census', *2001 Census of Population*, Catalogue no. 97F0004XCB01040.

married (Statistics Canada, 2002b). This suggests that there could be a substantial decline in the percentage of legally married couples in Canada in the future. As we saw in Table 1.1, there has already been a sharp decline in legal marriage with the rise in consensual unions.

Cohabiting relationships used to be viewed as temporary arrangements, but as they become more prevalent they look more like marriages. It is not always evident which couples are legally married and which are cohabiting unless you gain personal knowledge about them. They may refer to their 'partner' even when that person is actually a legal spouse. Some cohabiting women wear a ring on the fourth finger of their left hand, like a wedding band, while some married women wear no wedding ring and retain their maiden name. If we knew more about these people we might discover that some cohabiting couples share bank accounts while some married couples keep their money separate. Despite these similarities, researchers have found important statistical differences between the two types of relationships.

The first difference between cohabitation and legal marriage relates to the relative instability of consensual unions, especially among young people (Wu, 2000; Bradbury and Norris, 2005). Statistics Canada reports that first **common-law relationships** are twice as likely to end in separation as first marriages, but that first unions of younger couples are more likely to end in separation than those of older couples, regardless of whether they are married or cohabiting (Statistics Canada, 2002b). Furthermore, legal marriages preceded by cohabitation have slightly higher rates of dissolution compared to legal marriages in which couples did not cohabit before the wedding (Beaujot, 2000). This suggests that one reason for the relative instability of cohabitation relates to the youthfulness of people who typically live in these arrangements, but also that cohabiters may differ in some ways from those who never cohabit.

In statistical studies, cohabiting partners are more likely to report no religious affiliation and to have been previously divorced (Wu, 2000). Dempsey and De Vaus (2004) found that Australian cohabiters recorded in the 1996 and 2001 censuses included more men than women, more people with Anglo backgrounds, fewer Asian immigrants, and fewer people reporting a religious affiliation. Baxter (2002) noted that Australian women in cohabiting relationships were more likely than married women to be employed full-time, to have fewer or no children, and to expect an egalitarian division of labour. Baxter et al. (2005) also showed that cohabiting men do more housework than married men, while cohabiting women do less housework than their married counterparts. Although cohabiters are found to be less conventional than legal spouses, the differences between the two groups have been diminishing in recent years (Beaujot, 2000).

The dramatic increase of cohabitation among young people has prompted sociologists to ask whether this type of relationship merely represents a new form of 'courtship' or whether it signals a fundamental change in commitment or attitudes about marriage. Interpreting cohabitation as a new form of courtship may seem less dangerous from the viewpoint of social conservatives because it predicts that these couples will eventually marry as they mature. If cohabitation actually represents a more fundamental societal change, it may signify a diminishing respect for the church and state and increased emphasis on free choice in personal life, which would predict greater instability in future family relationships. These *are* fundamental societal changes that require some social adjustments, such as policy reform and new social services.

Researchers have also identified a new kind of relationship they are calling 'living apart together' (LAT). Couples in these relationships may be married but most would be cohabiting, spending allocated days together at regular intervals, such as weekends or holidays, but living apart the rest of the time, sometimes working in different locations. Although figures are unavailable for Canada, about 6 per cent of 35–44-year-old women in France and over 10 per cent of 25–34-year-old women in Austria report being in such a relationship (González-López, 2002). Although some male workers have always worked far away from their homes, especially forestry workers, sailors, and soldiers, more middle-class professional women are now commuting as well. This indicates that living arrangements are becoming more varied but also suggests that employment opportunities continue to influence family formation.

THE RISE IN SAME-SEX COHABITATION

The rise in cohabitation also includes an increase in same-sex couples living openly together, although the official numbers still remain very small. Statistics Canada (2002a) estimates that 0.5 per cent of couple households contain same-sex partners, but this includes only those who report their status to the census-takers and only those living in stable relationships. Some individuals who regularly have same-sex relationships live alone while others may identify as bisexuals and live in heterosexual marriages. American studies suggest that about 3 per cent of American men and less than 2 per cent of American women report that their sexual partners are exclusively of the same sex (Laumann et al., 1994; Black et al., 2000; Ambert, 2005).

In addition, Black et al. (2000) estimated that 30 per cent of gay men and 46 per cent of lesbian women had previously been married to heterosexual partners.

Are heterosexual and same-sex couples who share a home different in significant ways? In an Australian study, Sarantakos (1998) found that many of the gay and lesbian couples he studied did not differ significantly from heterosexual couples although they displayed less allegiance to **monogamy** and permanent relationships and less conventionality in sexual identity. Patterson (2000) found that same-sex couples who share a household in the United States report a more egalitarian division of labour than married heterosexual couples. In the American research by Kurdeck (1998, 2001), gay couples reported more autonomy in their activities, friendships, and decision-making than heterosexual married couples. They also reported less approval of their relationships from their birth families, lower levels of commitment between the couple, and higher rates of relationship dissolution than heterosexual couples.

Ambert (2005) reports a number of American studies that indicate gay men show less commitment to monogamy than either lesbians or heterosexual couples. She also reveals that cohabiting heterosexual partners showed less commitment to monogamy than married partners, although women are more monogamous than men. Another useful comparison in these studies is between same-sex couples and heterosexual cohabiters, as they also report lower commitment than married couples.

Some same-sex couples are happy to share a home without any legal recognition, but this means that if one partner is rushed to the hospital, the other might not have any visiting privileges if he or she is not legally defined as a 'spouse' or a 'family member'. If the couple has children, the other partner may not be seen as a 'parent' by school officials or by a family doctor. In many countries, same-sex couples have been fighting for certain forms of legal recognition, including acknowledgement as a 'spouse', permission to marry, and equal access to assisted reproduction services, child-fostering, and adoption (McNair et al., 2002; Weeks, 2002). As we will see in the next section, these issues remain controversial and have generated strong opposition from some religious groups and social conservatives.

THE SOCIAL AND POLICY IMPLICATIONS OF INCREASED COHABITATION

The rise in consensual unions has given policy-makers cause for considerable debate. First, they have had to decide whether these relationships should be considered similar to or different from legal marriage in terms of spousal entitlements and obligations during the relationship (Wu, 2000). One entitlement we mentioned is to be considered 'next of kin' if the partner is in an accident or in hospital. Another is to be eligible as a beneficiary to the partner's health insurance plan or retirement benefits. Second, if couples separate acrimoniously and ask the courts to divide their shared assets, should the state proceed in the same manner as for legal marriages? In many countries, legal reforms already require the equal division of family assets when marriage partners separate, unless doing so would create inequity or unfairness, but this legislation does not necessarily cover cohabiting couples.

Although some cohabiting couples have been demanding more rights, others want to keep their own personal arrangements outside any legal requirements. They may see cohabitation as a private choice that involves less commitment, fewer obligations to their partner or his/her kin group, a less gendered division of labour, and the option to leave without complications when the relationship is no longer mutually beneficial (Barber and Axinn, 1998; Elizabeth, 2000). Alternatively, they may see no practical advantage to legalizing their relationship or they may believe that the church and state have no right to intervene in their sexual or personal lives. The lack of legal protection, however, has sometimes left female partners with few assets and little income after separation. This is especially relevant for a cohabiting couple with children, where one partner has supported the family financially while the other (usually the woman) has provided unpaid domestic services and child care. If the relationship ends, these mothers and children could become impoverished unless the fathers continued to support them, the mothers were able to find paid work, or the state supplemented their incomes.

Some governments have resolved these issues by deeming heterosexual couples to be 'married' in terms of their rights, responsibilities, and the division of their joint assets after living together for a specified time (usually between one and three years, depending on the jurisdiction). If partners do not wish to divide their property upon future separation according to the same rules as married couples, early in their live-in relationship they become obligated to sign a legal contract to specify alternative arrangements. However, all states agree that parents must support any children they produce, whether or not they are legally married to their partners or living with the children.

Some countries or jurisdictions have recently changed their laws and regulations about these issues, while others continue to debate them. A number of jurisdictions have created a new category of relationship called a **civil union**, which provides some legal recognition and limited rights for cohabiting couples who are either same-sex or heterosexual. Civil unions may not share all of the same rights as legal marriage, but their creation represents a political compromise that offers some legal protection while respecting the traditional idea that marriage is a legal partnership between a man and a woman (Moore, 2003). Other jurisdictions have simply allowed same-sex couples the same marriage rights as heterosexual couples enjoy.

Belgium and the Netherlands legalized civil unions in 2001 (Arie, 2003). In 2003, the Canadian government drafted legislation to permit **same-sex marriage** but the legality of this bill was immediately challenged and sent to the Supreme Court of Canada, which unanimously determined in December 2004 that the federal government has the right to redefine marriage to include same-sex couples. This meant that federal and provincial laws and regulations could be amended, and the federal Civil Marriages Act of July 2005 formally legalized same-sex marriage. Stephen Harper's minority Conservative government, elected in January 2006, promised a free vote in the House of Commons on same-sex marriage, with the intent of either reversing the 2005 Act or satisfying its social conservative base. New Zealand's Civil Union Bill was introduced by the Labour-led government and passed in December 2004 with considerable opposition from religious groups and the (conservative) National Party. This law enables heterosexual or same-sex couples to register their unions with the state and acquire partnership rights, which includes being considered 'next of kin' if one partner is admitted to a hospital. In return, they would be considered legal partners for purposes of income tax, support obligations, or social benefits, but not legally married 'spouses' with automatic property rights or adoption rights.

The fight for civil unions has been led mainly by social reformers who argue that human rights are violated when long-term same-sex relationships are not acknowledged or respected by the state or employers. However, legalizing same-sex unions has been strongly opposed by a number of religious groups, including the Catholic Church and fundamentalist Christians as well as other social conservatives. Opponents tend to view civil unions and same-sex relationships as threatening to the institution of marriage, to public morality, to Biblical teachings, to stable patterns of reproduction and socialization, and/or to the norm of heterosexuality.

The rise in cohabitation is perceived by social conservatives as a negative trend, but having children outside legal marriage is considered a potential problem of greater proportions. In most Western industrialized countries, more babies are born outside legal marriage now than in earlier decades, although most are born to cohabiting couples. This dramatic increase in births outside marriage worries some policymakers because the lower stability rates of these relationships could have negative implications for the upbringing of children. In Canada, 31 per cent of live births in 2001 were to women who were not legally married, compared to 9 per cent in 1975 and 4 per cent in 1960 (VIF, 2004, 2000, 1994). Notable provincial differences are apparent in these statistics, with a high of 58 per cent of births outside marriage in Quebec and a low of 13 per cent in Ontario in 2002 (VIF, 2004: 48). The vast majority of these children are born to couples in their twenties and thirties who are living in non-legal relationships. Cohabiting couples who have produced children tend to have more stable relationships than younger childless couples (Wu, 1996).

When more couples enter consensual unions, relationships typically become less stable at the national level (Beck-Gernsheim, 2002). If these relationships are unprotected legally, separations could lead to disputes about how assets should be divided, whether financial support should be paid, and where any children born to the couple should live. Cohabiting fathers have a higher probability of separating from their partners than married fathers and subsequently of losing contact with their children. Goldscheider and Kaufman (1996) argued that although cohabitation usually represents a lower level of commitment to relationships, it also means that men are more likely than women to reduce their commitment to children. A father who is not living with his children can have a positive influence on them if he is involved, but the tenuous relationship with the mother on issues of parenting can also bring conflict into the children's lives. Goldscheider and Kaufman argued that more research is needed on the impact on children of parents' commitment to each other.

In a qualitative study in the United Kingdom, Lewis (1999) found that cohabiting and married parents both said that they made commitments to each other and to their children. However, the commitments of cohabiting couples tended to be private, while the married ones were public. The younger generation of parents talked about commitments as personal issues that were internally driven, whereas their own parents talked more about obligations that were externally imposed. Jamieson et al. (2002) found that legal marriage was seen as irrelevant to commitment by many Scottish young people (ages 20–9 years), although some saw marriage as important for children.

Cohabiting women are more likely than legally married women to be employed full-time (Baxter, 2002), which suggests they are more likely to have the financial resources to leave an unhappy relationship. Although some cohabiting relationships last a lifetime, most end in separation or legal marriage. One interesting question relates to why so many of the couples who decide to stay together eventually marry when there appear to be diminishing differences between cohabitation and marriage? Also, why do some cohabiting couples who subsequently marry arrange wedding ceremonies that retain many of the conventional symbols of traditional (patriarchal) marriage? We will try to answer these questions in the next section by providing some historical background on social and legal changes in marriage.

THE CHANGING MEANING OF MARRIAGE

Despite the increasing similarities between cohabitation and legal marriage, they are still perceived as different by many people, especially lawyers, government officials, parents, and older relatives. Legal marriage is seen as a public, long-term commitment to another person, with accompanying legal rights and obligations, while cohabitation is more likely to be seen as a transitional status involving relatively lower levels of commitment. Although many cohabiting couples make private commitments to each other, decisions to marry after a period of cohabitation might signal a desire to make a public commitment before parents and friends and to celebrate this important decision and transition (Lewis, 1999; Pryor, 2005).

A decision to legally marry might also represent a desire to produce children together with assurance that they will be considered 'legitimate' by their grandparents and other relatives as well as by the law. In addition, marriage after cohabitation could represent an attempt to gain legal protection in case of guardianship problems with children, of illness or disability that could draw on the partner's insurance, or of inheritance problems if one partner dies prematurely leaving a former spouse. Some of these issues seem more relevant for older people, which may partly explain why they are more likely than younger couples to legally marry.

Historically, both the church and the state viewed marriage as an economic and sexual partnership between husbands and wives that involved mutual dependency in the common endeavours of earning a living and raising children (Funder and Harrison, 1993). Particularly in agrarian and cottage industry-based economies of the eighteenth and nineteenth centuries, marriage was critical for economic and social survival. Both men and women typically worked long hours and needed a partner (or at least another household member) to help grow and prepare food, to make shelter and clothing, to protect and care for the home, to raise children, to earn money for household purchases, and to care for them when sick or frail.

Christian beliefs and practices required that the community, as well as the church, recognize potential marriage partners as 'legitimate' both in Europe and in the European colonies overseas (Baker, 2001b). This meant that marriage partners had to be legal adults, could not be close family members, and could not be simultaneously married to someone else. Colonial settlers could easily leave spouses behind in Europe or Britain but the church (and later the state) presided over wedding ceremonies to ensure that unions were legal and officially registered. In early Christian doctrine, the status of marriage had already been elevated from a private contract between individuals to a religious sacrament deemed to be indissoluble and beyond the scope of human will or law (Fletcher, 1973). Marriage contracts, unlike business contracts, were seen as sacred or blessed by God, and lasting until the death of one partner.

Among the early Europeans who settled in North America, Australia, and New Zealand, legal marriage was not as widespread as it later became in the twentieth century (Funder and Harrison, 1993; Baker, 2001b). The early fur traders in Canada, for example, created liaisons with indigenous women, who helped them survive in a harsh environment and provided them with the protection of their own kin group, sexual relations, companionship, and a temporary home and community. Yet these relationships seldom led to legal marriage, as the men often moved on. Even when European men legalized their marriages with indigenous women, the children of these unions were not always accepted as social equals in the European community (Bradbury, 2005).

The roots of marriage laws in English-speaking jurisdictions are found in English **common law**, while the French **civil code** provides the basis for family law in the Canadian province of Quebec. Under both these legal systems, the husband and father retained authority over his wife and children, and a wife had the legal status of a minor child. Women did not acquire political or civil rights until late in the nineteenth century—or later, in some jurisdictions—and a married woman could not sell or acquire her own property, but was expected to depend on her husband to control it for her. By today's standards, these colonial marriage laws were definitely sexist, but they were also Eurocentric, largely ignoring the traditional customs of the various tribes of indigenous people (Baker, 2001b: 183). Some of these tribes arranged marriages, used matrilineal marriage systems, accepted a less gendered division of labour between marriage partners, and were the guardians of tribal property rather than the owners of family land.

Early English common law viewed marriage as a heterosexual and gendered work partnership but not a partnership of work equals. A wife tacitly agreed to provide her husband with sexual intercourse, children, and domestic services in return for a home, protection, and economic support. Marriage was based on the public claim that marital roles were complementary but equal, although legal evidence indicates that the courts did not equally value women's unpaid contribution to marriage upon divorce (Funder, 1996; Greenwood, 1999).

The man was considered the head of the household under English common law, representing the family's interests to the larger community and making major decisions such as where they would live and at what living standard. Until the nineteenth

and early twentieth centuries, husbands also controlled their wives' income and property, voted on their behalf, and retained guardianship of any children resulting from
the marriage. Women gained the legal right to vote in national elections in New
Zealand in 1893, in Australia in 1902, and in Canada in 1918; but in Quebec, married
women were not permitted to vote in provincial elections until 1940 or to become the
legal guardians of their own children until 1964 (Baker, 2001b: 183).

During the Christian wedding ceremony, a woman used to promise to 'love,
honour, and obey' her husband while he promised to 'love, honour, and cherish' her
(ibid., 186). Until the 1960s, a Canadian husband had the right to establish the
couple's legal residence or 'domicile' and he was expected to provide his wife with
the 'necessities of life'; but the husband had the right to decide what was necessary
(Dranoff, 1977: 25). In contrast, a wife was expected to live wherever her husband
chose to live, maintain their household, care for their children, and be sexually available when he wanted. In recognition of these services, women were entitled to
'dower rights' or the right to one-third of his property under common law should
the marriage dissolve. In civil law, the wife could retain the property brought into
the marriage, but her husband controlled it for her. In both forms of European law,
the marital roles of men and women differed.

Growing dissatisfaction with the restrictions of marriage encouraged some
spouses to separate, and by the 1960s more couples were applying for divorces.
Backlogs of applications and concern about the outcomes for children and about
gender inequalities provided a strong impetus for divorce reform, including laws
relating to child support and custody. In the 1960s, divorce was legally complicated
but reformers had successfully argued that the marriage contract could be broken
with proof of a 'matrimonial fault' or a violation of the marriage contract. This
usually meant providing proof of 'adultery', but grounds were extended to physical
cruelty, to imprisonment for a specified period, to homosexual acts, and later to
'marriage breakdown'. Now, in many countries, marriages can be dissolved by
mutual consent, provided that partners sign legal documents to verify irretrievable
marriage breakdown. More details of these reforms are discussed in Chapter 6.

Marriage vows have also been modified since the 1960s. Few brides now promise to obey the groom and many couples marry outside a church or registry office.
The state has also certified marriage commissioners or celebrants, judges, justices of
the peace, and clerks of the court to carry out official marriage ceremonies, although
in 2001 Canadian clergy officiated at 82 per cent of first marriages and 66 per cent
of remarriages (VIF, 2004: 31). Weddings can now take place almost anywhere at any
time. A wedding industry has developed in which private companies attempt to
make a profit from helping couples to plan elaborate, unique, exotic, romantic, and
expensive weddings. The average cost of a traditional marriage, including a wedding
trip, has increased significantly in the past 50 years.

Although legal marriage is still portrayed as an important 'rite of passage', sig-
nifying maturity, responsibility, public commitment, and legitimacy, legal marriage
rates continue to fall in many countries. The decreasing social and legal distinctions
between marriage and cohabitation and the perceived instability of marriage clearly
inhibit some couples. In addition, low-income couples sometimes feel that they

cannot afford the type of idealized wedding they see in the media. They may postpone the legal ceremony until they save sufficient funds for a wedding celebration and trip, to buy a house, or until they stabilize their relationship, even when they already share a home and bear children together (Edin and Reed, 2005). For many of these couples, the wedding is postponed until it is too late, as the relationship has already dissolved. Edin and Reed's recent research (2005) suggests that the legal wedding has become an ideal but unattainable symbol of commitment, respectability, and prosperity for an increasing number of low-income couples in the United States.

CULTURAL PRACTICES IN MARRIAGE

All societies create rules about who is permitted to marry, who are preferred marriage partners, when the wedding should take place, what gifts are exchanged, who organizes and finances the celebrations, and where the new bride and groom should live. These rules may be cultural customs or traditions, but sometimes are written into law. For example, all societies develop rules against marrying close relatives (called 'incest taboos') in order to prevent inbreeding and congenital abnormalities in offspring and to limit conflict and jealousy within kin groups. In Western countries, parents, siblings, and (usually) first cousins are not permitted to marry and incest taboos include some relatives by marriage and adoption. In addition, people in Western or Christian countries are allowed to marry only one partner at a time although most states (but not all religious institutions) permit remarriage after legal divorce.

In many cultures, romantic love and sexual attraction are considered to be inadequate reasons for sharing a home and elder family members arrange marriages before young people have an opportunity to fall in love with an 'inappropriate' partner. In the Muslim Middle Eastern and African countries and parts of Indonesia and Pakistan, parents and older relatives feel that they are more qualified than young people to make these important family decisions that are expected to last a lifetime. Marriage is not about a personal or sexual attraction between the two individuals but instead is seen as an alliance between two families, designed to maintain and enhance their resources and reputation. It is a social institution for reproduction, child-rearing, and continuing the family line. Elder family members of either the bride or groom may make the initial inquiries and intermediaries sometimes help parents find suitable partners for their children. These intermediaries may be relatives, family friends, acquaintances with an extensive network of contacts, or professional marriage brokers who charge a fee for service (Baker, 2001b).

In arranged marriage systems, several potential partners might be identified, including the offspring of family friends. After some initial 'short-listing' by the young person and her/his parents, the best possible choice would be invited to a family meeting accompanied by his or her parents and perhaps other relatives. The potential partners would usually have a chance to meet, to talk with each other, and to see if they could feasibly develop a relationship leading to marriage. If the meeting does not progress well, another candidate might be interviewed with his or her family. When a match looks possible, the two families would meet again to discuss the future, to negotiate gifts and wedding expenses, and to make concrete plans for the wedding.

Box 3.1 A Personal View of Arranged Marriages

As an Indian-born immigrant living in New Zealand, I accepted the Western idea of free-choice marriage: falling in love, developing a relationship, and living together before marriage. Yet where I come from (Indian Muslim upper-middle-class background), such a concept is considered immoral and opposite to the way a relationship should progress.

In arranged marriages, two families with a marriageable son or daughter send out 'feelers' into the community through their social networks. This is usually through an *ism navesi* or personal resumé consisting of the qualifications and physical attributes of the man and woman as well as the names of parents, uncles, aunts and their occupations, qualifications and even property ownership. This forms the basis of the first screening and is done without personal meetings to avoid a 'loss of face' if an alliance does not materialize. Once the screening is completed, the family elders meet and 'size up' the other party for marriage compatibility. The prospective bride and groom are then introduced to each other and, if all goes well, become engaged. After several meetings and gift exchanges, they are married in a ceremony that symbolizes the union of two families rather than two individuals.

When I turned 20, my grandmother from India enthusiastically undertook the responsibility of finding me a husband. Until then, my life revolved around a government job and university study while my parents worked in Australia. Some of my friends had Indian backgrounds but others were New Zealanders with European, Maori, and Pacific Island backgrounds. My girlfriends and I regularly discussed heterosexual relationships and were open to the possibility of finding the 'right man'.

Once I turned 20, I began receiving *ism navesis* and photos of young men by e-mail and normal mail, accompanied by a letter or phone call from India from my grandmother, uncle, or aunt eliciting my feedback. At first I found the process humorous but also puzzling. How was I supposed to guess a man's virtue or suitability from a photograph or resumé? My friends and I used to discuss the man's attributes before dismissing them for real or imagined incompatibilities. I didn't think the process would come to much, given the unlikelihood that 'suitors' would be sent to meet me in Auckland.

One day they sent a photograph of a 28-year-old man with a university degree, who ran a computer training institute in India, and who I had met as a child because he was the son of my grandmother's cousin. The photo showed a man sitting on a sofa wearing an intense expression and for once I was unable to find any reasons to reject him. I reluctantly agreed to accept his phone call and one call led to another and then to an on-line chat. However, within six months our wedding date had been set in India. The news shocked me because unconsciously I was still expecting a romantic relationship to develop first. When I spoke to my uncle about how sudden it all seemed and how I was unprepared to go through with a wedding, he was aghast at my concept of a developing relationship and my Western ideas seemed quite foreign to him.

This conversation led to weeks of family pressure about how I would bring 'dishonour' to my family if I didn't go through with the wedding, and would insult the man's family after they had 'given their word' for the alliance. Since I didn't have any problem with the man in question, my relatives argued, why was I opposed to marrying him? By then I understood that their version of marriage involved love and commitment growing out of marriage while in the Western version, love and commitment came first. If I agreed to marry this man, I would be committed for life without even meeting him and would have to trust the family that the marriage would work out despite the culture gap and probable differences in our expectations. If I refused to marry him, I would be insulting a family who felt they were acting in my best interests. I also realized that choosing my own partner would provide no guarantee of a happy lasting relationship.

Ten days before my wedding, I reached India and found my grandparents' sprawling home full of relatives, cooks, tailors, jewellers, and others preparing for the wedding. The next day, I met my fiancé—Ayub. It was a strange meeting to say the least. Our phone and e-mail conversations had been private but this meeting included his mother, two sisters, and three aunts. I felt like I was on display and had to gain their approval. These ladies seemed very nice but asked personal and probing questions such as: Will you work after getting married? Do you cook? What do you do in your spare time? I was shocked at the personal questions but should have realized that the relatives have the right to voice their opinions about the potential partner in an arranged marriage system. However, I never had a decent look at Ayub, nor did I meet him alone, until we were married!

The wedding was a long process involving ceremonial visits and gift exchanges. Some gifts included jewellery and ornate clothes so I didn't have much to complain about. Muslim marriages also involve a marriage contract, in which the bride (or her male representative) stipulates conditions, such as money or property, that the husband is obliged to give her in the event of separation or divorce. Once the contract is signed, the marriage is complete and a reception or feast takes place. The next hurdle is the celebration of the marriage consummation, which by Muslim law should take place as soon as possible. The rationale behind this I think is that if one finds the other lacking in some respect, then the differences could be ironed out while the guests are able to help resolve the issue.

I need not have worried because my husband was very unlike the stereotypical Indian Muslim male I expected. He was articulate, pleasant, well-read, had very balanced ideas about gender roles that matched my own, and was willing to live in New Zealand. So the result has been that despite my misgivings and my friends' doubts, my husband and I have been happily married for the last four years and have a three-year-old son. I believe now that some arrangements are made in heaven!

Source: Personal correspondence with Nargis Ali, May 2006, Auckland, New Zealand.

Immigrants living in westernized countries might encourage their young people to return home to their place of origin in order to marry a partner already selected by family members still living there. Increasingly, young people expect to exercise some personal choice over their marriage partner or at least to acquire veto rights, especially if they live abroad, have obtained a Western education, or have travelled in Western countries. However, young people may also be pressured to abide by the marriage decisions of their elders, especially if they live in remote rural areas and have little formal education.

In Asian and African countries with arranged marriage systems, parents some-times make pre-marriage agreements or even child betrothals with other parents before their children reach puberty. These arrangements, which could be initiated when the children are under the age of 10, are sometimes seen as legal contracts that cannot easily be broken without some form of compensation between families. Making such promises early in their children's lives precludes less desirable marriage choices and prevents inappropriate love or sexual attachments from developing among young people (ibid.).

In arranged marriage systems, greater importance is placed on financial secu-rity, potential heirs, and extended family solidarity than on sexual attraction or love between the bride and groom. Potential marital partners are urged to respect each other and their family's wishes, and it is hoped that love will develop after partners marry and share a home. Both families maintain a stake in marital stability, so it is not surprising that arranged marriages less often end in divorce than is the case with free-choice unions. However, in these countries, divorce is often legally restricted, sometimes making it easier for men to divorce their wives than for women to divorce their husbands. In addition, women might be motivated to make the mar-riage work if they cannot support themselves outside marriage or must forfeit child guardianship rights to the husband or his relatives in a divorce. Increasingly, young people throughout the world are encouraged to seek a more intensive and egali-tarian relationship through the influence of Western education, international travel, foreign films, popular music, the Internet, and global advertising.

In Western countries, the law requires the consent of both bride and groom before a wedding can take place. Young people usually meet their future spouse in school, at work, at community functions, or somewhere in their neighbourhood. Friends and relatives may offer assistance by introducing potential partners but individuals make their own marriage choices based on their perceptions of compat-ibility and feelings of physical attraction and love. Similar interests and cultural backgrounds are valued in partners yet other social and gendered ideas influence our decisions, as we already discussed in Chapter 2.

Despite the apparent differences between arranged marriages and free-choice marriages, decisions are influenced by some of the same considerations. In Western marriages, couples expect to marry for 'love' but at the same time people marry for a variety of reasons, including companionship, emotional stability, regular and safe sex, the desire for children, and additional financial support. Being acknowledged as an adult and establishing a separate residence from parents may also be motivations for marriage, as the wedding is still considered an adult 'rite of passage' or social acknowledgement of the attainment of adult status, even when the couple has been living together. Love can certainly develop and thrive outside legal marriage, which suggests that people in all cultures marry for more than love.

Preferred Marriage Partners and the Exchange of Gifts

Some Eastern and African cultures have established preferential marriage rules that stipulate certain categories of people as the most socially desirable partners. In southern India, the cross-cousin or the child of the mother's brother or father's sister is considered to be the most desirable marriage partner, which helps to cement together the two families (Nanda, 1991: 231). Some countries permit more than one spouse at a time (called polygamy) although the typical pattern is for men to marry more than one wife (polygyny) but not for women to take multiple husbands (polyandry). In addition, most polygamous countries do not permit men with insufficient financial resources to marry a second wife, which means that polygamy remains a status symbol for wealthier men.

In some polygamous cultures, tradition specifies that a man should marry the widow of his dead brother even if he already has a partner (ibid.). This practice, called the levirate, provides some means of support for widows in cultures that do not encourage women to earn their own living. Marriage to a wife's sister (sororate) is encouraged in other cultures, especially if the first wife is infertile or dies prematurely. These customs indicate that marriage is conceptualized as a union or alliance between kin groups rather than as an intimate relationship between individuals (ibid.).

One legal spouse at a time is the law and custom in all Western countries, where 'bigamy'—marrying two partners simultaneously—is a criminal offence. The state's requirement of a marriage licence represents an attempt to eliminate bigamy, as does the Christian tradition of 'reading the banns', i.e., announcing the forthcoming wedding in church for three consecutive Sundays to see if anyone knows of any impediment to the marriage. The waiting period between obtaining the marriage licence and celebrating the wedding ceremony may be a few days to several weeks, which is designed to discourage hasty marriages. Now that legal divorce has been made easier to obtain in many places, an increasing percentage of the population marries more than once over a lifetime, referred to as **serial monogamy**.

In cultures with arranged marriage systems, dowries have sometimes been used to attract a partner for daughters, to cement alliances between families, and to help establish new households. Dowries involve payments of money or gifts of property that accompany brides into marriage and become part of marriage agreements. Although the types of payment vary considerably, they might include household furnishings, jewels, money, servants, farm or pack animals, or land. If a woman has a large dowry, she can find a 'better' husband, which usually means one who is wealthier, healthier, better educated, and from a more respected family. In some cultures, the dowry money becomes the property of the groom's family and in others it is used to establish the bride and groom's new household. Dowries have also been used to provide brides with some measure of financial security or insurance in case of partner abuse, divorce, or widowhood, but how effective this practice is depends on how much control women have over the money or property (Barker, 2003).

In **patrilocal systems** where the bride and groom reside with his family, the dowry money would make an important contribution to the household of the groom's parents. Clearly, this system encourages families to prefer sons over daughters, because males can bring new resources into the household through marriage settlements, males can more easily support the family through employment, and they also perpetuate the family name. Consequently, female fetuses have been aborted and female children and adults have been neglected or mistreated because of the economic stresses perpetuated in the dowry system. This system penalizes families with few resources if they must provide money or property in order to secure a husband for their daughter(s) but have no or few sons to attract dowries. For these reasons, dowries have been outlawed in India, although they continue to operate clandestinely in rural areas (Nanda, 1991).

In other cultures, the groom's kin group has been expected to pay a 'bride price' to gain permission to marry the family's daughter, to establish and secure alliances, and to compensate for the bride's lost labour or child-bearing potential in her birth community (Fleising, 2003). This pattern has been more prevalent in subsistent horticultural economies (such as sub-Saharan Africa), in patrilineal societies, and in places where the bride customarily moves to the groom's community. However, dowries and bride prices are disappearing as both men and women become educated and westernized, as more people live in urban areas, and as women gain opportunities to enter the labour force and become self-supporting.

Symbolic remnants of dowries and bride prices remain in traditional free-choice marriages even in Western countries. Trousseaus or 'glory boxes' consisting of special household items and fancy clothing are still collected by some girls and/or their families for their new home, their weddings, and the 'honeymoon'. Grooms sometimes purchase expensive (most often, diamond) engagement rings to assure their fiancées' consent to marry and give (usually, gold) wedding bands during the ceremony (although sometimes both partners exchange rings). Brides and their families generally make most of the wedding arrangements and sometimes pay for the reception meal, while grooms and their families often pay for drinks at the reception and for the wedding trip.

In Western countries, traditional weddings are redolent with symbolism that harks back to traditional practices and values of previous eras. The white wedding dress represents the virginity that used to be expected of brides. The bride entering the church on the arm of her father who then 'gives her away' to the groom symbolizes the patriarchal exchange of the woman from the authority of one man to another. The throwing of rice or confetti after the ceremony represents the community's wish that the marriage will be fertile and that the couple will be blessed with many children. The sharing of the reception activities and expenses represents the joining together of two families.

Many of these traditions are fading with the rising age of marriage and opportunities to create individualized wedding ceremonies. The prevalence of remarriages among older partners means that many of the financial costs are now paid by the

bride and groom themselves rather than their parents. Although many couples eliminate some traditions from their weddings, a considerable number of couples marry
in church, brides wear white dresses and are 'given away' by their fathers, and friends
and relatives throw confetti. This may be done even when the couple doesn't attend
church, the bride is no longer a virgin and rejects patriarchal practices, and they plan
to remain child-free. These wedding practices often represent either a desire to
maintain cultural traditions or social pressure to retain some practices, regardless of
their original meanings.

Relations with Kin, Surnames, and Residence

Marriage systems sometimes require either the bride or the groom to relocate and live
with one kin group, leaving her or his own family of origin behind. Rules of patrilo-
cality and patrilineal descent require the woman to move to the community or home
of her husband's family and give priority to his kin group. The important kinship ties
are passed from father to son to grandson, which is the most prevalent pattern with
a long history in both Eastern and Western civilizations (Leslie and Korman, 1989:
48). Within this system, a wife would marry into her husband's family, and their children would become members of his kin group. With **matrilineal descent**, relationships are traced through the female line, downplaying the importance of the father's
relatives. Matrilineal descent and **matrilocality**—living with or near the bride's kin
group—were practised by some indigenous people in North America, including the
peoples of the Iroquois Confederacy at the time of European contact (Brown, 1988).

If newly married couples are considered to be equal members of both kin groups,
called **bilateral descent**, they might participate in the family activities of both the bride
and groom and could inherit from either side of the family. Both kin membership and
inheritance are based on bilateral descent in most Western countries, but among the
British upper classes, primogeniture was the rule for inheritance. This meant that the
first-born male child inherited the family home or estate and subsequent children
received an annual income or smaller amounts of family resources. This system of
inheritance maintained the integrity of large landholdings but encouraged younger
sons to move away, take on business or professional jobs, become career military offi-
cers, or emigrate. Throughout the colonies, younger sons of wealthy British families
emigrated and were known as remittance men, after the regular remittance of
allowance that was sent to them. The system also assumed that daughters would marry
and be supported by their husbands, although rich daughters often entered marriage
with private incomes from their fathers' estates. The system of primogeniture perpetuated legal inequalities that were sometimes resented by sons and daughters.

Upon marriage, surnames have traditionally passed through the male side of
the family in the English-speaking or common-law countries, although this was
often done through custom rather than law. The bride and the couple's subsequent
children took the groom's family name because he was the legal head of the household and his name symbolized their legal and social union. Most couples still maintain this pattern because it seems easier, they think it is a legal requirement, or one
name acknowledges their legal union. However, a name change may mean that
the bride loses her professional identity or acquaintances who did not know of her

marriage or her new name. In Quebec, married women are legally required to keep their birth names, although they may add their husband's surname to it, but in Ontario brides may choose either their (father's) surname or their husband's at the time of marriage (Baker, 2001b). In addition, anyone may create a new name for himself or herself by going through a legal name change or simply by adopting a new name, as long as this is not done for purposes of fraud.

Since the 1970s, more women have retained their birth name after marriage. This is sometimes a professional decision for those who want to maintain a profile with colleagues, customers, or (in the case of politicians or public performers) their followers or fans. It might also be a feminist statement about unwillingness to lose a former identity. A few women actually choose new surnames that do not relate to their father or husband. However, many women continue to take their husbands' name upon marriage, often to the surprise of professional colleagues and kin. This may involve a conscious effort to discard a difficult or unpopular name, or a public statement about being married as opposed to cohabiting, or a statement about their unity in marriage. Alternatively, some people either feel that life would be too complicated with a different name for husband, wife, and children, or they want to emphasize their new relationship or rite of passage.

Newly married couples in Western countries usually try to establish a residence apart from both kin groups after marriage, which is called a **neo-local residence**. Most young couples prefer this arrangement even if it means accepting a lower living standard and later forgoing live-in child-care services. Although many couples with European backgrounds reside with parents at some point in their marriage, especially when they are in financial difficulty, most would define this living arrangement as a temporary and undesirable hardship. However, certain cultural groups are far more likely to live in extended families, seeing this arrangement as cost-effective, a solution to child-care problems, socially desirable, and culturally appropriate.

These cultural variations indicate that all social groups create customary expectations relating to marriage and weddings, although many of them are unwritten or even unspoken. Such customs evolve over time but individuals sometimes experience family opposition when they try to ignore cultural traditions or attempt to create their own. Social pressure and the law ensure that couples intending to marry abide by at least some of these rules or practices. Although people have more choice about weddings and marriage partners than they did in the past, they still cannot marry more than one person at a time if they live in a Judeo-Christian country. The law also requires people to reach a certain age in order to marry (the age of majority) and stipulates that some potential partners are unsuitable (close relatives). Declining legal marriage rates suggest that more people are choosing to create their own consensual unions outside of matrimony, but if they legally marry, they often embrace at least some of the traditional practices.

MARRIAGE RATES

Since the 1970s, the crude marriage rates (defined as the number of new marriages in a specified year per 1,000 in the total population) steadily declined in many countries. The decline in legal marriage is often attributed to the rise in informal living arrangements and the fading relevance of legal marriage as a form of financial security (OECD, 2005b: 33). Cross-national differences are apparent in marriage rates but declining rates have created noticeable differences between generations and income groups, with older and wealthier people much more likely to marry.

Marriage rates also fluctuate with the rise and fall in living costs, the availability and cost of residential housing, the pressures of war, employment opportunities, and the availability of contraception. The Canadian marriage rate reached a low point of 5.9 marriages per 1,000 people during the Great Depression of the 1930s because couples could not afford to marry and establish separate households. However, the rate rose sharply during World War II, to 10.9, when people had more money and wanted to cement their unions in order to gain emotional security, sexual freedom, and possibly state income support if the husband was killed or injured. After the war, the rate declined until 1961, increased to over 9 marriages per 1,000 people in 1971, and then fell again. The Canadian marriage rate continued to decline from 5.5 in 1994 to 4.7 in 2001 as more people cohabited without legalizing their relationship (Statistics Canada, 2003).

The average age of first marriage has also increased in many countries since the 1970s, influenced by rising educational requirements for employment and higher housing costs. In Canada, the average age of first marriage in the 1960s was 22 years for women and 25 years for men, but this increased to 28 for women and 30 for men by 2000 (McDaniel and Tepperman, 2004: 109; Statistics Canada, 2003). Because so many people now divorce and remarry, the average age of all marriages in Canada was 31.9 years old for brides in 2001, up 5.7 years from 1981. The average age of grooms in 2001 was 34.4, up 5.6 years from 1981 (Statistics Canada, 2003). Table 3.2 shows some comparative marriage statistics for Canada and Australia.

The growing secularization of society has encouraged more people to view marriage as a contract that can be broken under certain circumstances. Individualism and the idea that people are entitled to satisfying relationships have discouraged couples from staying together out of duty or concern for family reputation. Furthermore, more effective contraception has permitted people to separate sex and reproduction, and the decline in fertility—with fewer children per family—has made divorce easier. Separation and divorce also became more economically feasible when more women could support themselves from their earnings and when

Table 3.2   Marriage Trends in Canada and Australia

Country	Consensual Unions (% of all couples)		Legal Marriage Rate in 2001 (per 1,000 Population)	Average Age of First Marriage, 2001	
	1991	2001		Brides	Grooms
Canada	6.3	13.8	4.7	28.2	30.2
Australia	8.0	12.4	5.3	29	31

Sources: Baker (2001b); Wu (2000: 50); Statistics Canada (2003); Australian Bureau of Statistics website; VIF (2004).

governments began paying income support to low-income households led by mothers. More liberal divorce laws also contributed to rising divorce rates.

Lower marriage rates, declining fertility, and rising divorce rates are viewed by many social conservatives as trends that demonstrate the decline in the family as a social institution. However, others view these trends as indicators of greater choice and personal freedom in society, permitting more people to recreate satisfying relationships. Although legal marriage rates are declining and the age of marriage is rising, most people continue to live in couple relationships. For example, over three-quarters of Canadian women aged 35–44 years live with a partner, either legally married or cohabiting (Statistics Canada, 2002b). This suggests that 'marriage' remains very popular if we define it in broader terms.

THE QUALITY OF MARRIAGE

Although academic studies tend to focus on relationship conflict and separation, researchers have also tried to understand why so many people see marriage as a desirable living arrangement. In one popular motif, 'scheming' women are said to push reluctant bachelors into marriage; however, several studies have suggested that men see marriage as desirable and benefit more from marriage than women do. Jessie Bernard (1972) first popularized the research finding that married men in the United States experience fewer psychiatric problems and less physical illness, and also tend to live longer than single men, but found that this trend was less apparent for women. Bernard argued that men do well in marriage because they have someone to care for them physically and emotionally, to keep their households function-ing, and to look after their children. In contrast, women marry at some cost to their own physical and emotional health because they are expected to continually cater to other people's needs as well as to their own.

De Vaus (2002) used this earlier American research as a starting point to see how marriage impacted on the well-being of men and women in Australia. When a range of mental disorders were considered (including mood swings, anxiety, drug and alcohol abuse), he found that married people were less likely to experience these problems than single people. De Vaus concluded that regardless of whether they are married or not, women are more at risk of mood and anxiety disorders than men, but men are more at risk of drug and alcohol disorders. Marriage and child-rearing do not increase the risk for either men or women. In fact, married people are less likely to report these problems than never-married or separated/divorced people. Although people with these disorders may be less likely to marry in the first place or to stay married, De Vaus concluded that having a close relationship seems to act as a buffer to health-related problems.

Using recent American data, Waite (2005) demonstrated statistically that on a wide range of indicators of health and well-being, legally married people are healthier, happier, and live longer than never-married people, but only if they rate their rela-tionship as 'moderately good' or 'excellent'. Although acknowledging that unhealthy or unhappy people are less likely to marry and stay married, she also argued that a close intimate relationship assists people to fight against stress and poor health. How-ever, a poor and unsatisfying relationship can damage people's health and well-being.

Researchers have also tried to understand how relationship satisfaction varies throughout the duration of marriage and what makes some relationships last while others end in separation. It is difficult to assess the merits of some of the research because many studies from the 1980s were based on retrospective reporting and involved couples in therapy rather than a random selection of the population (Parker, 2002). It is widely accepted in the family research that marital satisfaction tends to follow a U-shaped trajectory: satisfaction is usually high in the early years but often declines during the middle or parenting years, rising again after children leave home (Van Laningham et al., 2001). In fact, satisfaction seems to decline in the middle years even when there are no children present (Clements et al., 1997), although exceptions have been found to this trend. Gender and individual differences are also apparent.

Marriage satisfaction research is usually based on a cross-sectional design done at one point in time, with few studies following the same couples over periods of more than 10 years. This is because longitudinal studies are expensive and difficult when people move away or withdraw from the research project. However, Karney and Bradbury (1995) surveyed 100 longitudinal studies of marriage from which they created a model to explain why some survive and others dissolve. They called it the 'vulnerability-stress-adaptation' model. These researchers noted that marriage satisfaction and stability are influenced by a combination of individual factors, family variables, and life events. The 'enduring vulnerabilities' are the strengths and weaknesses that each spouse brings to the marriage, influenced by their upbringing, social background, and their attitudes. Stressful life events are incidents, transitions, or circumstances that can impinge on their relationship and create tension or stress. Adaptive processes refer to the ways that people cope with stress and conflict, and how couples communicate and support each other. The authors concluded that the strategies for dealing with life events and resolving conflicts vary by these factors, which then influence marital satisfaction.

Mackey and O'Brien (1995) identified five factors that appeared to be important for marital longevity: containment of conflict; mutuality of decision-making; quality of communication; relational values of trust, respect, understanding, and equity; and sexual and psychological intimacy. Their research was based on interviews with 60 American couples who married from the 1940s to the 1960s, and whose youngest child had completed high school. The themes of adaptability, resilience, and commitment recurred throughout the interviews. While some of the attitudes and values of these people changed over the years, their views of marriage as a permanent commitment of love and fidelity held fast.

Alford-Cooper (1998) collected data on 576 American couples living on Long Island in New York, whose marriages were intact for 50 years or more. Based on questionnaires as well as interviews with a smaller subsample, it was found that only 56 per cent reported being 'very happily married' but a further 37 per cent reported being 'happily married'. Although 21 per cent had at some point concluded that their marriages had failed, they had stayed together because they wanted to remain with their children, they did not believe in divorce, or they lacked the financial resources or social support to leave. When asked which relationship characteristics helped them stay together, the most common ones were trust, a loving relationship, and willingness to compromise. They also reported mutual respect, a need for each other, compatibility, children, and good communication.

Sharlin et al. (2000) conducted a study of non-clinical couples from eight countries (United States, Canada, Israel, Chile, Germany, Netherlands, Sweden, and South Africa) who had been married, or in the case of Sweden had been living together, from 20 to 46 years. The study included 610 couples obtained through the authors' networking, which created a sample somewhat biased to the middle or upper-middle classes. Love, mutuality, and sharing emerged as bases for long-term marital satisfaction, and a number of qualities such as mutuality of trust, respect, support, give and take, and the sharing of values, beliefs, interests, philosophies, fun, and humour all arose across cultures. Couples said that they stayed in the relationship because of commitment to the partnership and love of their spouse, but those who expressed lower levels of happiness reported staying together for the children and to honour their commitment to a lifelong relationship.

These studies reveal a set of characteristics or attributes influencing marriage stability, but Wallerstein and Blakeslee (1996) saw happy and lasting marriages as the product of a series of processes. Based on interviews with 50 married couples in the United States who reported their marriages as 'very happy', the researchers identified four different types of marriage that were not necessarily mutually exclusive, which they called 'romantic', 'rescue', 'companionate', and 'traditional' marriages. Each of these was based on different assumptions and dynamics, suggesting that there is no single way to create a happy and lasting marriage. Wallerstein and Blakeslee argued that marriage is 'always a work in progress' (p. 269) that requires ongoing maintenance, including negotiation and compromises.

Some research suggests that couples married for a long time can impart their wisdom to the younger generation whose marriages are far less likely to last (Parker, 2002). However, the current cohort of young married couples is experiencing very different social, economic, political, and cultural circumstances than those married for many years. Nevertheless, marriage preparation courses and marriage counselling are becoming more prevalent, as therapists, policy-makers, and older couples express increasing concern about high rates of relationship breakdown, especially in the United States. Most of these courses, however, are targeted to those who are planning to marry and those whose marriages have already broken up. Few formal supports exist for ongoing relationships despite the fact that the research suggests that rewarding and lasting marriages require regular and intentional maintenance (ibid.).

BARRIERS TO LEGAL MARRIAGE

Policy discussion, especially in the United States, has often suggested that the plight of lone mothers living on low earnings or social benefits would be resolved if they simply married their male partners. Public campaigns have tried to convince low-income Americans of the value of marriage, and state income-support programs have been made less generous to encourage unmarried couples receiving social benefits to legalize their relationships. American research suggests that those with higher educational qualifications and higher incomes have much higher marriage rates than poorer and less-educated people. In contrast, the 'disadvantaged' are only half as likely to marry but more often cohabit. When disadvantaged people do marry, their divorce rates tend to be higher, and these rates have been rising in recent years (McLaughlin and Lichter, 1997).

Qualitative and quantitative studies have uncovered a number of barriers to legal marriage among the 'disadvantaged'. Edin and Reed (2005) reviewed the recent American research and found that disadvantaged men and women highly value marriage but are unable to meet the high standards of relationship quality and financial stability they believe are necessary to sustain a marriage and avoid divorce. Many see marriage as 'sacred', more committed than cohabitation, and something they want to do 'some day'. Many cohabiting partners with low income and low education are already parents and have had a child by another partner, although this child was not usually planned. Nearly a third of poor American women aged 25 and older have had a child outside marriage compared to 5 per cent who were not poor (Hoffman and Foster, 1997).

American research suggests that low-income men and women do not view marriage as a prerequisite for child-bearing but they often say that children are better off when raised within marriage (Edin and Reed, 2005). However, the ideal of marriage remains unrealized because of the complexities of their lives. Their relationships are often conflict-ridden and involve partner violence and frequent separations. Furthermore, the stigma of divorce is deemed greater than the stigma of having a child outside marriage. Both men and women struggle to find employment that can pay the bills, and many couples experience bouts of unemployment and low-paid jobs. Before they can marry, many feel that they need a secure income, enough money for a mortgage on a modest home, some furniture, a car, some savings in the bank, and some money for a 'decent' wedding (Edin and Kefalas, 2005).

Over the past few decades, legal marriage seems to have lost some of its instrumental value as more women become self-supporting, contraception and abortion are widely available, premarital sex and cohabitation have become more socially acceptable, and marriage is no longer necessary for women's social or legal status (Edin and Reed, 2005). In fact, legal marriage would make little difference to the daily lives of many mothers and fathers who are already cohabiting. Yet American research has found that the symbolic value of marriage remains. Edin and Kefalas (2005) argued that marriage has become a symbol of status and luxury rather than of necessity. It has become a relationship that carries much higher expectations of relationship quality and financial stability, and many of the poor cannot meet this higher marital standard.

CONCLUSION

Although more people now cohabit without the blessing of religion or the legitimation of the state, the majority of people eventually marry and stay together for life. In both Western and Eastern countries, people marry for a variety of reasons, and many remain married even when their relationship is not particularly satisfying, either emotionally or sexually. Two can live cheaper than one, few parents want to forfeit the daily companionship of their children, marriage partners derive satisfaction and esteem from other aspects of their lives, and most married people want to grow old with their families intact.

Nevertheless, satisfaction seldom remains the same over the years of marriage, as children come and go and personal circumstances change. Levels of satisfaction tend to be the highest at the beginning of marriage as well as after many years of life together, but the middle years seem more prone to disappointments. Some of the problems in middle age are related to difficulties dealing with adolescent children, but even child-free couples report lower levels of satisfaction at this time. However, marital roles are changing as more mid-life women are employed full-time, while more men are able (or forced) to change jobs, return to school, or create their own businesses. Some of these transitions may strengthen levels of satisfaction but they may also push marriage partners towards separation.

Some couples who stay together into old age have always been satisfied with their marriages while others manage either to adapt to their disillusionment or to reinvigorate their relationship. Over time, most relationships are cemented with shared understandings, memories, children and grandchildren, and mutual love, caring, and companionship. Although social scientists tend to focus on conflict and marriage breakdown, most couples in reality remain together for life. Yet this is seldom reiterated in the media or in academic research.

SUMMARY

This chapter shows that marriage remains the choice of lifestyle for most people, but that a growing portion of young people are choosing to live together before settling with a more permanent partner. However, the kind of relationship that young people choose tends to reflect their social-class backgrounds, culture, and educational and employment opportunities.

Questions for Critical Thought

1. Why are younger and poorer people more likely than older and richer ones to cohabit rather than legally marry?
2. What difference does it make if women take their husband's surname upon marriage?
3. Why are gifts typically exchanged as one part of most marriage ceremonies?

Suggested Readings

Ambert, Anne-Marie. 2005. 'Same-Sex Couples and Same-Sex-Parent Families: Relationships, Parenting and Issues of Marriage', Vanier Institute of the Family, at: <www.vifamily.ca>. Ambert surveys the literature on same-sex relationships and discusses the relationship between sexual preference, commitment, and family practices.

McDaniel, Susan A., and Lorne Tepperman. 2004. *Close Relations: An Introduction to the Sociology of the Families*, 2nd edn. Scarborough, Ontario: Pearson/Prentice-Hall. An introductory textbook to family studies, designed for a Canadian audience.

Wu, Zheng. 2000. *Cohabitation: An Alternative Form of Family Living.* Toronto: Oxford University Press. This book examines the implication of rising rates of cohabitation from academic and policy perspectives, using Canadian data.

Suggested Website

Vanier Institute of the Family
www.vifamily.ca
The Vanier Institute provides news items and research on various aspects of Canadian families, including cohabitation and same-sex relationships.

Chapter 4

Child-bearing, Child-rearing, and Childhood

Learning Objectives
- To understand national trends in fertility and the timing of childbirth.
- To distinguish between social expectations or professional practices and personal choices in childbirth and parenting experiences.
- To understand how the experience of childhood and adolescence has been influenced by larger societal changes, such as educational requirements, patterns of work, greater use of technology, and new ideas about childhood.

Chapter Outline

This chapter discusses demographic trends including declining fertility and smaller families and households. It also presents research findings about the social history of childhood, changing child-rearing advice to parents, the medicalization of childbirth, and new patterns of parenting.

Introduction

In this chapter, I explore how the decisions and experiences relating to pregnancy and childbirth have changed over the past few decades and whether childhood in the twenty-first century is much different from what it used to be. These questions can be approached by examining social research and academic theories, as well as public controversies and media representations about having children and raising them. Generally, the research suggests that having children has become more of a choice but that in many countries the experience of childbirth is now dominated by the medical profession and technological interventions. Second, perceptions of childhood, parenting styles, and the life experiences of children and youth have varied over the decades with changes in the economic value of children to families, new ideas about child development, different forms of supervision, more influence from the media and technology, and broader socio-economic changes in the larger society (Synnott, 1983; Wall, 2004).

Children's upbringing is increasingly influenced by television, videos, video games, advertising, the Internet, other children, and non-family care providers, as well as by the actual care and supervision from parents, siblings, and other close relatives. In addition, educational experiences, expectations, and opportunities have increased for all children but especially for those from lower-income families. Nevertheless, the research indicates that children's **socialization** and life chances continue to be influenced by their gender, the socio-economic circumstances of their parents, the cultural background of their family, and the economic environment and social programs in their country of residence.

If we want to understand how cultural, social, and economic changes have influenced child-bearing, child-rearing, and childhood, the central questions are: how much change has actually occurred and what factors continue to influence parenting and growing up in liberal welfare states today? Let us begin by examining changes in fertility rates because they illustrate some of the broader societal influences on personal life.

DECLINING FERTILITY, SMALLER FAMILIES

In recent decades, fertility rates have declined considerably in most OECD countries, as Table 4.1 indicates. Demographers estimate that if each married couple produced about 2.1 children each, population stability would be maintained and countries could replace their deaths with new births. However, the total fertility rates (or the average number of children per woman who has completed child-bearing) are now below replacement levels in all OECD countries except in Mexico and in Turkey (OECD, 2005b: 28). In Canada, the total fertility rate was 1.52 in 2002, well below the replacement rate (ibid.). The rate in Korea has plummeted even further to 1.17 in 2002 (ibid.). Even the Southern European countries now experience low fertility rates. Both Italy and Greece had total fertility rates of 2.4 in 1970 but by 2002 their rates had declined to 1.26 in Italy and 1.25 in Greece (ibid., 29). The recent figures for Southern Europe obscure any previous statistical association between high fertility, Catholicism, and traditional family values (Castles, 2002).

Policy-makers are concerned about declining fertility rates because they lead to 'population aging'—a higher percentage of elderly people compared to younger ones in the future population. In addition, lower birth rates could signal future labour shortages and insufficient taxpayers to finance the needs of the higher proportion of seniors. Despite these recent concerns, fertility rates have actually been declining since the late 1800s, influenced by modernization, industrialization, urbanization, and the rising cost of raising children. Infant mortality rates began to decline in the 1920s with improved living standards and better health care, permitting couples to produce fewer children because more were expected to reach maturity (Chesnais, 1992).

The cost of raising children also increased, while the benefits of having a large number of children per family gradually declined, especially for those living in towns and cities. The financial cost of having children is now calculated in terms of women's lost earnings, the need for more spacious accommodation in better school zones or

Table 4.1   Fertility Rates in OECD Countries, 1970 and 2002
             (births per woman)

Country	1970	2002
Australia	2.9	1.75
Canada	2.0	1.52
Denmark	2.0	1.72
Finland	1.8	1.72
France	2.5	1.89
Germany	2.0	1.31
Greece	2.4	1.25
Ireland	3.9	1.97
Italy	2.4	1.26
Korea	3.0*	1.17
Netherlands	2.6	1.73
New Zealand	3.3	1.90
Portugal	2.8	1.47
Spain	2.9	1.25
Sweden	1.9	1.65
United Kingdom	2.4	1.64
United States	2.0	2.01
OECD Average for 27 countries	2.7	1.60

*1976 figure

Source: OECD (2005b: 29), based on data chart GE3.2. Decline in completed fertility and increase in mean age of mother at first childbirth. © OECD 2005.

safer areas, as well as the direct costs of children's food, clothing, care, and education. Few parents now rely on their children to care for them in old age because most OECD countries provide some form of old age security. Also, children are required to attend school until the age of 16 in most countries and cannot be asked from a younger age to support the family. Declining fertility is also related to improvements in contraception (especially since the mid-1960s), access to legal abortion, personal choices for smaller families, and the difficulty mothers experience combining employment with child-rearing (Hakim, 2000; McDonald, 2000; Weston and Parker, 2002).

Recent fertility trends indicate that these rates are no longer related to women's labour force participation rates, as they were a few generations ago (Castles, 2002). Current employment trends in OECD countries suggest that most women cannot afford or no longer wish to refrain from paid work in order to raise large families (ibid.). Yet fertility rates are moderately high in countries such as France and Sweden with formal care provisions for preschool children and flexible workplace arrangements for employed parents. Rates are also relatively high where cultural minorities value reproduction but birth control is less accessible and child care is relatively inexpensive, such as in the United States where child-care services are largely unregulated by the state but nevertheless are affordable. In contrast, women tend to have fewer children when they must struggle to earn a living, such as through low wages, job discrimination, few child-care services, or public discourse that makes them feel guilty about 'neglecting' their children if they seek employment.

Fertility has also declined because women are now bearing their first child later in life, at around 28–30 years of age (OECD, 2001: 25). The growing tendency to postpone childbirth has some advantages for women, who are able to complete their education and find paid work before childbirth. A period of continuous, full-time employment is often required before women become eligible for maternity benefits; however, postponing motherhood until later in life sometimes makes conception more difficult, pregnancy riskier, and contributes to lower fertility rates at the national level. This suggests that delayed fertility may be beneficial to women but at the same time be perceived as a problem for the nation.

Teenage birth rates have also declined in the past 20 years, from an average of 34 births per 1,000 women aged 15–19 in 1980 in OECD countries, to 16 in 2002 (OECD, 2005b: 86). Comparisons further back in time are more dramatic. For example, the fertility rate for first births for Canadian women aged 15–19 declined from 45.6 in 1957 to 17.56 in 1998 (Ram, 1990: 83; Bélanger et al., 2001: 96). For all

Table 4.2   Teenage Birth Rates in 2002 (births to mothers aged 15–19 per 1,000 women aged 15–19)

Country	Teenage Birth Rates
Korea	2.7
Japan	6.2
Denmark	6.6
Sweden	6.9
Italy	7.0
Netherlands	7.7
Spain	8.7
Norway	10.3
Finland	10.9
Greece	11.3
France	11.4
Czech Republic	11.5
Germany	13.2
New Zealand	14.0
Poland	14.6
Australia	18.4
Ireland	19.3
Portugal	20.4
Hungary	21.7
Canada	21.9
United Kingdom	28.6
United States	43.0
Mexico	51.1

Source: OECD (2005b: 86). Based on CO4.2, Large cross-country differences in teenage birth rates. © OECD 2005.

teenage births, the rate in Canada was 21.9 in 2002, compared to 51.1 in Mexico and 2.7 in Korea (OECD, 2005b: 87). This suggests that cultural, socio-economic, and social service factors influence these rates.

The decline in teenage pregnancy is usually applauded because early pregnancy is often associated with disadvantage. Statistical analysis shows that family poverty encourages early pregnancy, which can then contribute to the perpetuation of low income throughout life. Many studies have found a strong correlation between teenage pregnancy, early family formation, and poor life chances for both parents—but especially mothers—and their children (Hobcraft and Kiernan, 2001). Cross-national variations in teenage birth rates are influenced by trends in sexuality, access to contraception, social ideas about women's roles, and the percentage of poor and deprived groups in the population (OECD, 2005b: 86). Teen fertility rates remain relatively high in countries such as the United States with large percentages of visible minorities (African Americans and Hispanics) with low household incomes, few employment opportunities, and lack of access to contraception. These disadvantaged minorities tend to cohabit and marry at younger ages and to place a higher value on parenthood as an indicator of adult status and love between partners (Edin, 2003; Mink, 1998).

Births outside marriage have also increased in many OECD nations, but most are to cohabiting couples in which the woman is between 25 and 35 years old. Lewis (2003: 28) noted that the extramarital birth rate in the United Kingdom increased from 5.9 per 1,000 single, divorced, and widowed women (ages 15–44) in 1940, to 39.6 in 1995. Ex-nuptial birth rates in 1997–8 were the highest in nations such as Sweden (55 per cent of all births) and Denmark (45 per cent), both countries with high rates of non-marital cohabitation. In contrast, such rates were relatively low in countries such as Italy, with lower rates of cohabitation (ibid.).

Researchers and policy-makers generally agree that lower teenage birth rates are socially beneficial but do not always acknowledge the advantages of fewer children for individual women, families, and their communities. Large families often require state income supplements, so fewer children per family would help ensure that parents are able to support their children on their own earnings. Fewer children also enable women to pursue their educational goals and retain paid employment, which raises the standard of living for many families as well as providing income tax revenue for the state. Theoretically, fewer children per family would also enable each child to receive more parental attention.

In the 1960s, the United Nations began to encourage governments to support the policy of 'zero population growth' and to provide reproductive services such as therapeutic abortion and contraception. Now, as total fertility rates drop farther than anticipated, more OECD countries are expressing concern about the national economic consequences of declining fertility. At the same time, developing countries attempt to counteract overpopulation and high urban growth rates by developing family planning strategies and urging citizens to comply. This suggests that having children is not always seen as a personal choice or the couple's decision but as something governments want to control for the good the nation.

Decisions to reproduce and unexpected pregnancies are influenced by personal and family circumstances, employment prospects, regional and national economies, and prevailing social attitudes. In the next section, I examine some historical changes in attitudes about parenting and childhood, as well as the impact of socio-economic circumstances on having and raising children.

PARENTING AND CHILDHOOD IN THE PAST

In the nineteenth century, parenting experiences differed considerably by gender, age, social class, and culture, as they do today. However, they were particularly influenced in the past by **gendered roles**, the assumption of heterosexuality, unreliable contraception, and limited life options once people married and reproduced. As we noted in the previous chapter, marriage functioned as a legal partnership to promote heterosexual co-operation in work and reproduction. The husband was expected to become family earner and decision-maker, while it was assumed that the wife would care for the children and provide or manage domestic labour.

Marriage, as a legal institution, involved economic co-operation and the containment of sexuality and reproduction. Marriage often implied that the wife was sexually available to her husband on a regular basis. Nevertheless, unless couples used some form of contraception or abstained from sexual intercourse, many wives spent a considerable amount of time during their pre-menopausal years in pregnancy, lactation, and miscarriage. Contraception has been available for hundreds of years but in the past it was less reliable, difficult to purchase, and, in some social circles, considered unacceptable or frowned upon. The common view was that child-bearing and child-rearing were sufficient vocation for a woman, although some women who could afford to developed larger spheres of influence in reform movements (prison, prostitution, temperance, orphans, women's suffrage, etc.), in the arts, in church work, and even in business. However, using contraception and especially remaining childless were interpreted by some as a rejection of normal gendered behaviour, of religious values, and of traditional marriage.

Husbands were encouraged to reproduce in order to continue the family line and to become reliable family heads through earning household income. Men were also expected to be the main disciplinarians of children in their families. While many wives became conscientious and nurturing mothers, others struggled with the lack of alternative occupations, the heavy domestic responsibility and workload, and the social isolation of housework, especially among the lower classes. Couples who were unable to reproduce were pitied by their relatives and neighbours, but childless married women were not always encouraged or even permitted to accept full-time paid jobs. However, some were able to help run the family farm or participate in family businesses while others became involved in artistic pursuits, voluntary community work, or temporary paid jobs.

Both men and women were expected to marry and reproduce. Those who did not want to become parents often avoided marriage, but single adults were continually pressured to find a partner and 'start a family' unless they joined a religious order that promoted celibacy or were ill or disabled. Employment options were limited, even for single women, and some were expected to help care for their aging parents or sibling's children; thus, they lived with relatives with little autonomy or status, instead of developing independent lives. In rural districts, some sons remained on the family farm to assist their frail fathers and therefore found fewer opportunities to meet potential wives. When men did marry, however, they had to be prepared to support not only a wife but also a new baby within the first year of marriage.

Households in the nineteenth century generally contained more children than today but also more relatives, servants, and paying boarders. In working-class families, pregnant women needed to carry on with their domestic chores right up until childbirth unless they could find relatives to stay and help with the work of the household and the new baby. Although infant and maternal death rates were higher than today, working-class mothers and babies were at relatively greater risk because of their harsh living conditions, poor diet, and lack of health-care services.

As soon as working-class children were old enough, they were expected to contribute to the family economy in some way, first helping around the house and garden and later contributing their labour or wages to support the household. Nineteenth-century children sometimes worked in dangerous jobs as factory workers, miners, and chimney sweeps until laws were enacted to abolish child labour and institute compulsory education for children to 16 years of age. However, low-income families sometimes withdrew their children from school periodically if they needed their labour, or permanently if they could obtain permission from education authorities after the child turned 14. In other words, childhood and especially adolescence in some respects were not much different from adult life in nineteenth-century low-income families.

By contrast, middle-class families usually could afford to hire servants to help with farm chores, housework, and child care but the wife/mother was responsible for household management, including the quality of the furnishings and meals, and the hiring and disciplining of servants and care providers. Middle-class parents sent their children to public schools to learn to read and write but also to learn the value of hard work, discipline, sportsmanship, religious values, and obedience. The wealthy hired private tutors to come to the family home and give the young children lessons in literacy, arithmetic, foreign languages, religion, and science. Some children were sent to expensive private boarding schools to learn academic subjects as well as debating skills, sports, and good manners. Gender and social class influenced the content of children's education because the future roles of boys and girls were expected to differ, especially in privileged families.

Unlike the poor, wealthy parents could afford to pamper their children and idealize them as symbols of innocence, because they did not need their labour or the income they might produce (Coveney, 1982: 45). Early childhood was a time of play, but upper-class parents were rarely fully involved in the daily care and supervision of their children. Babies were seldom breast-fed by wealthy mothers but rather by 'wet nurses' hired for this purpose. The wealthy family home contained adult-only areas that were separate from the children's rooms where nannies and servants catered to their physical and emotional needs.

Wealthy parents hired nannies and tutors to educate their children until they were sent to school. While boys sometimes boarded at the school, girls were more often educated only at home. During the daytime, these parents pursued their own occupations and interests, seeing their children for short periods each day or during school holidays. At night, the children of the rich were cared for by their nurses or nannies at home, or by school employees if they boarded at a residential school. While some people today believe that young children 'need their mums' during the daytime, they forget that many children from wealthy families were raised largely by servants and teachers in the past. However, some of the nannies stayed with the children throughout their entire childhood and even continued working for the family for more than one generation.

Prior to the late nineteenth century, neither the churches nor governments protected children or granted them legal rights because they were considered the property of their parents. Adults learned to parent from their own parents and relatives, with some assistance from doctors, religious leaders, and teachers. British parents were discouraged from praising their children or allowing them to express themselves verbally because children were expected to be 'seen but not heard', to obey their parents and other elders, and to abide by parental rules until they left home. Physical punishment was freely used to discipline children, both at home and in schools. Extensive schooling was reserved for boys from wealthier families. These residential schools provided a classical education with some training in sports and sportsmanship, leadership, debating, and manners, and were run with rigid and hierarchical rules attuned to the larger class-based society (Clement, 1975; Houston and Prentice, 1988).

By the end of the nineteenth century, values had shifted from emphasizing children's economic utility to focusing on love, companionship, and enjoyment (Cameron, 1997). Children's economic contributions to families and their potential to support parents in old age became less important with urbanization, compulsory education, and the development of old age pensions. Redefinitions of motherhood later influenced how children were valued, particularly the new maternal ideologies that focused on the mother's natural duty to support the health and well-being of the child and to raise 'quality' children. The value of children was further enhanced by government programs that focused on children's welfare and rights rather than simply on their discipline and education (Kedgley, 1996). The economic utility of children has now been replaced with the new ideology that children are a form of social capital and an investment in the future of the nation (Cameron, 1997: 109; Jenson, 2004).

Child-rearing Advice

State intervention in families began to increase around the 1920s and 1930s (Ursel, 1992; Baker, 1995; Gauthier, 1996). High infant mortality and maternal death rates in the former colonies as compared with Northern and Western Europe led to considerable public discussion about the causes of this premature mortality and how these rates could be reduced. Male professionals expressed concern that mothers themselves were promoting child health problems by their lack of knowledge about sanitation, nutrition, and child care. They strongly criticized the expertise of mothers by suggesting that the worldly ambitions of the 'new woman', who desired education and paid work, would lead to the deterioration of family life (Strong-Boag, 1982: 161).

Child-welfare agencies and state officials produced written advice about child-rearing and domestic matters, promoting bottle-feeding and 'scientific' infant formula (Baker, 2001b). Governments also established special clinics for expectant mothers and babies as part of a campaign to reduce infant mortality and to improve baby care. Fathers still were not expected to be involved in physical parenting, especially with infants, but they were urged to be understanding of the mother's responsibilities and to provide economic security for the family. Strict scheduling was recommended for infant and child care, which meant that if babies were hungry before the designated feeding time, they often were left alone in their beds to cry. Parents thus desensitized also might neglect children's cries for other important reasons.

In 1946, Dr Benjamin Spock's *Baby and Child Care* first appeared, encouraging a more permissive approach to parenting and advising mothers to trust their 'common sense' and enjoy their babies (Wall, 2005). In addition, developmental psychology, especially the work of John Bowlby (1953, 1958, 1969) on maternal deprivation and attachment, began to influence child-rearing advice. He argued that the absence of the mother during the early years, even for temporary periods, had profound negative effects on the child's development and adult personality. Throughout the 1950s, women's magazines in North America and Australasia also celebrated 'maternalism' and homemaking for married women.

By the 1960s and 1970s, ideas about infant and child care became more flexible. Husbands were encouraged to take more interest in their wives' pregnancies and to be present at the birth of their children. Both parents were encouraged to pick children up when they cried, to cuddle them when they wanted attention, to be verbally expressive in their affection, and to assist each child's self-development. At the same time, more married women were being drawn into paid work by changes in the labour market, which created problems with child care. Lacking a public system of child-care services, many mothers nonetheless felt guilty about leaving their children in the care of relatives or neighbours. Feminists and other social reformers who supported the importance of higher education and earned income for women's equality with men challenged the gendered division of labour both at home and in paid work. They lobbied for public child-care services with government regulation and subsidies, and also encouraged husbands to become more involved in childbirth, housework, and child-rearing (Benoit et al., 2002).

Wall (2005) discussed the recent proliferation of educational material designed to convince parents of the importance of secure attachments and adequate stimulation in their child's early years. She argued that the current approach to parenting is intensely child-focused, compared to the pre-World War II idea that children should fit into an adult-centred home. Mothers now are taught that their own behaviour can influence the development of their fetus as well as their young child's social and intellectual development. Technological advances have enabled the fetus to be monitored and photographed, and fetal imagery and the discourse of fetal rights have encouraged people to view a pregnant women as an 'ecosystem for a growing child' rather than an individual person. Canadian research by Knaak (2005) on the changing discourse of breast-feeding supports this conclusion, arguing that the discourse shapes the choices of new mothers but does not necessarily coincide with scientific

research findings. Weir (1996) referred to the recent focus on public and expert regulation of the behaviour of pregnant women as the 'remoralization of pregnancy'.

Attitudes towards childbirth have been influenced by prevalent ideas about gender, family, and self-fulfillment but they have also been altered by changes in living
standards and the economy. In the early twentieth century, infant mortality rates fell
with industrialization, modernization, and rising prosperity. From 1970 to 2002,
infant mortality in OECD countries continued to decline from 28 deaths per 1,000
live births to 7 (OECD, 2005b: 74). Countries with lower infant mortality rates tend
to have higher levels of income, more equal income distribution, and affordable
health-care services (ibid.). Declining infant mortality may encourage couples to
reduce their family size because they can be confident that more babies will reach
maturity.

Over the years, fertility rates declined with higher living costs, greater marriage
instability, and pressures on women to contribute to the family income as well as to
the larger community. More adults can now decide whether or not to reproduce
because more effective contraception and legalized abortion are available, also
enabling parents to more successfully space their children according to personal
needs. When reproduction becomes more of a choice, some couples opt for no children while others pamper their offspring and view them as luxuries and status symbols. However, having fewer children is not always an explicit choice but reflects
personal circumstances and changes in the larger society, as the costs and benefits of
reproduction vary with gender and socio-economic and cultural circumstances
(Beaujot, 2000; Weston and Parker, 2002).

REPRODUCTION: A DELIBERATE CHOICE?

Raising children into well-adjusted, socially responsible adults is a difficult task
requiring vision, commitment, and years of hard work. Nevertheless, researchers
have found that most parents see pregnancy and childbirth as a natural outcome of
adulthood and marriage rather than as a conscious choice. In attempting to explain
why people continue to reproduce despite the well-publicized hardships of child-
rearing, sociologists gloss over parental instincts or biological explanations and
focus on two major social reasons. One relates to expectations and pressures, and the
other emphasizes perceptions of the costs and benefits.

Since the 1970s, sociologists have argued that people reproduce largely because
having children is perceived as sign of maturity, normality, sexual competence, and
psychological stability. These conclusions are reached after questioning parents and
studying people's reactions to those who choose not reproduce or cannot have children. When parents are asked why they have had children, they usually portray the
experience in positive terms. They talk about the opportunities to relive the joys of
childhood, to pass on their values and knowledge, and to receive unconditional love.
They also mention desires to expand their social networks, to create their own social
group, and to pass on their family name and genes (Veevers, 1980; Callan, 1982;
Cameron, 1990; Morell, 1994; May, 1995).

Studies from Australia, Canada, New Zealand, and the United States have
found that individuals who deliberately choose *not* to reproduce or to bear only one

child tend to be stigmatized by others (Veevers, 1980; Magarick and Brown, 1981; Morell, 1994; May, 1995; Cameron, 1990, 1997). People who choose to remain childless (or 'child-free') are viewed as selfish, maladjusted, unloving, irresponsible, unnatural, immature, materialistic, individualistic, career-oriented, lonely, unhappy, child-haters, and even psychologically unstable. Younger people tend to view this choice more liberally, yet it is still widely accepted that married couples *should* produce children.

The social pressure to have children comes from many sources: religious leaders, government officials, family, friends, and even strangers. The churches historically have viewed the purpose of marriage as reproduction, and after the wedding cere- mony friends and family often symbolize this expectation by throwing confetti or rice (symbols of fertility) on the couple. Governments, employers, and community leaders continue to see children as necessary because they will become the future gen- eration of taxpayers, voters, workers, and consumers. Parents often want grandchil- dren to amuse them and later watch over them in old age, and siblings want nieces and nephews to expand the family group. Parents want to share their child-related experiences with their friends, as well as stories about the joys and problems of child- rearing. Consequently, many parents, professionals, and policy-makers romanticize child-rearing and downplay the disadvantages. Representations in the media, espe- cially advertisements for household cleaning products and fast food, show happy parents (usually mothers) interacting with healthy, smiling, active, and loving chil- dren. These images encourage us to see child-rearing as desirable and rewarding.

Another theory about why people reproduce is that they believe children will enhance their lives in ways that compensate for the expenses and hard work of child- rearing. Parents say they receive pleasure, fulfillment, and a sense of achievement from watching their children develop, and that producing children enhances par- ents' personal and sexual identity (Willen and Montgomery, 1996). Cameron (1990) studied why New Zealanders reproduce and found that over half the respondents felt that companionship and the simple enjoyment of children were important rea- sons. Seventy per cent agreed that having children provided a sense of continuity after death. Women emphasized passing down ideas and knowledge about family history while men focused on having sons to carry on the family name and family line (ibid., 42).

New Zealand parents also said that having children reinforced adult status and identity, strengthened marital relationships, and made individuals 'complete' (Cameron, 1990: 60). Reproduction is associated with maturity because it provides visible evidence of sexual and social competence. It also serves as a rite of passage or transition from childhood to adulthood, and fulfills dominant conceptions of mas- culinity and femininity. Cameron's research found that parents stated that the disad- vantages of having children focused on the amount of time, the cost, and loss of personal freedom. Nevertheless, most people highlighted the social and psychological rewards, and clearly believed that parenthood was superior to a childless marriage.

Raising children is expensive. Microeconomic theories of fertility tend to devote considerable attention to the economic costs and benefits and to view children as 'social capital', downplaying the social and psychological costs and rewards. They also argue that the cost should be measured as a percentage of family income rather than as an absolute figure because the wealthy spend more than the poor on all aspects of living costs, including raising their children. For example, Douthitt and Fedyk (1990: 29) showed that two-child families in Ontario, regardless of their income, typically spend at least 18 per cent of their gross income on their children. Parents meet these costs by working longer hours, increasing the amount of time spent on household work rather than hiring help or using labour-saving devices, reallocating income from other potential expenditures to child-related goods, or decreasing their savings (ibid.). Parents tend to spend less than child-free couples on restaurant meals, recreation, tobacco and alcohol, adult clothing, and gifts, and they save less money.

Other researchers have tried to estimate the average cost of child-rearing in absolute terms. In Canada, for example, researchers have estimated that the average cost of raising a child from birth to age 18 was about $164,000 in 2003 for families living in Winnipeg. This included paying for shelter, home furnishings, food, clothing, recreation, child care, school needs, health care, personal care, and transportation (VIF, 2004: 120). Researchers also found that it is more expensive to raise a child in its first year of life, when an average of $10,000 was spent (ibid., 119). Of course, this average child-rearing cost based on Winnipeg prices is lower than for larger Canadian cities such as Toronto and Vancouver, which have much more expensive accommodation costs. Also, young people today normally stay at home beyond the age of 18.

Social patterns are apparent in who reproduces, with some people less likely than others to become parents. Research from many countries indicates that individuals who decide to remain childless tend to weigh the advantages and disadvantages and discuss the issues at some length with their partner, family, or friends before finalizing their decision (Ramu and Tavuchis, 1986; Cameron, 1997). Women with post-graduate education and high incomes are less likely to marry and have children compared to educated men or women with lower levels of schooling and income (Beaujot, 2000). However, Gillespie (1999) argues that women who choose not to procreate have to account for their choices in ways that women who choose to be mothers obviously do not.

Conception problems seem to be increasing in urban industrialized societies with higher levels of pollution, more stressful lifestyles, higher rates of obesity, more substance abuse, and delayed attempts at conception with older marriages. Those experiencing fertility problems are now more likely to seek medical treatment, although the live birth rates from reproductive procedures tend to be low and the price of treatment is high. The fact that some couples are willing to spend huge sums of family money on medically assisted conception illustrates the continuing importance attached to having children in postmodern society (Baker, 2004c).

CHILDBIRTH, SPECIALISTS, AND TECHNOLOGY

The timing of birth and childbirth experiences always have varied with social, economic, and cultural circumstances, such as the woman's age and marital status, her physical and emotional health, the family's socio-economic situation, and the

Box 4.1 Infertility, Childlessness, and Social Exclusion

In Baker's study of couples who seek fertility treatment in New Zealand (Baker, 2004c, 2005b), most participants said that they took it for granted that they would reproduce when they became adults. A 29-year-old woman in this study commented that she always assumed she would have children:

> When I was about thirteen, from that age, I started collecting things for my future children . . . things like baby clothes, baby toys, always only little stuff to go in the glory box ['hope chest' or trousseau] . . . . So it was always going to be my destiny at some stage.

A 36-year-old factory worker, in reply to a follow-up question about whether she had always wanted to have children, exclaimed:

> Oh yes, always! I had a really good friend that lived across the road from me and she had children very young . . . I was always living at her place and dreaming that her kids could be my kids—that's all I wanted to do was get married and have children.

A 34-year-old married businessman said:

> I never envisaged that I would be [in an infertile marriage]. It doesn't fit the model, you know, the socialization you go through. I mean, I come from a family of four . . . and so family to me has always been in the back of my mind. . . . I never for one moment thought I would be without children . . . (I imagined) being married at 30, director of a company by the time I was 33 and financially I wanted to be in the position, by the time I was 35, to have children . . . so I had it kind of formally mapped out in my mind.

A number of people we interviewed told us that their inability to reproduce made them feel frustrated, worried about marital stability, and excluded from 'normal' adult life, especially when their siblings and friends were having children. For example, a 34-year-old wife said:

> I have a lot of guilt because I perceive it is my fault that we don't have any children. (My husband) doesn't and he gets quite upset when I say it. So I have a lot of anxiety about him leaving me for somebody who can have children.

A 38-year-old husband commented:

> You definitely miss out on something [if you don't have children] because a lot of my friends have got kids and . . . you gradually get further and further away. . . . When we've gone out with couples who have got kids and we haven't and the couples with kids talk kids, it's all kid talk and we, you know, we can't contribute . . . .

One 38-year-old woman in a cohabiting relationship said:

We've had nine friends in the last two months who told us that they're pregnant and only four of those I think it was planned as such. So we've very quietly and privately struggled with that. . . . Deep down, we're saying 'What about us? What about us?'

Source: Baker (2005b: 521–43). Reprinted by permission of the publisher.

presence or absence of the father. In recent decades, a number of social changes in the larger society have influenced childbirth practices, including the rising age of first births, more hospital births involving obstetricians, and more technological interventions.

In the nineteenth century, most births took place at home with the assistance of midwives or experienced married women who lived nearby. Gradually, medical practitioners persuaded the public that safer childbirths required the sterile conditions of hospitals and medical interventions (Tew, 1998). In recent decades, more babies have been born in hospitals although the percentage varies by country. In England and Wales, for example, about 97 per cent of births occurred in hospitals in 1997 compared to 62 per cent in 1961 (ibid.). In the United States, less than 1 per cent of births take place at home, a trend remaining essentially unchanged over several decades (US Department of Health and Human Services, 2002: 16). In hospitals, general practitioners used to deliver most babies but now more specialist obstetricians have taken over, which has altered childbirth practices in many countries.

Childbirth now involves a variety of medical interventions that may include electronic fetal monitoring, anaesthetics, episiotomies, the induction of labour, and routine procedures such as pelvic shaves and enemas. Caesarean deliveries have also become more prevalent and the rate now exceeds 20 per cent of all births in the liberal welfare states (Baker, 2005c). Rates of Caesarean deliveries vary by the age, social class, and ethnicity of the mother, with older, wealthier, and 'European' or 'white' women more likely to experience such deliveries in Canada, the United States, Australia, and New Zealand (ibid.).

Considerable controversy exists over the rising rate of Caesarean births, which are increasing partly because women are having their first baby later in life and medical practitioners tend to define these births as 'high risk' (Bosch, 1998; Health Canada, 2000: 23). Doctors and nurses view childbirth as risky if women are over the age of 35 or if there are indications of medical problems, and argue that these women and their fetuses require technological monitoring and medical intervention. Doctors use Caesarean deliveries to limit the risks of vaginal birth but also to reduce their potential legal liability if the birth becomes complicated. However, Caesareans also can be conveniently scheduled in advance and command higher fees because they require more medical expertise. For this reason, some critics wonder if these expensive and invasive operations are being overused.

Some older and wealthier women may ask their doctors for a Caesarean delivery because they are encouraged to believe that they are safer, but also because they can be scheduled in advance. Some journalists have suggested that a few women are convinced that elective Caesareans provide aesthetic and sexual benefits over vaginal births (i.e., an abdominal scar is seen as a lesser disadvantage than a 'loose vagina' from vaginal birth that may impede sexual satisfaction). This has led to media articles about women who are 'too posh to push' (Asthana, 2005). However, elective Caesareans not only are more costly than vaginal births but also require a longer recovery time for the women undergoing this surgery (Tew, 1998). For these reasons, elective Caesareans remain options for wealthier patients who are able and willing to pay the additional costs and whose doctors are willing to accommodate them.

The steadily increasing rate of Caesarean births over the last century has become one of the most contested issues in maternity care (Walker et al., 2002). The World Health Organization, which has firmly stated that medical interventions such as Caesareans should be performed only with medical justification, suggests that the optimum rate should fall between 5 and 15 per cent of births (WHO, 1998: 77). However, few countries have rates below this level. In some regions of a number of countries, Caesarean rates range from 25 per cent to 45 per cent of all births (Walker et al., 2002: 28).

Even with normal births, midwives are less likely than doctors to rely on technological monitoring, drugs, and other interventions. Consequently, the clients of midwives require less postpartum care and recovery time, and their services are less costly to public health-care systems (Tew, 1998). However, comparing hospital births to home births by midwives gives a false impression of the consequences of each option. Higher-risk maternity cases are accepted by obstetricians rather than midwives and riskier births usually take place in hospitals, which raises the neonatal mortality rates of hospital births delivered by obstetricians compared to home births attended by midwives.

If a doctor cautions a pregnant woman that vaginal birth could be risky for her, few patients would have the means of evaluating this medical advice and most would be likely to accept a recommendation of a Caesarean. Doctors, as well as pregnant women and their families, do not want to take unnecessary risks in childbirth. The medical profession remains powerful in many liberal welfare states and has been able to lobby governments to accept their practices and also to limit the powers of alternative practitioners in childbirth. The fact that Caesareans are more often performed on wealthier women who are paying for private care suggests that doctors may have chosen to benefit financially from these operations without necessary medical grounds for the procedures (Walker et al., 2002; Ford et al., 2003).

Some governments restrict the use of Caesarean operations. The health-care funding system in the Netherlands, for example, requires normal births to be midwife-attended and to take place at home (Tew, 1998). In the Netherlands and in Sweden, rates of Caesarean deliveries have remained at about 10 per cent since the 1980s, much lower than in the liberal welfare states (Walker et al., 2002: 29). Both of these countries provide extensive prenatal care and enjoy among the lowest maternal and infant mortality rates in the world (UN, 2000).

The medicalization and bureaucratization of childbirth have concerned many patients and their families, and have forced health officials and hospital administrators to improve birthing facilities. Private hospitals and birthing centres offer more luxuries to patients who can afford them; however, cost-cutting measures are widespread in both private and public institutions. In the 1940s and 1950s, women could expect a two-week 'confinement', but now they are expected to give birth and leave the hospital within a few days. This short stay is justified for health reasons, but also has served as a cost-cutting measure (Tew, 1998).

In addition, health-care services are being regionalized in some countries and responsibility is being shifted from public institutions to informal networks and unpaid caregivers (Armstrong et al., 2002). Benoit et al. (2002) argued that non-urban women in British Columbia view the recent regionalization of maternity-care services in a largely negative light. They complain about the lack of choice in care providers, discontinuous care across the birthing period, and inadequate quality of care. However, many politicians believe that it is more important to try to reduce the cost of public health care, especially as more services will be needed in the future as the population grows older. As the birth rate falls, health-care providers might be tempted to give priority to services for older citizens rather than to pregnant women and children. Yet the rising cost of childbirth is only one concern. As more mothers enter the labour force, many families and policy-makers worry about who will care for the children.

REARING AND SUPERVISING CHILDREN

Families remain important places for children and young people to develop a sense of identity, to distinguish what is important in life, to clarify ideas about desirable futures, and to develop optimism about the future. Young people implicitly learn from their parents and siblings how to get along with others, or how to argue and fight. From observing their own parents and those of their friends, children and adolescents develop impressions about what it is like to be married, to become a parent, to negotiate and make compromises, and to resolve interpersonal differences. These may be negative, ambivalent, or positive lessons and sometimes leave young people confused.

Despite the pressures on mothers to contribute to household income, some choose to care for their children at home, seeing this as their vocation or, at least, as a temporary but worthwhile job. This option is especially available for those with a partner who earns an income that is adequate for the entire household. Other mothers might remain home from work for the first two years because affordable infant care is expensive and difficult to find. Even if infant care is available, parents want to ensure that the number of staff is sufficient to keep the infants clean, fed, stimulated, and free from infectious diseases and that care providers are well qualified. Finding a skilled care provider to come to the child's home or who will welcome an extra child in her home is also difficult. Licensed family homes are available in most urban jurisdictions, but child minders or sitters usually operate outside these regulations. Informal care seldom is regulated by any level of government yet remains the most prevalent type of child care for employed parents in the liberal welfare states (Baker, 1995: 235; Millar and Rowlingson, 2001).

When mothers leave full-time work for childbirth, the couple's previous division of labour often changes. Although many mothers enjoy the flexibility with time, household tasks that might have been shared before childbirth often become the woman's responsibility. The longer a mother stays at home, the more traditional the division of labour becomes, although neither partner may notice any change at first (Cowan et al., 1985). Furthermore, isolation and depression are sometimes a problem for new mothers.

Kedgley (1996: 299) noted that 10 per cent of new mothers in New Zealand were diagnosed with post-partum depression, but 30 per cent who were not employed outside the home reported that they felt depressed. These feelings arose from overwork with routine tasks, from losing touch with adult activities and labour force requirements, from social isolation, and from perceived lack of recognition for their hard work. Reported depression increased to 70 per cent among those whose child displayed behavioural problems or who experienced marital disharmony (ibid., 300). Isolation for new mothers may be a lesser problem in countries where most mothers remain at home with young children, but a more serious problem in Canada and the United States, where most mothers are now at work during the daytime.

In a recent American study, Evenson and Simon (2005) confirmed that parenthood is not associated with enhanced mental health and that non-parents report lower levels of depression than parents. Their research and other studies also conclude that depression levels are particularly high among lone parents, those with low incomes, and parents residing with minor children, which suggests that these factors serve as stressors. However, they conclude that the emotional disadvantages of parenthood are not greater for women than for men, although women typically report higher levels of depression.

Married fathers who care for their children at home while their wives work for pay may actually experience more problems than mothers do because they do not fit into existing support groups or children's play groups. Unemployment seems to lower men's decision-making power in the household and raises marital conflict (Cherlin, 1996; Beaujot, 2000). Neighbours and relatives often criticize a 'house husband' for not accepting the masculine role of breadwinner and family head. Consequently, social pressure and financial constraints discourage men from caring for their children at home except for temporary periods. Most Canadian fathers who care for their children at home on a full-time basis are unemployed and have not chosen housework and child care over paid employment (Marshall, 1998).

Considerable research focuses on how children are socialized to become adults. For years, academics argued about the influence of 'nature' (biology) versus 'nurture' (culture) in human behaviour, and these debates continue today in a slightly different form with increased interest in the genetic basis of social behaviour and health outcomes. However, pre-1950 ideas about the biological basis of gendered behaviour in children were challenged in the 1960s and 1970s with **social learning theory** and the growing body of research about how children are socialized into 'sex roles' (later called 'gender roles'). Sociologists and social psychologists demonstrated that male and female infants may be born with different bodies but that these differences are usually enhanced and augmented by social practices that vary by culture.

In cultures with a British origin, parents treat girls more gently, dress them in pink, give them dolls to play with, and protect them from dirt and rough play. In contrast, male infants are often dressed in blue and as they grow older are given active toys, encouraged to become independent from their mother at a younger age, and are expected to engage in rough physical play with other boys and men. Girls are encouraged to see their mothers as **role models** as they grow up, to help her around the house, and to become interested in fashion, appearances, and relationships. In contrast, boys are seldom expected to perform much housework but are encouraged to mow the lawn, help their father, focus on their education and employment training, and develop sports-related skills. By the 1980s, many researchers were investigating the impact on children of gendered practices in the home, in schools, and in the media. In Chapter 5, I discuss how parents 'perform gender' at home through their unpaid work, and the potential this has to shape children's attitudes and behaviour.

Lundberg and Rose (1998) showed that household specialization associated with parenting declined in the United States from 1980 to 1992. Nevertheless, the first birth reduced mothers' paid working hours by 45 per cent but did not alter fathers' hours. In fact, fathers' wage rate *increased* by 9 per cent after the birth of a child, while mothers' wage rate fell by 5 per cent (ibid.). In 2000, only 2.9 per cent of employed fathers aged between 25 and 54 worked part-time, compared to 28.7 per cent of employed mothers with one child and 36.6 per cent of mothers with two or more children (OECD, 2002: 77). Clearly, having children alters women's employment patterns more than men's in OECD countries.

SAME-SEX PARENTING

In Canada, about 15 per cent of lesbian couples and 3 per cent of gay couples are raising children (Ambert, 2005). Most of these would be raising children from previous heterosexual relationships although some lesbian women have undergone donor insemination in private fertility clinics or on their own (Patterson and Chan, 1997). In lesbian families, both partners could be mothers who bring children into the household from previous relationships or from insemination. Ambert (2005) reports that same-sex couples who are parents often create a network of 'fictive kin' or friends, former partners, and willing relatives who offer social support and provide role models for the children.

How does same-sex parenting influence children? Meezan and Rauch (2005) reviewed the American research since 1970 and found that the children studied are doing about as well as children normally do. Gay and lesbian parents are as likely as heterosexual parents to provide healthy and supportive environments for their children. Generally, the results of the research suggest that the development, adjustment, and well-being of these children do not differ from those of heterosexual parents. However, methodological problems are inherent in studying small populations that are difficult to locate, and the research does not yet show whether the children studied are typical of the general population of children raised by gay and lesbian couples. In examining how same-sex marriage might influence the lives of children already raised by gay and lesbian couples, the authors note that it could help ensure children's financial well-being and the stability of their parents' relationships, as well as increase the social acceptance of their household arrangements. Same-sex marriage is relatively new in the United States, but the fact that different states offer different legal arrangements (Meezan and Rauch, 2005) provides a useful setting for future research.

PROLONGING ADOLESCENCE

Social historians and sociologists have investigated historical transitions in the life cycle and noted that the distinction between childhood and adolescence has been augmented as young people tend to remain in school longer and more of them depend on their parents for accommodation, meals, and financial assistance. Generally, parents grant to their adolescents more autonomy and privacy than to younger children, allowing teenagers more privileges and rights, offering them additional choices in their daily life, and including them in family decision-making. Parents usually encourage their adolescents to develop adult skills and to want to establish their own households separate from their parents. This involves encouragement to become educated and to develop job skills, to expand their confidence and interpersonal skills, and to develop good judgement about personal relationships.

Older people often think of adolescence as a time of hope, anticipation, and preparation for the future but some young people are depressed by world events, their parents' relationship, their family's poor socio-economic circumstances, and perceived constraints to their future employment and personal happiness. They may demand more autonomy than their parents are willing to give them, and when they are constrained they may engage in acts of rebellion in an attempt to show that they are individuals able to make their own choices (Baker, 1993: 206).

Some families with adolescents experience considerable conflict. Numerous studies show that at this stage in the family life cycle, parents reach their low point in life satisfaction and marital satisfaction (Lupri and Frideres, 1981; Van Laningham et al., 2001). If parents have been married for years, interactions between them may become less person-oriented and more associated with household tasks and obligations. Financial obligations also increase as teenage children grow and develop their interests, and some parents also acquire responsibilities for aging parents at this stage. Both husband and wife are likely to work in the labour force in mid-life and their jobs may require more commitment and time as they gain seniority. At the same time, teenage children are often critical of parents' values, lifestyles, and appearance and friction may also occur between the parents over how to deal with their teenage children.

Many parents have experienced the breakdown of their marriages by the time their children reach their teen years. Some have re-partnered and live in stepfamily situations, but others (especially women) remain alone, struggling with financial constraints as well as with rearing children at this difficult stage. Those who have re-partnered may feel that they are caught between their current partner and their biological children, who do not always get along with their step-parent (Pryor and Rodgers, 2001).

Some parents with adolescent children find that rearing them is a complex task requiring patience and understanding. Teenage mood swings may also coincide with mothers' menopausal symptoms or other forms of mid-life crisis of either parent. Some adolescents are confused and distressed, turning to alcohol, drugs, or promiscuous sex. Many refuse to talk to their parents about their feelings, partly because they are unsure of how to express their concerns but also because their peers may discourage them from confiding in parents or other adults. Peer pressures remain strong and belonging to a peer group is often given precedence over family co-operation.

Adolescents have to deal with physiological and emotional changes, educational choices, relations with friends, new dating experiences, and imminent occupational decisions (Baker, 1993: 207). They tend to be caught between childhood and adulthood, and sometimes feel that social expectations are unrealistic. While many are physically mature, they have not completed their education or found full-time work, and therefore find it financially difficult to leave home. They may resent parental restrictions, feel that their parents are unreasonable and old-fashioned, and yearn for independence.

Many adolescents and young adults now work part-time while they attend school and university but fewer seem to be required to pay 'room and board' to their parents. Their earnings are seldom enough to become self-financing although young people may be expected to pay for some of their educational expenses, their clothes, and their leisure activities. They may also receive some income from parents, as gifts or in return for household chores. As young people attempt to separate themselves from their parents and become individuals, they may engage in sudden outbursts of anger or sullen periods of self-exclusion from family activities.

Adolescence may also be a time of questioning about family history and parents' earlier activities and relationships. More young people live with only one parent or in stepfamilies, and may want to know details of their parents' past, including reasons for their marriage breakdown. About 1 per cent of babies are born from assisted conception, including sperm donations or donated eggs (Ford et al., 2003), but this percentage is expected to rise in the future. Undoubtedly, these young people will want to know something about their backgrounds and may press their parents for answers. As children grow older, they tend to question parental authority and want to establish the superiority of their own ideas and knowledge. Despite these conflicts, most parents derive considerable satisfaction from seeing their children grow into thinking individuals and watching them blossom into physical maturity. A minority of parents despair at the way their young people have turned out, and may blame themselves, their spouse, or former partner for the outcomes.

Young people from immigrant families often face a wider gap between peer expectations and the values of their parents and older relatives. Many are taught to respect their elders, to obey parental advice, to protect the family's privacy and reputation, and to reduce family conflict. Those who come from cultures favouring arranged marriages may be fearful of the prospect of dating, as their parents would disapprove, but at the same time be unable to accept their parents' choices for them.

Forced to act as family translators, some young people from immigrant families feel caught between two cultures.

As children mature, they are continually confronted by media representations and advertisements for consumer goods that encourage them to aspire to material wealth, fashionable clothing, international travel, and personal fame. Many students feel compelled to work part-time in order to afford this kind of lifestyle but paid work may interfere with their studies. Part-time employment earns them spending money and may provide useful job experience for the future, but many of the jobs available to youth are low-level service jobs with wages below the adult minimum.

From the earlier discussion of family life in previous eras, we have seen that the creation of adolescence as a separate stage in the family life cycle is relatively recent historically. This stage was possible only after the abolition of child labour, the legislation of compulsory education, and the necessity of young people to prolong their education in order to find paid work. The trend towards delayed marriage and high accommodation costs encourages prolonged dependence on parents even though young people are physically mature and sexually active. Compared to the 1970s, young people now continue to live with their parents and siblings for several more years, which could cement relationships or perpetuate conflict.

CONCLUSION

Although parents may see their children as their pride and joy (or the bane of their existence), policy-makers now tend to view children as a form of 'social capital' or a future resource to the nation (Jenson, 2004). Some governments have increased the level of child benefits, extended maternity benefits, and introduced larger subsidies for public child-care services. However, fertility rates continue to decline in many places as becoming a parent has considerable consequences for employment opportunities, living costs, and lifestyle. Especially mothers are expected to juggle the timing of child-bearing with the demands of paid work, and many struggle to combine employment and family responsibilities.

Having children is becoming more of a choice for women or couples, but childbirth is also becoming less natural and influenced more by technological monitoring and medical interventions. Pregnant women are expected to be mindful of fetal health and well-being, and to regulate their own behaviour to ensure that they bring no harm to their unborn babies. Potential parents can view their fetus before birth and these images may enable decisions to be made about whether or not to continue with pregnancy. Policy-makers and lobby groups also use these images to consider whether fetuses have legal rights.

All this suggests that having and raising children today is considerably different now than was the case in decades past. As infants and toddlers, children are thought to need more extensive adult attention and intellectual stimulation, and as they grow older we expect them to acquire more schooling. Children are now given more opportunity to develop their identities and to express their personal views. More mothers are employed now, so many children receive at least some daily care from other relatives, paid child-care workers, teachers, and organized recreation workers.

In addition, parents seem to have less influence over their children now that they watch television and videos, play video games, have access to the Internet, and interact with other care providers.

As more mothers accept full-time jobs, the supervision of their children becomes more complicated during parental working hours. School authorities still expect parents to take an interest in their children's education and to participate in school activities, but many employed parents have limited time to do so. More parents now depend on organized after-school activities and paid care providers to supervise their children while they are at work. At the same time, communities are perceived as more dangerous in terms of vehicle traffic, sexual predators, illicit drugs, and negative influences from the Internet, television, and videos. This suggests that the expectations of parenting and typical parenting experiences have changed over the past few decades, causing additional stress for all parents but especially for those with low incomes who live in dangerous neighbourhoods. In the next chapter, issues of employment and family money are examined in more detail.

SUMMARY

The desire to have children and actual patterns of reproduction are influenced by other opportunities in the larger society, such as education, employment, income, wealth accumulation, and family and cultural activities. In addition, the experience of being a child has been transformed by new expectations about parental supervision, the growing trend for non-parental care, access to various mass and interactive media, and the perceived need for prolonged education among youth.

Questions for Critical Thought

1. How have child-rearing professionals modified their advice to parents since the 1950s?
2. Why are more medical specialists now involved in conception and childbirth?
3. Are there differences in outcome for children raised by same-sex parents compared to heterosexual parents? What factors might influence the child-rearing experiences of same-sex parents?

Suggested Readings

Doucet, Andrea. 2006. *Do Men Mother?* Toronto: University of Toronto Press. Based on the narratives of over 100 Canadian fathers who are primary caregivers of children, this book explores the interplay between fathering and public policy, gender ideologies, social networks, and work-family policies.

Fox, Bonnie. 2001. 'The Formative Years: How Parenthood Creates Gender', *Canadian Review of Sociology and Anthropology* 38, 4: 373–90. This article is based on the author's study of a group of heterosexual couples as they make the transition to parenthood. It illustrates the way particular versions of mothering and fathering are negotiated.

Friendly, Martha, and Jane Beach. 2005. *Early Childhood Education and Care in Canada*, 6th edn. Toronto: Childcare Resource and Research Unit. This monograph provides cross-Canada data and information on regulated child care, kindergarten, and maternity and parental leave together with relevant demographic information.

Wall, Glenda. 2005. 'Childhood and Child Rearing', in M. Baker, ed., *Families: Changing Trends in Canada*, 5th edn. Toronto: McGraw-Hill Ryerson, 163–80. This chapter focuses on the social construction of childhood through an examination of twentieth-century child-rearing advice in Canada. Wall also discusses the structural realities and social policies relating to children.

Suggested Websites

Statistics Canada
www.statcan.ca
Statistics Canada provides a wide range of census documents and statistics relating to fertility rates, families, and households.

Childcare Resource and Research Unit
www.childcarecanada.org
The website for this research centre at the University of Toronto includes Canadian and cross-national research and other material on child-care issues.

Centre for Families, Work, and Well-Being
www.worklifecanada.ca
This University of Guelph centre provides information about child-care research projects.

Chapter 5

Family Work and Family Money

Learning Objectives
- To understand how families divide their labour within the household.
- To acknowledge that opportunities to earn, borrow, spend, and save vary by age and gender.
- To trace the impact of changing patterns of paid work on family life and domestic labour.

CHAPTER OUTLINE

This chapter discusses patterns in the household division of labour of cohabiting and married couples, as well as their access to 'family money'. It also acknowledges the impact of parenthood on the type of work that men and women do, their hours of work, and the relative rewards they reap from employment. The chapter ends with a discussion of how recent labour market trends and employment-related policy changes have influenced family life.

INTRODUCTION

In this chapter, I argue that patterns of work tend to change for both men and women when they marry and become parents. Fathers usually increase their commitment to paid work, spending longer hours earning money to support their wife and children, while mothers tend to reduce their hours of paid work in order to spend more time on child care and domestic work. In recent years, these gendered work patterns have begun to converge slightly. More mothers work full-time, which increases household earnings but reduces time for household tasks, child care, and leisure. Some fathers retrain or become unemployed or self-employed, enabling them to share some of the child care and housework. However, husbands and fathers are far more likely than single men and all women to work full-time and overtime, and wives and mothers are far more likely than men or single women to work part-time and take responsibility for child care and housework. Although parents might willingly accept these gendered patterns of work, they can impede mothers' opportunities to become self-supporting, distance fathers from their children and home activities, and provide children with gendered role models.

In this chapter, I also show that changing patterns of paid work in Western industrialized countries, including the '24-hour economy' and deregulated labour markets, impact many aspects of family life. New patterns of paid work alter the organization of housework and child care, the management of family money, the scheduling of family activities, and even personal ambitions. With these employment trends, the work lives of husbands and wives are beginning to look more similar even though large differences remain. This suggests that personal choices about developing a career, supporting a family, and caring for children are constrained by wider socio-economic conditions and vary by gender, marital status, age, culture, and socio-economic circumstances.

COHABITATION, MARRIAGE, AND HOUSEWORK

When couples share a home, a number of maintenance tasks are necessary to sustain the household, including cooking, cleaning, laundry, shopping, and household repairs, as well as personal care. Some of these tasks can be creative but others might seem mundane or even tedious even though they must be done. If a couple owns a car or buys a house with a garden, the level of maintenance work increases. When children arrive, the workload rises exponentially, with more food preparation, cleaning, laundry, and constant child care. Most couples search for ways of reducing domestic labour but this usually costs more money. For example, some parents occasionally use takeout meals to reduce the cooking and washing up, but these meals are often lower in nutritional value and more costly. Families with higher incomes can afford to eat out more frequently as well as to hire outsiders to clean their homes, to do household repairs, and to help care for the children. However, most families cannot afford hired help and must do the housework and much of the child care themselves. As more mothers work longer hours, most couples find that managing two full-time jobs as well as the housework and child care remains very challenging and time-consuming.

Individuals initially develop their standards of cleanliness and orderliness from observing or reacting to their parents, and they further develop or alter these habits over the years. When couples first move in together, how do they establish a division of labour? Studies from many countries indicate that who performs domestic tasks is not always based on joint decision-making but often coincides with conventional ideas about 'doing gender', as well as being influenced by upbringing and the availability of household resources. In moderate-income and lower-income families, women continue to do most of the indoor household tasks and caring work, while men do much of the outside work, including maintenance and repairs (Dempsey, 1997; O'Connor et al., 1999; McMahon, 1999; Beaujot, 2000). This indoor/outdoor split even includes women cooking in the kitchen while men cook outside on the barbecue. In higher-income families, couples often contract outsiders for most of the housework and household repairs, send their young children to high-quality preschools, or hire nannies or housekeepers to live in their home. However, these couples often retain a gendered division of household labour for other household tasks.

Before the 1970s social scientists seldom analyzed patterns of housework and child care, but when they did they saw these tasks as part of women's 'role', suggesting that the division of household labour was determined mainly by biology but also by culture. For example, many of the early structural functionalists, such as British anthropologist Bronislaw Malinowski (1884–1942) and American sociologist Talcott Parsons (1902–79), argued that the nuclear family was universal and based on a biological division of labour that subsequently led to different psychological characteristics and social roles (Luxton, 2005). 'Maternal instincts' and women's ability to lactate were thought to make them more suited biologically and psychologically to perform other domestic tasks.

Men in preliterate societies were considered to be more suited physically to warfare, hunting, and protecting their kin group because of their larger size and superior strength. Academics argued that men rather than women typically supported families in industrialized societies because men were stronger, more rational, and more 'task oriented' than women (Parsons and Bales, 1955). Furthermore, early social scientists argued that the father's physical presence within the family was no longer required after conception whereas the mother continued to breast-feed each subsequent child. In other words, biology shaped their destiny.

In the 1960s, American writer Betty Friedan (1963) identified the isolation of the suburban housewife and her lack of meaningful work as major causes of women's malaise and 'oppression'. This book contributed to the rebirth of the North American feminist movement but also encouraged social researchers to study domestic labour and caring work more systematically. Until the 1970s, few sociologists had studied housework although they had investigated many other occupations. The first sociological studies of housework include Helena Lopata's American study, *Occupation: Housewife* (1971), and Ann Oakley's British research, *The Sociology of Housework* (1974). These sociologists redefined housework as 'work' rather than a natural extension of women's role or an activity motivated by love, and noted its characteristics as gendered, unpaid, potentially isolating, low-status, and not always chosen by the incumbents (Baker, 2001b).

Throughout the 1970s and 1980s, sociologists in many countries investigated the household division of labour. For example, Fletcher (1978) revealed a traditional gendered pattern of household work in New Zealand families in the 1970s, noting that wives rather than husbands accommodated their housework around their employment. Luxton (1980) examined family life in an isolated Canadian mining town, arguing that housework was 'more than a labour of love', involving gendered and class expectations and power relations. Hochschild (1989) showed that American mothers working full-time often experience a 'double day' or a 'second shift' when they arrive home to unpaid housework and caring responsibilities.

Considerable research has also shown that men and women disagree about how much housework husbands actually do, and that many wives (but fewer husbands) see the division of labour at home as unequal and unfair. Bell and Adair (1985) found that 30 per cent of the women in their New Zealand sample reported that they did all the housework in their homes and 80 per cent said that they did most of it. Only five per cent of the women reported that their partners had increased their contributions to housework over the past decade even though most men in their study said that they had. Phillips (1988) noted that women have grown increasingly resentful as they intensify their work by becoming more efficient and disciplined with their time.

Parents usually encourage their children to share some of the housework to help them develop 'responsibility' but research suggests that their contributions are rather slim. Goodnow (1989) and Goodnow and Susan (1989) studied children's work in Australian families, examining what children do, why they do it, who organizes and supervises their work, and how it impacts on the household. This research found that parents expected their children to share some of the household work, but mothers expended more time and energy encouraging their children to do this work than it took mothers to do the work themselves. If a child failed to perform a designated task, it usually fell to the mother rather than another child or the father to do it. The Australian Time Use Survey found that for every hour of work done by a son, a daughter does 1.3 hours, a father does 2.75 hours, and a mother does 6.5 hours. When mothers take on full-time employment, teenage children do 18 extra minutes of housework each day but sons do only two-thirds of the unpaid work done by daughters and most of it is done outdoors (Bittman, 1991: 19).

Data about unpaid work are often derived from time-use or time-budget studies. This kind of research asks participants to record their activities at regular intervals during specific days, usually on a weekday and on a weekend day. Analysts then make statistical comparisons between various categories of participants, such as men and women, married and single people, the young and old, and those working full-time and part-time. The fact that husbands and wives perform different household tasks is not necessarily a problem but in recent years most wives have increased their hours of paid work. Time-budget studies can tell us whether or not men do more housework when their wives increase their paid work, and if younger couples create a different sort of division of labour than older couples.

All the governments of the liberal welfare states have developed studies of unpaid work and some have been carrying out this kind of research long enough to draw conclusions about changes over time. For example, the Australian Bureau of Statistics has completed extensive time budget surveys since the 1970s and has found that women perform about 70 per cent of unpaid domestic work, and this percentage is largely unaffected by their increasing employment rates. No matter how many hours of paid work an Australian wife does, her husband's contribution remains relatively constant (Bittman, 1991; Baxter, 1994; Bittman, 1995; Baxter and Bittman, 1995). Despite the increasing use of dishwashers, microwaves, automatic washers, and clothes dryers, Australians in the early 1990s spent about the same time in the kitchen and laundry as they did in 1974.

From 1974 to 1991, Australian women lost one hour of leisure time per day because they were working more for pay but they generally retained responsibility for domestic duties. By 1991, men were doing more work in the kitchen and laundry but many of these men were single, reflecting higher separation and divorce rates and older ages of marriage. Furthermore, two-thirds of men's unpaid work was done outdoors and many of the tasks were occasional ones rather than daily chores

(Bittman, 1991). Using the 1997 Australian Time Use Survey, Bittman and Rice (1999) continued to show that husbands have *not* taken up the slack even though wives have increased their hours of paid work. Instead, 'domestic outsourcing' or the purchase of market substitutes for domestic labour helps Australian women resolve the time pressure created by an increasing commitment to paid work.

Canadian studies of unpaid work have found that wives who are employed full-time tend to perform less housework than those who work part-time or are outside the **labour force**. Wives employed full-time either lower their housework standards, encourage other family members to share the work, or hire someone to clean their houses or care for their children. Having a larger number of children clearly represents more work for mothers. Yet, many women continue to retain all or most of the responsibility for indoor housework and child-rearing tasks, including the hiring and supervision of cleaners and care providers (Baker and Lero, 1996). Women with less than high school graduation and older women are more likely to accept sole responsibility for housework (Marshall, 1993, 1994). The Canadian research suggests generational and social class differences in patterns of housework, as well as gender differences.

Gazso-Windle and McMullin (2003) used 1995 Canadian social survey data to explore the relationships among time availability, relative income, gender ideology, and the time spent on housework. They concluded that there is some evidence that partners, but especially husbands, 'trade off' the time they spend in housework by doing more paid work. However, women and men with higher incomes and education spend less time on housework and more time on child care. Ironically, wives spend *more* time on housework when their wages are higher or closer to their husband's, which suggests that being a successful family earner means something different for men and women. Some women may feel that they have to compensate for their success in the (male) breadwinning role by performing extra domestic tasks. Alternatively, the husbands of high-earning women may resent their 'intrusion' into family breadwinning and consequently may resist sharing domestic work. These researchers concluded that egalitarian notions about gender behaviour are more likely to influence Canadian men's participation in child care than in housework.

Many researchers have confirmed that mothers rather than fathers accept the responsibility for caring work even when they work full-time (Bittman and Pixley, 1997; Potuchek, 1997). However, globalizing labour markets are becoming even more competitive, making it difficult for employees to take time off work for child-bearing and child-rearing. If mothers quit their jobs, they may not be able to find comparable work again when they are ready to re-enter the labour force. Even if they take an extended **parental leave**, they may find themselves back in a job with similar wages but not necessarily the same position or one that is as rewarding.

Marriage and child-rearing usually encourage fathers to take their earning obligations seriously but mothers often reduce paid work and increase unpaid work after bearing children. When mothers with several children accept a paying job, they tend to work weekends, part-time, or alternate shifts with their husbands in order to integrate paid work and family life (Marshall, 1994; Drolet and Morissette, 1997). Yet family conflict is highest if couples work shifts over which they have no control because co-ordinating child care, leisure, and other family activities becomes more difficult (Marshall, 1998). Employment leave is sometimes the only way to deal with family emergencies, but mothers are far more likely than fathers to disrupt their work schedules to balance this conflict (Akyeampong, 1998).

People who live in countries with liberal market regimes (including Canada, the United States, the United Kingdom, Australia, and New Zealand) tend to work longer average hours than those in other types of welfare regimes. However, there is little variation in the gender division of domestic labour or time spent in leisure activities (Gershuny and Sullivan, 2003). Work-life stress has been found to be more prevalent among mothers than fathers and among parents with more children at home (Crompton, 2004). Work-life stress is also more prevalent in certain countries rather than others, depending on labour conditions such as hours of work, holidays, family leave entitlements, and public child-care services. Crompton (2004) found that employees who reported that they shared housework and child care, and those who worked shorter hours and lived in countries with institutional supports for employed parents (such as Finland and Norway), reported lower levels of work-life stress. This suggests that the stress related to balancing employment and family responsibilities can be lessened by couples sharing their domestic work and by governments ensuring that employees are entitled to family leave, child-care services, and adequate time off work.

Among heterosexual couples, indoor housework and child care remain women's responsibility throughout much of the world, although husbands will 'lend a hand' if their wives are pressed for time. Furthermore, women who have attempted to resist the gendered consequences of marriage by cohabiting without legal marriage often find that they slip back into conventional arrangements (Elizabeth, 2000). However, some research indicates that the division of labour among gay and lesbian couples is more egalitarian than among heterosexual couples (Ranson, 2005). Although biological mothers in lesbian households might do more mothering tasks, the housecleaning and cooking is more likely to be evenly shared on the basis of individual tastes and abilities (Dunne, 2000; Nelson, 1996, 2001). These findings support the idea that housework and child care are sites for 'doing gender' and for reinforcing the biological and social differences between heterosexual men and women.

HOUSEHOLD MONEY AND WEALTH ACCUMULATION

Sociologists and political economists often argue that wealth is developed and passed on through families, who protect their resources through careful investments and strategic marriages. They also argue that knowledge of people's social class background (or the income and wealth accumulation of the family of origin) is crucial to understanding their ambitions, desires, and lifestyle choices. Sociologists also argue that 'new money' is different from 'old money'. The very notion of 'nouveau riche' implies that those who recently acquired money often feel the need to show off their success through 'conspicuous consumption' with their cars, homes, and furnishings (Veblen, 1899). The concept of the 'trophy wife' further suggests that rich men can afford to marry much younger and beautiful women who enhance their status through their fashionable and youthful appearance.

Gilding (2005) used the *Business Review Weekly*'s list of the 200 richest people in Australia to examine how families accumulate and transmit their wealth. He noted that family businesses that grow and survive often develop into larger impersonal corporations but most small and medium enterprises remain as family businesses. Furthermore, family relationships are still pivotal in the transmission of wealth across generations. Wealthy families protect their assets through business partnerships with trusted relatives and pass on their assets to spouses and children. They also create holding and investment companies and 'family trusts', which help to minimize the payment of taxes. In fact, Gilding argues that the Australian taxation system encourages the formation of 'family entities', which limit the dispersal of family fortunes.

Home ownership is one of the ways that ordinary families can accumulate wealth (VIF, 2004: 117). About 68 per cent of all Canadian households (including individuals and families) were homeowners in 2002, but access to home ownership varies by age, marital status, and household income. Senior couples (aged 65 and over) have the highest rate of home ownership at 88 per cent, compared to 44 per cent for unattached older persons. Among the richest 20 per cent of households, 91 per cent owned their own home compared to only 37 per cent of the poorest households.

About 16 per cent of Canadian homeowners spend more than 30 per cent of their income on shelter, including mortgage payments, property taxes, and/or condominium fees, a level that is considered to be financially stressful (ibid., 117–18). Affordable housing is a growing problem for families living in urban conditions, especially those with more than three children, new immigrants, and mother-led families. In Canada, low-income families are most likely to live in rental accommodation and most of these pay market rents. Welfare advocates have argued that reliance on the private housing market means that many low-income families are forced to live in unhealthy, overcrowded, and unsafe accommodation, which can encourage the development of respiratory ailments, the spread of infectious diseases, and depression and anti-social behaviour. Substandard housing can have negative and permanent consequences on children's health, behaviour, and development (Jackson and Roberts, 2001).

Lack of affordable housing can also keep women and children living in abusive households and create overcrowded conditions that heighten family tensions. Moving too many times through inability to pay the rent also has detrimental consequences for children's school performance as well as their peer relationships. Transition housing provided by voluntary organizations and sharing accommodation with relatives and friends are temporary solutions to problems of affordability. However, in many countries, the state has helped to expand housing stocks and to improve the quality and affordability of housing because governments often equate home ownership with family and community stability and well-being.

Access to income clearly influences opportunities to own a home, enjoy comfortable accommodation, and accumulate family wealth. In recent years, researchers have also compared rates of **child poverty** and used them as an indicator of the relative generosity of parental wages and social benefits for families in each country.

The United Nations Children's Fund and the Organization for Economic Co-operation and Development regularly publish comparative statistics on the percentage of children living in households with 'low' incomes, usually defined as less than 50 per cent of the median income in that country, after taxes and government transfers and adjusted for family size. These figures show that poverty rates tend to be high in the liberal welfare states, such as the United States, Canada, and New Zealand, and much lower in the social democratic countries, such as Denmark, Finland, and Sweden (OECD, 2005b: 57). However, poverty rates are much higher when children live only with their mother. Table 5.1 shows the child poverty rates for single-parent and two-parent households in selected countries.

Since the 1960s, social researchers have also explored the connection between who earns household money and decisions about how it is spent. They concluded that the social meaning of money is important because who brings it into the household and how it is distributed relate to ideologies of gender and marriage (Pahl, 1995). Since the beginning of wage labour, husbands have been the primary earners in most households with European origins. The ideal of the **family wage** spread until, by the early 1900s, it meant that married men were paid a higher wage than single men or women. This wage was supposed to be sufficient to permit male breadwinners to support themselves, a wife, and two to three dependent children. As this employment practice was implemented, wives' earnings became viewed as less significant, as supplementary income for extras, and essentially disposable, regardless of how much they earned (Zelizer, 1994).

Although husbands earned most 'family money' in the past, they did not always manage it on their own. Often they kept some for themselves but gave the rest to

Table 5.1   Poverty Rates among Children by Household Type, 1999–2001

Country	All Children	Children in Single-Parent Households	Children in Two-Parent Households
Australia	11.6	38.4	6.8
Canada	13.6	42.1	8.5
Denmark	2.4	7.2	1.9
Finland	3.4	10.5	2.5
France	7.3	26.6	5.1
Italy	15.7	24.9	14.1
New Zealand	16.3	47.5	8.8
Portugal	15.6	32.5	12.4
Sweden	3.6	9.3	2.0
United Kingdom	16.2	40.7	8.7
United States	21.7	48.9	14.5
OECD (24 countries)	12.1	32.5	8.7

Note: 'Poverty rate' is defined as households with less than 50 per cent of national median income, after taxes and transfers, and adjusted for family size.

Source: Based on data in OECD (2005b: 57, chart EQ3.2, Poverty rates are much higher for families with jobless parents). © OECD 2005.

their wives, who then purchased the necessities for the entire household. Sometimes husbands and wives managed their money jointly. When husbands managed their earnings themselves, they usually gave their wives a set amount of 'housekeeping money'. If wives earned their own money, they often used it to buy food or clothing for the children or to purchase household items; but some wives saw their personal earnings as their own money and kept it separate from household money. Current research suggests that the idea of the **male breadwinner** continues today even though most wives are also earners (Pahl, 2005).

The organization of family money is not always consciously discussed or decided but is influenced instead by cultural factors, by gender ideologies, and especially by the relative earnings of husbands and wives. Money is not the only valued resource in the **family economy**, nor is it equally valued in all households. Studying money allocation patterns reveals important cultural differences in access and control over family resources. For example, Fleming's New Zealand research (1997) concluded that Maori and Pacific Island couples often lived within a wider family group where the use of their earnings could be dictated by the extended family. For couples with European origins, control over money is related to the relative amount earned by each partner and is more influenced by the notion that the husband should be the provider. In Maori and Pacific Island families, the provider role was not necessarily associated with power or authority, as other sources of male authority were available. Fleming (1999) also found that money allocation patterns in stepfamilies differed from first marriages, particularly with regard to supporting the other partner's children.

Although most wives are now employed, husbands typically earn considerably more than their wives. In British research, most married men and women defined their personal earnings as 'family money' but husbands were more likely than their wives to express this view (Pahl, 1995). Although there are several different ways of managing money, most couples pool their resources, and this money could be managed jointly, by the wife, or by the husband. Increased female employment is associated with the greater pooling of earnings that are managed jointly. In fact, the higher women's earnings are relative to their husbands, the more say wives have in how their combined earnings are spent (Vogler and Pahl, 1994). This suggests that longer hours of paid employment have enhanced wives' control over family money.

Despite more dual-earner families, few couples keep their earnings in separate bank accounts; however, this pattern is becoming more prevalent. In the 1990s, research found that only about 3 per cent of British couples kept all of their earnings separate but more recent research suggest that over a quarter of young British couples manage most of their earnings separately and combine only some designated for household expenses (Pahl, 2005). Independent money management was particularly characteristic of younger couples, those without children, and those where the woman was in full-time paid employment. Cohabitation rather than legal marriage also influences patterns of family money. New Zealand and British studies have found that women who cohabit are more likely than legally married women to have their own earnings and to keep their money separate from their partner's in order to maintain their independence (Elizabeth, 2001; Pahl, 2001).

Spending responsibilities also differ by gender. Canadian and British research suggests that wives and mothers tend to be responsible for buying food for the household, clothing for themselves and their children, and child care and school expenses. Men/fathers spent more money on meals out, alcohol, motor vehicles, repairs to the house, and gambling. Responsibility for other items of spending was more evenly distributed (Phipps and Burton, 1992; Ermisch, 2003; Pahl, 2005). With gendered differences in income, women often can raise their living standards by sharing a residence with an employed man, especially if they pool their earnings. However, if they keep their money separate and she continues to be responsible for spending in the above areas, the financial outcome might not be equitable (Elizabeth, 2001; Pahl, 2005). Consequently, some heterosexual couples arrange to pay a percentage of their earnings rather than an equal amount into their joint account.

Another indication that relative income between partners is important for the control of family money arises out of studies of families living on state income support. In low-income families, especially those on social assistance, women tend to have more control over how the money is spent (Fleming and Easting, 1994; Christopher et al., 2001). This finding probably relates to the fact that women's incomes are essential for the survival of low-income households, but are not always necessary in higher-income households. In addition, governments often pay income support directly to the mother on behalf of the children or to both partners equally. Generally, women gain decision-making power as their income approximates that of their partners. As more women have their own full-time earnings, their willingness to accept male management of household resources declines.

Children learn about the social and cultural value of money from their parents early in childhood but also from their peer group and the media. Increasingly, young people are using access to money and consumption to create an identity. A recent New Zealand survey found that two-thirds of parents give their children allowances or pocket money (averaging $20 per week) and three-quarters of 12–19-year-olds have, or have had, part-time jobs (McFadden, 2005). Many children are expected to do family work for their allowances, such as setting the table, cleaning their rooms, and caring for younger siblings. When New Zealand teens are employed outside the home, they often work from 10 to 20 hours a week, earning between $10 and $15 per hour. Yet, unlike previous generations, these teenagers seldom return any of this money to their parents and many see their earnings as their own. Although some save for their education or a car (especially boys), many spend it quickly on non-essentials, such as cellphones and designer clothes, which have become status symbols, as well as magazines, CDs, and snacks. Despite having access to more money, McFadden argued that the current generation of New Zealand youth are falling into debt attempting to pay off their cellphone and credit card charges. Those who continue their education are also paying off student loans.

Access to credit is increasingly important to lifestyle but this access varies by age, gender, and employment status. In addition, the 'easy money' available to today's youth sometimes leads to a lifetime of poor money management and debt, especially as youth are often targeted by advertisers (ibid.). Within adult couples, men are more likely than women to acquire access to credit with their higher incomes, but wives who work full-time are more likely than homemakers to use credit cards and electronic money transactions (Pahl, 2001). Greater use of credit cards is associated with youth, full-time employment, and higher education. Unemployed and retired people are less likely to use credit cards, but among the retired, men are more likely than women to use them, reflecting differences in income, confidence in using new technologies, or a tradition of male dominance in marital finances among this age group. Credit cards can be used as status symbols, especially when the colour gold or platinum reveals the holder's income and credit levels (ibid.). Access to financial services is clearly constrained by income, employment status, age, gender, and location of residence.

Despite the emphasis that economists give to rational decision-making in financial transactions, discussions of family money often involve such strong emotions as anxiety, guilt, or pride. Singh (1997) differentiated between 'marriage money', which is domestic and co-operative and typically held in a joint account, and 'market money', which is impersonal and subject to contract. The difference between the two is particularly important if couples divorce or if they use their family home as collateral for a husband's business loan. When the divorce settlement is finalized or the bank demands repayment of the loan, the financial arrangements that had represented trust and love suddenly become impersonal and contractual (Pahl, 2001), not to mention acrimonious and expensive. Lawton (1991: 7) uses the concept of 'sexually transmitted debt' to discuss the ways that financial co-operation within marriage can end in serious problems if the trust is broken or the relationship sours.

Although credit cards are used mainly by younger people, net worth usually increases with age. In Canadian households in 1999 where a male was the main earner, net worth reached a peak between the ages of 55 and 64 years. However, it declined after separation and divorce for both men and women, and was especially low for households in which a woman was the main income recipient (VIF, 2004: 122). Two incomes per family have become the norm in many countries and increasingly necessary to pay the bills. From 1980 to 2002, the after-tax incomes of most Canadians increased, even after accounting for the effects of inflation, largely because more households had acquired two earners (ibid., 91). However, personal savings are at record low levels and debt is rising relative to income (ibid., 92).

The growing gap between rich and poor families in many countries has been attributed to higher rates of separation, neo-liberal restructuring of income support programs, and global labour market conditions that pay some people very high wages while encouraging low minimum wages and temporary or part-time jobs for others. Couples with two full-time incomes, high levels of education, and no children tend to have the highest incomes, while lone-mother households and large 'visible minority' families tend to experience both low income and debt. In the next section, I discuss how labour markets have changed in recent years and what this means for families with children.

Changing Labour Markets

Increasingly, both men and women work for pay regardless of their marital or parental status, but labour market conditions have changed considerably in the last

45 years. After the 1960s, the service sector of the economy expanded in many countries, wages and aspirations increased, and employers began to demand higher qualifications from new employees. As more people gained the required credentials, employers continued to raise the entry-level qualifications for many jobs. For example, in the 1950s, to become a school teacher a high school graduate used to attend a year-long training course, but by the 1980s, in many jurisdictions new teachers were expected to graduate from university before beginning their specialist education training.

In the mid-1970s, the world economy experienced a downturn and more employers became concerned about restricting financial losses, reducing the numbers of permanent employees, maintaining national competitiveness, and/or developing new international markets. Governments signed new trade agreements that permitted employers to make or sell their products in other countries, including places with lower production costs and higher productivity gains. This raised unemployment rates in industrialized countries with higher wages. Less often, new trade agreements permitted workers to cross borders and seek employment in other countries, such as in the European Union. Generally, the use of global markets increased the competitiveness of local labour markets as employers began to advertise nationally and internationally for new workers.

Especially since the 1980s, some manufacturing jobs that were previously unionized and nationally based have shifted outside the borders of Western economies and lost both their legislative and trade union protections. In addition, the service sector expanded, but by providing more temporary and part-time positions than full-time, year-round jobs (Banting and Beach, 1995; Edwards and Magarey, 1995; Van den Berg and Smucker, 1997). Today, compared to the 1970s, a higher percentage of adults are working for pay, but more are also working longer hours. Nevertheless, families are not necessarily better off, either financially or in terms of the quality of their family life or in opportunities to be with their children. Many workers have been expected to retrain, to work in the evenings and on weekends, to become self-employed, or to take early retirement. The lives of men and women, as well as youth, have been influenced by these labour market changes (Baker, 2001b).

At the same time, increased advertising and consumerism have heightened personal aspirations and expectations. People expect their homes to have the latest equipment—microwave ovens, dishwashers, and personal computers—and new forms of credit have been created to enable people to aspire to this higher standard of living. While the cost of some consumer goods such as televisions and computers has fallen relative to average wages, the cost of housing has skyrocketed in the major cities, meaning that even those who work longer hours continue to struggle to pay the rent or mortgage and the credit card bills. More parents are working longer hours now than in the 1960s and many expect their adolescents to earn money to help pay for their own expenses, even while they are still in school.

In summary, work patterns have changed because employers are placing new demands on their workers with changes in the conditions of production and trade, but also because families now need more than one wage to pay for basic living costs.

However, material aspirations have also increased and more people expect some luxuries. Increasingly, what used to be considered a luxury is considered essential, such as two-bathroom homes, two cars per household, one or more home computers, and a personal cellphone. However, labour market changes have not impacted equally on men and women, especially if they are parents.

GENDER AND WORK

Patterns of paid work are beginning to converge for men and women, as employment rates have decreased slightly for men and increased substantially for women since the 1950s. Men's rates have decreased because youth now remain in school longer as employers require higher certification as a qualification for many jobs. In addition, more men work on short-term contracts, work part-time, or are self-employed rather than working a full week and continuously for the same employer. From the 1970s to the 1990s, many men were able to retire before the age of 65 as a consequence of improvements to both public and private pension plans and private savings from better wages and higher interest rates (Myles, 1996). However, in such countries as Canada, male wages from the 1970s to the 1990s did not always keep pace with rising living costs, and successive waves of men are now earning less than their elders at every stage in their work lives (Beaudry and Green, 1997). Consequently, the age of retirement for men is once again rising.

Although the husband still is the major breadwinner in most families, women's increased earnings and the time spent in the workplace are beginning to alter their expectations about marriage, children, and the household division of labour. Women's employment has increased dramatically in many countries, especially among mothers with children under six years of age (OECD, 2005b), as work patterns have been influenced by economic, ideological, and technological changes. First, the **service sector** of many national economies has expanded since the 1950s and 1960s, creating more clerical and service positions in education, retail sales, hospitality industries, health care, and the growing government bureaucracies. Many of these new jobs were thought to be appropriate for women because they were clean and safe and performed indoors. Some were also part-time, allowing mothers to retain most of their domestic and caring duties (Baker, 2001b).

Women's employment also increased because families needed wives' wages to counteract the spiralling cost of living after the 1960s, especially where men's real wages were declining relative to living expenses in Canada and the United States, among other countries (Torjman and Battle, 1999). Throughout the 1970s and 1980s, unemployment rates also increased and more families needed additional income to pay household bills. This included the consumer products that advertising campaigns induced people to buy, such as two cars and modern household appliances, as well as longer periods of formal education for the children. Furthermore, a shortage of employment opportunities has encouraged more young people to stay in school, often while continuing to live in the parental home, increasing financial pressure on all members of the family (Kobayashi, 2007).

The third reason for rising employment rates among women was that feminist ideologies, revived in the 1960 and 1970s, encouraged them to continue their schooling and use their education to contribute directly to household earnings and to the larger society. North American feminists in particular argued that women should gain financial independence from their fathers and husbands in order to 'liberate' themselves emotionally, to develop self-confidence, to achieve equality with men, to realize their potential, and to establish an autonomous household if they so wished (Friedan, 1963; Pierson et al., 1993). At the same time, feminists in Britain, Australia, and New Zealand focused more on gaining government support for mothering at home, portraying women as different from men in their life goals and personal experiences (Land, 1980; Baker and Tippin, 1999). More North American women chose to find paid work in order to use their education, further their ambitions, earn their own money, raise their bargaining power in marriage, and contribute to household purchases and public life.

Fourth, more effective contraception permitted women to better control their pregnancies, especially after the contraceptive pill was marketed in the mid-1960s. Effective contraception enabled women to continue their education and work outside the home throughout their fertile years. Widespread use of contraception also meant that fewer employers worried about unexpected pregnancy among their female staff and were therefore willing to hire and promote women workers. Generally, modern contraceptives have enabled women to acquire higher education, reduce their fertility, and plan for a lifetime of paid work, if they so choose.

Despite these changes, women's employment rates remain much lower than men's in most OECD countries. Some gender convergence is apparent in the type of jobs and the hours of work, but men and women continue to perform different kinds of work and men are more likely to work full-time, overtime, and in positions of responsibility. Women are far more likely than men to accept part-time employment in all OECD countries, as Table 5.2 indicates (OECD, 2005a: 253), and part-time work is much less likely to lead to seniority or higher lifetime wages. Instead, it creates short-term solutions and long-term problems for women.

Table 5.2 shows an increase in men's part-time work in all of the countries included and an increase in women's part-time work except in Denmark, Norway, and Sweden. In Canada, about 27 per cent of women and 11 per cent of men worked part-time in 2004, but other countries such as Australia, Germany, the Netherlands, and Switzerland have much higher rates of part-time work among women. In the Netherlands, for example, 60.2 per cent of female employees worked part-time in 2004, which is well above the OECD average of 25.4 per cent (ibid.).

Women's employment rates are lower than men's and their average earnings are also lower. Despite anti-discrimination and pay equity legislation in most OECD countries, a gender gap remains in the wages of both full-time and part-time workers. In Canada, women working full-time earned 82 per cent of the amount earned by men in 2001, which is slightly below the OECD average (OECD, 2002: 97). This wage gap reflects the different jobs that are often accepted by men and women but also men's longer working hours and greater acceptance of responsibility for earning family money. Women are more likely to reduce their paid work to deal with family commitments, to have lower bargaining power with their employers, and to suffer discrimination when they attempt to progress through the ranks.

Table 5.2   The Incidence of Part-time Employment in Selected OECD Countries
as a Percentage of All Female and Male Employment, 1990 and 2004

Country	1990		2004	
	Women	Men	Women	Men
Australia	38.5	11.3	40.8	16.1
Belgium	28.8	4.4	34.1	6.3
Canada	26.8	9.2	27.2	10.9
Denmark	29.7	10.2	24.3	11.6
Finland	10.6	4.8	15.0	7.9
France	22.5	4.5	23.6	4.8
Germany	29.8	2.3	37.0	6.3
Hungary	4.0	2.0	5.1	2.2
Italy	18.4	4.0	28.8	5.9
Japan	33.4	9.5	41.7	14.2
Luxembourg	19.1	1.6	33.3	1.7
Netherlands	52.5	13.4	60.2	15.1
New Zealand	34.8	7.9	35.4	10.7
Norway	39.8	6.9	33.2	10.3
Portugal	12.8	3.9	14.0	5.8
Spain	11.5	1.4	17.2	2.6
Sweden	24.5	5.3	20.8	8.5
Switzerland	42.6	6.8	45.3	8.1
United Kingdom	39.5	5.3	40.4	10.0
United States	20.2	8.6	18.8	8.1
OECD average	19.7	5.0	25.4	7.5

Source: From OECD (2005a: 253, Table E, Incidents and composition of part-time employment). © OECD 2005.

Although we have focused on gender differences in paid work, middle-class 'white' men have been most likely to experience career advancement leading to higher earnings and better employment-related benefits (such as retirement pensions). In contrast, working-class men and members of certain cultural minorities, as well as many women, have worked with fewer expectations of advancement, pay increases, or fringe benefits, except when trade unions intervened on their behalf. Generally, men have been more likely than women to work full-time and overtime, to progress through the ranks into senior managerial or professional positions, and to earn high wages (Bittman, 1998; Vosko, 2000). How do these comparative statistics relate to family responsibilities?

EMPLOYMENT AND PARENTHOOD

In Canada, men and women with neither spouse nor children have similar rates of full-time employment, but the presence of spouse and children tend to push men and women in opposite directions (Beaujot, 2000). Mothers make more concessions than fathers to the integration of earning and caring as unpaid domestic work is one of the important sites for 'doing gender' (ibid.). New mothers often remain outside the labour force or accept temporary and part-time work to enable them to supplement the household income while they care for their children. Some mothers consider that earning family money is secondary to their main job as care provider and homemaker.

Women in some countries see working part-time as a solution to the problems of combining earning and caring, but the feasibility and desirability of working part-time varies cross-nationally. Mothers might be forced to work full-time if the cost of living is high, if male wages are low, if part-time jobs are difficult to find, if separation and divorce rates are increasing, or if the state provides little or no support for those outside paid work. We find considerable variation across countries among mothers employed part-time whose youngest child is under six years; for example, in 2002, in the Netherlands 79 per cent worked part-time, in Canada 30 per cent, and in Denmark 5 per cent (OECD, 2005b: data chart SS4.3). These cross-national variations in part-time employment rates suggest that local labour market characteristics, social programs, and cultural attitudes about 'good mothering' shape women's employment behaviour, rather than women's personal choices alone creating these patterns.

Women are also more likely than men to work in temporary jobs in almost all OECD countries (ibid., 35). The average OECD incidence of temporary employment as a percentage of all employment was 15.2 per cent for women and 13 per cent for men. However, in some countries, the rates are very high for both men and women. In Spain, for example, 33.5 per cent of women and 28.6 per cent of men work in temporary positions (ibid.). Although women's continuing responsibility for caring work contributes to the steady supply of part-time and temporary workers, local labour market conditions clearly influence these figures.

Increasingly, more family members work at varying schedules from each other. According to the 1995 Canadian Survey of Work Arrangements, nearly 40 per cent of those dual-earner couples who are working full-time also work shifts outside the traditional nine-to-five time frame, including 10 per cent working at completely different times of the day (Marshall, 1998). These working hours affect family mealtimes, the household division of labour, and child-care arrangements.

Low-income Households with Children

Rapid labour market changes can lead to larger gaps between high and low earners and among those whose income derives from different sources, such as wages, salaries, state support, or investments. With globalizing markets and increased competition, caring for children at home without earning money has become a luxury affordable by fewer and fewer women, including those married to high earners or those who are independently wealthy. In Table 5.1 we saw that children living in single-parent households have the highest poverty rates, but Table 5.3 clearly shows that in many countries families need the wages of the wife/mother. For example, children living in one-earner, two-parent families have poverty rates of 22.9 per cent in Canada and 30.5 per cent in United States, but these rates dwindle to 3.5 per cent in Canada and 8.3 per cent in the US for two-earner families (OECD, 2005b: 57). In some countries, few mothers with young children can afford to opt out of paid work because this would deepen the family's level of poverty (ibid., 40).

Table 5.3   Poverty Rates for Children by Work Status of Their Parents, 1999–2001

Country	Total Single Parents	Single Parent Not Working	Single Parent Working	Total Two-Parent Family	Two Parents, No Worker	Two Parents, One Worker	Two Parents, Two Workers
Australia	38.4	58.7	11.7	6.8	43.3	5.4	3.3
Canada	42.1	89.7	27.7	8.5	75.3	22.9	3.5
Denmark	7.2	22.2	4.0	1.9	19.0	6.4	0.7
France	26.6	61.7	9.6	5.1	37.9	6.3	1.6
Mexico	35.0	45.6	32.6	20.7	37.9	26.2	15.4
Netherlands	30.3	42.8	17.7	5.2	50.7	7.8	1.7
New Zealand	47.5	87.6	21.3	8.8	43.3	14.5	4.1
Norway	9.9	24.7	2.8	1.7	38.0	2.8	0.1
Sweden	9.3	34.2	5.6	2.0	13.7	8.2	1.1
United Kingdom	40.7	62.5	20.6	8.7	37.4	17.6	3.6
United States	48.9	93.8	40.3	14.5	77.9	30.5	8.3
OECD (24 countries)	32.5	58.0	20.6	8.7	41.6	13.7	4.3

Note: 'Poverty rate' is defined as households with less than 50 per cent of national median income, after taxes and transfers, and adjusted for family size.

Source: From OECD (2005b: 57). Based on EQ3.2. Poverty rates are much higher for families with jobless parents.
© OECD 2005.

Despite higher rates of maternal employment, low-wage work is more prevalent among women than men, among mothers than fathers, among lone mothers rather than partnered mothers. Many of the 'new poor' (such as lone mothers with pre-school children and men made redundant from previously secure manufacturing jobs) require state income support at least for a transitional period until they can find a job or an additional income in the household. In many countries, 'welfare' requirements now press more categories of people into employment, making paid work the normal life course for fathers, mothers, and young adults.

When parents are offered state income support, their benefit levels often are set below the minimum wage and below the poverty line, especially in the English-speaking countries. Table 5.3 shows that in the United States, for example, 93.8 per cent of children with 'non-working' single parents live below the poverty line. These families are either ineligible for income support payments or the benefits are set at a very low level. In most countries, poverty rates are much higher for families with 'jobless parents' than for those who are working for pay (ibid., 57). Notice that caring for children is no longer considered to be a 'job' in the language of the OECD, although it was a few decades ago.

Studies concerning the long-term implications of living in poverty suggest that these children experience poorer health and more behaviour problems than children from higher-income families (Hobcraft and Kiernan, 2001; Roberts, 1997; Ross et al., 1996). Living on a low income can permeate all aspects of child-rearing. Wealthier parents can purchase child-care services, after-school lessons and recreational activities, counselling, and preventive health care for their children. Low-income parents cannot afford to visit the doctor if they must pay for each consultation or pay to fill prescriptions, even if these services are partially subsidized by the state. A lack of adequate transportation, or its cost, also affects the ability of low-income parents to access medical services even when, as in Canada, basic health care and drug care for social assistance recipients are covered by the state. In addition, without household savings, parents cannot prepare for emergencies. Research from several countries suggests that low-income, lone mothers, especially, suffer from anxiety and depression related to previous relationships, the heavy responsibility of child care alone, and despair about the future (Curtis, 2001; Sarfati and Scott, 2001; Whitehead et al., 2000).

In many countries, mothers with young children at home are more likely to work for pay if they live with a partner. Full-time work requires either unpaid child care by a family member or paid child care by a service provider. Lone mothers are less likely than partnered mothers to have either a family member available or the money to pay for care. Lone mothers' full-time employment rates also vary cross-nationally and are lower in some of the liberal states (such as Australia and the United Kingdom) because social programs have permitted these mothers to care for their children at home (Baker and Tippin, 1999). In addition, demographic and socio-economic differences exist between lone and partnered mothers. For example, lone mothers tend to be younger when they bear their first child and to have lower educational attainment and less employment experience. Vast differences are also apparent among lone mothers depending on their route to lone parenthood: those who have never been married generally have the lowest socio-economic status and poorest job prospects (Dooley, 1995; Hunsley, 1997; Goodger and Larose, 1999; Millar and Rowlingson, 2001).

Typically, lone mothers have lower skill levels and less education than either fathers or partnered mothers, and consequently they find mainly low-paying jobs without flexible work hours, paid sick leave, or extended health benefits (Edin and Lein, 1997; Vosko, 2000; Millar and Rowlingson, 2001). Few have worked long enough with the same employer to be entitled to sick leave. Some lone mothers also experience emotional problems from marriage breakdown, continuing disputes with their children's father, and children's behavioural problems that interfere with finding and keeping paid work (Pryor and Rodgers, 2001).

Some lone mothers understandably view the opportunity to receive welfare while caring for their children at home as more viable than struggling on low wages with piecemeal child-care arrangements (Baker, 2004a). However, recipients of state income support are increasingly encouraged into employment by the need to pay the bills and the desire to become role models for their children, as well as by a desire and need to develop new social contacts. The stigma attached to being a 'welfare mom', the constant scrutiny by case managers and neighbours, and low benefit levels motivate many mothers to retrain and find employment. However, part-time work is often more manageable than full-time work because it allows mothers to improve their incomes while retaining their caring responsibilities.

Parenting on a meagre income is clearly challenging, especially without a partner or affordable child care. The lone mothers in our New Zealand study (Baker, 2004a; Baker and Tippin, 2004) typically felt that being a 'good mother' required constant supervision of their children, especially because so many lived in overcrowded and 'high-risk' neighbourhoods. They believed that paid work brought poor financial returns but left them with a myriad of household problems and child-care dilemmas, especially during school holidays or when the children were sick. The three factors of poverty, stressful work, and lack of social support seem to impede effective coping mechanisms.

When policy-makers reform income support programs, they often focus on saving public resources and encouraging good work habits. However, they also need to consider the interaction among lone parenthood, poor health, child-care problems, and the ability to find and retain a job. Caring for children on a very low budget with little assistance demands emotional strength, parenting skills, and considerable time. Furthermore, living in low-income neighbourhoods often augments parental concerns about child safety. Expecting mothers to become wage earners as well as care providers under these conditions often increases stress levels and promotes poor family health.

Box 5.1 Changing Labour Markets and Welfare-to-Work Programs

The personal interviews by Baker and Tippin (2002) illustrate how lone mothers have been affected by new retail opening hours, factory closures, their qualifications and employment experience, and employers' preferences for employees without family responsibilities. A lone mother with a school-aged child recounted how—from her perspective—flexibility diminished when her supermarket employer moved to 24/7 trading hours:

> I have been working at a supermarket . . . and was made redundant again because they wanted me to start earlier or finish later which, with my daughter, I can't start at 6:40 in the morning. [She was working 9–2.] You think a supermarket would be quite a good place to work because they have students who come in and work on school holidays, but they are all changing. They want people who can work shifts and start early and finish at 3 p.m. or start later and work late nights. They don't even want to look at you if you can't work those hours. . . . I am honest and work hard . . . but because of the hours, they would rather let you go!

Another lone mother told us:

> I . . . managed to get more hours in my job so I got rid of the income support and I was working full-time. I did that for four years . . . but had to go back on welfare. . . . I started being harassed. . . . [My supervisor] would give me all the dirty jobs and my life became a misery working there in the end. I started getting sick because I started stressing out. . . . Social welfare have offered me a cleaning job and I don't want to go back to cleaning because I have done it for years. They offered me work . . . where you get pooled on a casual basis. You might be working on the roads and I don't want to do that. They ring me and say 'You have to work today', but I have done all that hard labour.

Several women talked about how employers can discriminate against welfare recipients:

> The supermarket man [employer] who was interviewing me told me quite plainly that he treats women on welfare differently and that he doesn't like to employ them. . . . He said that I didn't have a 'support network' so if I had a child that I had to get up to in the night, then in the morning I would be the only one there and he said for that reason he didn't like employing anyone on welfare because they were unreliable.

Case managers reported that they use 'staircasing' strategies for clients who are not seriously ill but have physical or emotional health problems. At the time, clients in New Zealand could undertake an 'activity' (such as a course of study) for a minimum of 15 hours a week without immediately being pressured into coping with paid employment. In our interviews, many sole mothers appreciated this training but others strongly doubted whether it would lead to employment or even if it was appropriate to their interests or needs. One woman (Pakeha [European New Zealander], two children) expressed it like this:

> I have signed a form saying that I am looking for work and they are looking for work for me . . . I am currently studying a [computer and accountancy] course . . . I imagine that [the welfare office] thinks I am going to get a job. I feel that, as I don't have any child care support at all and because we live out here [in a remote area], then I have no school holiday child care or after-school care. I feel it would be difficult for me to work . . . .

Another Pakeha woman explained her personal and family dilemmas in the welfare-to-work transition:

> I hadn't worked since just before [my son] was born. I wasn't able to work afterwards because he was sick [with asthma, allergies, a heart problem, and now behavioural problems]. The main reason I can't get back into the workforce now is, [even though] I am doing a computer course to upgrade my skills . . . the biggest problem is that, although I am very experienced and qualified in an office, I am [in my fifties]. I have a child who, when he is sick, I have to stay home. During the school holidays I have to stay home, as there is nobody to look after him. He has nobody but me.

Source: Baker and Tippin (2002: 345–60). Reprinted by permission of Sage Publications Ltd. from *Journal of Sociology*, Copyright © TASA the Australian Sociological Association, 2002.

Employment Leave and Families

Before the 1970s, employment practices in most countries assumed that workers were men with wives at home to cook their meals, wash and iron their clothes, clean the house, and care for their children. However, the influx of women into the labour force meant that laws, policies, and practices had to change to take into consideration women's child-bearing capacity, the health benefits of breast-feeding, and the care and supervision of children whose parents are employed. Offering paid leave for female employees during the interval surrounding childbirth has a long history in some European countries but dates back only to the 1970s in Canada. In 1971, the Unemployment Insurance program first included maternity benefits, but over the years parental benefits were added for adoptive parents and for biological fathers. Changes were also made to eligibility rules and to the length of time that benefits could be drawn (Baker and Tippin, 1999).

In the 1990s, further reforms removed some of the obstacles and patriarchal biases from maternity/parental leave legislation. In Canada, employment leave is under provincial jurisdiction but maternity/parental benefits are paid by the federal government, and thus several Canadian provinces reduced or eliminated the requirements of a lengthy employment record to enable more women to qualify for leave, as women are more likely than men to work part-time or in temporary positions. The reformed Employment Insurance program (EI) in 1996 began to base eligibility for maternity/parental benefits on the number of hours previously worked rather than the number of weeks. This could help non-standard workers to become eligible for EI, except that benefit levels were reduced in the process (Baker and Tippin, 1999: 97).

The Canadian government also extended the length of parental benefits from 10 weeks to 35 weeks in January 2001, which brings the combined total of maternity and parental leave to 50 weeks with up to 60 per cent of previous wages (Lawlor, 2003). In contrast, the United States and Australia offer no statutory right to paid employment leave for new parents, and New Zealand introduced 12 weeks of paid leave only in 2002 (raised to 14 weeks in 2006). The New Zealand scheme requires one year's continuous employment with the same employer and pays the same rate to all eligible recipients. Back in 1952, the International Labour Organization required governments to provide 12 weeks of paid leave and has since increased this to 14 weeks (UN, 2000: 133). While Canada and most European nations have adopted this recommendation, the United States and Australia could be seen as 'welfare laggards' in this regard.

When parenting is divided, fathers usually assume economic parenting, acquiring full-time paid work. Mothers are more likely to engage in practical parenting, performing routine household tasks and caring for the children because they want to, because it is still seen as 'women's work', but also because women are less able to find permanent full-time jobs that pay high wages and likely because they are acculturated to and feel confident in that role. If only one parent at a time is permitted to take parental leave, which is usually the case, the family is better able to survive on the father's higher earnings. In addition, both men and women view mothers as the logical choice because they are already taking employment leave for childbirth and recovery.

Most governments provide some funding for child-care services if they are required for employment. Some offer tax benefits for parents who are able to show receipts for employment-related child care or they subsidize services for low-income working parents. Compared to the other liberal welfare states, the Canadian government offers a relatively generous tax deduction for working parents using non-family child care, while the provinces subsidize care for low-income children using some federal money. In 1997, the Quebec government (under the Parti Québécois) introduced a child-care program that required parents to pay only $5 per day for care whether or not parents were in paid work (later raised to $7 per day). The provincial government also increased the number of spaces, the wages of educators, and its child-care budget at a time when neighbouring provinces were making cuts. However, in 2003 the Parti Québécois lost the election to the Liberals, who soon announced that they intended to slow the expansion of the child-care program, increase parental fees, and encourage for-profit child care (CRRU, 2003). This suggests that politics and financial decisions, rather than parental need or the benefits to children, influence the development and restructuring of child-care services.

Paid childbirth leave and affordable child care are necessary for women's employment equity, but these programs alone will not resolve the gender-based inequalities in work. The structure of paid work needs to be altered to remove the assumption that it is separate from personal life. The design of leave programs must acknowledge that women's feelings of obligation to children and partners have encouraged them to accept part-time or temporary employment, limit overtime work, take unpaid leave, relocate with their partner's occupation, and accept lower wages. Therefore, social programs need to focus on providing affordable and accessible child care, improving pay equity, raising girls' interest in occupational achievement, and increasing the participation of both boys and men in child care and housework. However, reforms that cost public or employer dollars are less likely to occur under neo-liberal restructuring of labour markets and social programs.

CONCLUSION: THE GROWING IMPACT OF PAID WORK ON FAMILY LIFE

Throughout much of the twentieth century, married men were the main family earners while married women cared for the home and children. Women usually worked in the formal labour force before marriage but not always afterwards, working fewer hours than men, earning lower wages, and more often earning money at home. Today, most women are employed regardless of their marital or parental status but noticeable differences remain between the paid and unpaid work patterns of mothers and fathers.

In recent decades, globalization, technological change, freer trade agreements, and new government policies have altered labour markets and employment patterns both for men and for women. Women's employment rates still are influenced by the financial need of their households, the age of their children, ideologies about women's role, opportunities to work part-time, and the availability of affordable child-care services, but they are also affected by national or local employment conditions. Some workers have benefited from globalizing labour markets, including young educated men and women who are childless and geographically mobile. Yet lone mothers and certain cultural minorities remain disproportionately represented among low-wage workers and low-income households.

In the past two decades, many firms, especially in the manufacturing sector, have downsized to remain competitive in a world of freer trade and the rapid movement of capital. Governments in the liberal welfare states no longer provide the same level of statutory protections for employees and unemployed workers, and labour forces have consequently become more polarized. Some families are 'work poor' or the adults are unemployed or marginally employed, while others are 'work rich' but have insufficient time for caring activities or leisure (Bittman, 1998; Torjman and Battle, 1999). The neo-liberal restructuring of paid work and the welfare state continues to aggravate the problems of the working poor, especially youth and lone mothers. Some governments have restricted eligibility to income support, arguing that nothing should prevent the rational unemployed person from finding and keeping work. Welfare-to-work programs imply that paid work is the answer to family poverty—but this can be true only when the job market is booming and wages are adequate relative to living costs.

Taylor-Gooby (2004) argued that new social risks have arisen from the decline of the male breadwinner family, labour market changes, and the impact of **globalization** on national policy-making. These new risks create challenges especially for women, youth, and those without job skills, as well as for governments. They include balancing paid work and family responsibilities, being called on to care for a frail elderly relative, lacking the skills to find paid work with adequate wages, having skills that become obsolete, and using private provision that supplies insecure or inadequate services. Although balancing work and family is not exactly a new risk for women, the extent of the problem certainly has increased over the last generation as more married women have joined the workforce, as male wages have not kept up with living costs, and as the number of mother-led families continues to grow.

Although welfare states were established to deal with the risks of unemployment, sickness, disability, and retirement, the new risks provide complex challenges for governments (ibid.). They could expand public care for children and the elderly, promote more equal opportunities, and reduce employment poverty; but these solutions require agreement about the issues, considerable state intervention in the economy, and co-operation among governments, employers, unions, and voluntary organizations. New public spending would also require considerable political will to counteract the strong lobby from the political right that continues to argue for less government intervention and lower taxes.

Although governments are encouraging families to derive more of their income security from full-time work, parents with the major responsibility for child care and housework enjoy few incentives to seek full-time employment or promotion (Bittman and Pixley, 1997). Many mothers cannot accept job assignments that involve moving to another city or country because they have to consider their partners' and their children's lives. In addition, women's lower lifetime earnings increase their chances of poverty in old age, requiring state income support for many older unattached women. For this reason, governments are encouraging both women and men to see a lifetime of paid employment as normal; but not all women can easily do this unless family leave and caring arrangements are in place.

SUMMARY

In this chapter, we see that who earns the money makes a difference to entitlement to spend it. Men normally have greater access to earnings than women but employed wives are more likely to maintain control over a portion of family money as well as their own earnings. The time that women typically spend on caring activities reduces access to earnings and personal savings, but employed mothers are often caught in a 'time crunch'. As family members work longer hours for pay, family time becomes precious and more focused around employment needs while some household tasks and caring work are purchased on the market.

Questions for Critical Thought

1. Are wives entitled to the same family privileges as husbands when they are successful family breadwinners?
2. How have global labour markets altered family life?
3. Do children and young people contribute their fair share to household chores? Why not?

Suggested Readings

Atlantis: A Woman's Studies Journal. 2004. 'Never Done: The Challenge of Unpaid Work', special issue 28, 2. This issue of a Canadian women's studies journal focuses on the value, gendering, and organization of unpaid work.

Beaujot, Rod. 2000. *Earning and Caring in Canadian Families.* Peterborough, Ont.: Broadview Press. Beaujot analyzes the tensions for both men and women between earning a living and accommodating family and children.

Pahl, Jan. 2001. 'Couples and Their Money: Theory and Practice in Personal Finances', in R. Sykes, C. Bochel, and N. Ellison, eds, *Social Policy Review 13*. Bristol: Policy Press, 17–37. Pahl's research shows that access to 'family money' is influenced by gendered expectations, age, and earning capacity.

Ranson, Gillian. 2005. 'Paid and Unpaid Work: How Do Families Divide Their Labour?', in M. Baker, ed., *Families: Changing Trends in Canada*, 5th edn. Toronto: McGraw-Hill Ryerson, 99–120. Ranson shows how shifts in the economy and how people earn their living affect the way that family life is organized. She also discusses the gendered division of caring work in Canada.

Suggested Websites

Childcare Resource and Research Unit
www.childcarecanada.org
This University of Toronto site includes academic research and media coverage relating to child-care issues.

Statistics Canada
www.statcan.ca
The Statistics Canada website includes extensive information about paid and unpaid work, employment, and family status.

Vanier Institute of the Family
www.vifamily.ca
The Vanier Institute site offers information about employment trends of men and women, as well as material on family spending and debt.

Separation, Divorce, and Re-partnering

CHAPTER OUTLINE

This chapter begins with a discussion of the rising rates of separation and divorce and the reasons for these trends. It also traces reforms in family and divorce laws—including those related to property, child custody, and child support—and examines the research on the outcomes of divorce and on experiences of living in stepfamilies.

INTRODUCTION

In the previous chapter, we saw that changing patterns of paid work have altered expectations about education and employment, the timing of marriage and childbearing, and the division of labour between couples. More adolescents and parents now work longer hours, including evenings and on weekends, and aspirations for material wealth and career progression have increased. The opportunities for young men and women have expanded, requiring more choices about what and where to study, the kind of job they should accept, and where they want to work. Despite these new opportunities, the kind of work people do continues to be influenced by their gender, age, and social class background. Furthermore, the nature of paid work influences the availability of family time and the household division of labour. When both spouses are employed, the household division of labour is more often contested, although many wives continue to accept responsibility for routine housework and child care.

The growing percentage of the population working in temporary and insecure jobs and the increased choices about where to work also contribute to the impermanence of relationships. In recent years, the legal termination of marriage is more often viewed as an acceptable conclusion to a relationship that has already broken down, and more people have come to appreciate that relationship dissolution does not necessarily arise from the misbehaviour of one partner. Instead, it stems from a variety of social and economic factors as well as personal ones, including less economic necessity to stay together if the marriage is unhappy and both partners can support themselves. Growing time pressures and perceptions of an unfair division of labour at home also contribute to resentment (especially from employed mothers) and in some cases lead to marriage dissolution.

In this chapter, we explore why a higher percentage of couples now separate, why legal marriages span shorter periods of time than in previous decades, and how the experiences of children, mothers, and fathers differ in the 'post-divorce family'. These issues are not entirely academic ones as many of us have experienced either parental separation or the dissolution of our own marriages, while others have witnessed the separation of friends or siblings. These personal experiences may help to shape our understandings of the consequences of divorce, but we need to keep in mind that our own experiences may not be typical. However, personal knowledge might enhance our curiosity about the research findings relating to the separation and divorce outcomes of other people.

WHY ARE SO MANY COUPLES SEPARATING?

When people get married, they usually intend to stay together for life. However, marriages are not lasting as long as they used to. A number of personal characteristics are correlated with higher rates of divorce, such as marrying someone from a different social background with varying ideas about the nature of marriage or preferable lifestyles. The probability of divorce also rises when couples marry early in life, household income is low, partners come from families with divorced parents, the woman gains high levels of education and income, partners are not religious, and when they cohabit before marriage (Wu and Schimmele, 2005; Bradbury and Norris, 2005). Bibby (2004–5) found that most Canadians look for certain characteristics in a partner and marry for a variety of reasons. However, the most prevalent reasons given for divorce were 'different values and interests' and 'abuse', as Table 6.1 indicates. This suggests that some partners either do not meet premarital expectations or grow apart during marriage.

Couples have their own personal reasons for separating but rates of separation and divorce and the average duration of marriages that end in divorce vary regionally and cross-nationally, suggesting that societal factors alter these rates. For example, 38 per cent of all Canadian marriages compared to 50 per cent of marriages in the province of Quebec can be expected to end in divorce before the thirtieth wedding anniversary (VIF, 2004: 33). The first year of marriage is often quite satisfying for couples but the likelihood of divorce rises abruptly in Canada until the fourth year of marriage. The mean duration of legal marriage is 14.2 years in Canada but only 8.3 years in Australia and 10.2 years in the United States (OECD, 2005b: 33).

Table 6.1   Desired Characteristics in a Partner and Reasons for
            Marriage and Divorce

The Ten Top Characteristics That People Want in a Partner

1. Honesty
2. Kindness
3. Respect
4. Compatibility
5. Humour
6. Dependability
7. Love
8. Values
9. Religious commonality
10. Communication

The Top Eight Reasons Why People Want to Marry

1. Feeling that marriage signifies commitment
2. Moral values
3. Belief that children should have married parents
4. It is the natural thing to do
5. Financial security
6. Religious beliefs
7. Pressure from family
8. Pressure from friends

The Top Five Reasons Why People Want to Divorce

1. Different values and interests
2. Abuse—physical and emotional
3. Alcohol and drugs
4. Infidelity
5. Career-related conflict

Source: Bibby (2004). Reprinted by permission of the publisher.

As we will see later, cross-national differences in divorce rates and the duration of marriage are influenced by legal restrictions, cultural conditions, and religious considerations (ibid.).

From 1970 to 2001, average **divorce rates** tripled in OECD countries from 14.3 divorces per 100 marriages to 40.9 (OECD, 2001: 32; 2005b: 33). As Table 6.2 indicates, there is considerable variation in the divorce rates by country, from a low of 8.6 in Mexico to a high of 69.6 divorces per 100 marriages in Belgium in 2001 (ibid.). In addition, divorce rates stabilized during the 1980s and 1990s in some countries (such as Canada) as cohabitation became more prevalent and legal marriage rates declined. Generally, separation rates (without legal divorce) are not available from government statistics because partners can walk away from their relationships without reporting the dissolution to the authorities. Nevertheless, demographers have estimated that if separations were added to current divorce

Table 6.2   Divorce Statistics in Selected OECD Countries, 2001

Country	Divorces per 100 Marriages	Mean Marriage Duration at Divorce
Australia	53.6	8.3
Belgium	69.6	13.0
Canada	48.5	14.2
Denmark	39.9	11.0
Finland	54.6	12.4
France	39.1	13.3
Germany	50.7	12.1
Ireland*	14.7	—
Italy	15.4	19.1
Mexico	8.6	—
Netherlands	46.6	12.2
New Zealand	48.5	13.0
Portugal	32.3	13.1
Spain*	18.2	16.1
Sweden	58.8	11.7
United Kingdom	54.8	10.9
United States	47.6	10.2
OECD average	40.9	11.9

*Spain passed divorce legislation in 1981 and Ireland in 1996.

Source: OECD (2005b: 33). Based on GE5.3. The ratio of divorces to marriages increased in most countries from 1995 to 2001. © OECD 2005.

rates, the figure could be four times as high as the official divorce rate, especially if we included separations from cohabitation (Beaujot, 2000: 110).

Higher rates of relationship breakdown have been influenced by a number of societal changes, including growing opportunities to live together outside marriage, changing attitudes about the 'right to happiness' in marriage, and liberalized divorce laws. Before the 1950s, both men and women needed marriage to survive economically, but since then the expansion of women's employment opportunities, public child-care services, and governments' income support programs have made it possible for both women and men to leave unhappy relationships and live outside marriage. Although women are more likely than men to initiate the separation (Amato and Previti, 2003; Hewitt et al., 2005), many separated mothers with young children struggle to make ends meet without a male earner in the household. Consequently, most governments have created state income support programs that enable lone mothers to recover from the emotional and financial trauma that often accompanies separation and to support their children while searching for paid work. Also, it is now easier for separated partners to live alone due to the availability of appliances, convenience food, self-contained apartments, and a variety of domestic services available on the commercial market.

Greater expectations of personal happiness and freedom of choice encourage people to leave unhappy relationships. People now feel less obligated to stay with their partners to fulfill their marriage vows, to please their parents, or to protect their reputations or those of their family. **Marital breakdown** has also become prevalent with increased geographic mobility and contact with people from different cultures. More **exogamy** or marriage outside one's social or cultural group means that an increasing percentage of partners enter marriage with different ideas about what constitutes a good couple relationship, positive relations with other family members, and a favourable lifestyle, which could augment marital conflict and eventually lead to separation.

Another reason for increased marriage breakdown is that laws in most countries now permit couples to divorce if one or both partners agree that their relationship has irretrievably broken down. Previously, divorce laws in common-law countries required legal proof presented in court to show that a partner had violated the marriage contract before the other partner could petition for divorce. This was a stressful, time-consuming, and expensive process. Now in many places, divorce is granted if the former partners state in writing that their marriage has broken down, as long as they wait a necessary period before applying for a divorce.

Reforms dealing with the division of matrimonial property, **child custody**, and **child support** have taken place in all the liberal welfare states. However, these legal changes have been controversial for a number of reasons. (1) They highlight deep-seated resentments about the different contributions husbands and wives typically make to family resources. (2) Children in the 'post-divorce family' often live in impoverished households, despite recently acquired legal rights in all these countries and international conventions on the rights of the child from the United Nations. (3) Parents often re-partner and scarce resources need to be shared among two or more households including biological and stepchildren. (4) Some critics suggest that liberalized divorce laws discourage couples from working harder to make their marriages work and argue that the grounds for divorce should be tightened.

In summary, more relationships and marriages now end because women and men have gained more opportunities to live outside marriage and because reformed divorce laws (combined with fewer children) make it easier for couples to separate. More people believe that they have the right to a satisfying marital relationship. If their current marriage is unhappy, they feel that they should not be forced to stay together and should be permitted to try again with a new partner. The rise in consensual relationships may have led to a stabilization or slight decline in divorce rates in some countries since the 1980s, but this does not mean that fewer relationships are dissolving. As we noted in Chapter 2, cohabiting couples have higher rates of separation than legally married couples. As more people cohabit, they contribute to family instability in the larger society (Beaujot, 2000: 125; Beck-Gernsheim, 2002).

SEPARATION OUTCOMES

Since the 1970s, the consequences of separation and divorce for men, women, and children have become controversial and the object of considerable public debate and policy research. Despite widespread agreement that spouses should not be forced to live together against their wishes, marriage and divorce trends have led to a number of concerns. These include the negative implications for children's behaviour and emotional well-being, the high poverty rates of mother-led families, and either the large percentage of 'fading fathers', who fail to visit their children and pay child support, or the alleged court bias against fathers in custody and access awards.

After separation, most parents make their own decisions about child custody; if the courts in the common-law countries are asked to decide, they are expected to base their decisions on 'the best interests of the child'. However, who can best decide what is best for children and how do they arrive at this decision? In practice, most children continue to live with their mother after separation and divorce for a variety of reasons, discussed below. The minimum child support payment required by the state is usually kept at a low level to encourage and enable low-income fathers to pay, but this means that it is often too small to pay the bills for the child's household. Furthermore, in the liberal welfare states many fathers fail to pay the required amount of child support and about one-third of fathers lose contact with their children altogether (Smyth, 2004). In most of these countries, the majority of divorced men re-partner and some produce additional children with new partners. Yet many fathers cannot earn enough to support two households with children.

Despite legal reform throughout the 1980s and 1990s, the courts have been unable to compensate for the gendered nature of paid and unpaid work during marriage, which clearly creates economic and social inequalities after separation. In addition, the courts are unable to compensate for the fact that two adult incomes increasingly are necessary to cover current living expenses and that the one-earner household remains disadvantaged unless it relies on an above-average income. Households led by lone mothers usually struggle on low incomes even when these mothers are employed (OECD, 2005b). Even when child-care services are unaffordable or unavailable, mothers in the liberal welfare states are still expected to care for their children while they are earning money or to depend on relatives or neighbours to help them. This means that many mothers with young children work part-time or rely on some level of state income support that seldom pays an amount equivalent to the minimum wage (Baker, 2004a). Consequently, the average earnings of mothers supporting young children are lower than men's earnings or the earnings of women without children at home (OECD, 2005a).

In most Western countries, divorce has become easier both legally and socially, especially among childless couples and those with fewer children. In countries such as Canada and New Zealand only about half of divorces involve children under 18 (Baker, 2001b: 181); nonetheless, parents and the state need to consider their emotional and economic well-being also. Although researchers tend to focus on the harmful effects of separation and divorce on children, it is also apparent that the perpetuation of an unhappy marriage can be more detrimental than separation and divorce both to adults and to children (Amato and Booth, 1997; Pryor and Rodgers, 2001: 239). Some lone mothers provide strong and positive role models for their children with their capacity to manage the household and earn money to support the children. However, social policies and reformed family law increasingly assume that lone mothers can pay household bills on their own earnings, even when they cannot.

FAMILY AND DIVORCE LAWS

Divorce laws vary cross-nationally but two main systems of law are used in the liberal welfare states and in European countries. English Canada, the United States, Australia, and New Zealand have based their legal systems on common law, originally brought from England and still used in the United Kingdom, while Quebec and many European countries use variations of civil law (Harrison, 1993). In federal states such as Canada and the United States, jurisdiction may be further divided by province or state.

In Canada, the federal government retains jurisdiction over divorce, including the legal right to remarry, and also establishes guiding principles for child custody, access, and financial support (Bala and Clarke, 1981). The provinces hold jurisdiction over marriage, the division of family assets upon the separation of spouses, and laws pertaining to the granting and enforcing of child custody, access, child support, and spousal support (Wu and Schimmele, 2005). This means that the laws and practices relating to custody and support vary by province, as well as between Quebec and the rest of Canada. This division has led to some enforcement issues and unequal living standards for mother-led households in different parts of the country. Generally, common law relies more on custom and precedents from judicial decisions while civil law emphasizes legal statutes, basic principles, and the written contracts made by cohabiting partners regarding their own wishes.

Marriage, child-rearing, and divorce under common law are considered to be mainly the concerns of family members rather than the broader community (Harrison, 1993: 35). Although spouses are permitted to own and control property acquired before marriage, they are expected to share the income they earn and the possessions they acquire during marriage (such as the marital home, their furnishings, and the family car). Historically, patterns of ownership differed for husbands and wives because their access to earnings and family money was not the same.

Marriage, Gender, and Property

In common-law jurisdictions, a legal wife was entitled to 'dower rights' or one-third of her husband's property should the marriage dissolve. In return, a husband was expected to support his wife financially until her death or remarriage, but he retained the right to establish their legal residence (or domicile) and their standard of living. If couples divorced before the 1970s (and few did), family assets typically were divided according to dower rights, in a way that reflected who purchased them or whose name was on the deed.

A former husband could be required by the pre-1970s courts to pay **alimony** or lifelong financial support to his former wife if she had not committed a **matrimonial fault**. The most prevalent matrimonial fault or reason for a wife to forfeit financial support was adultery or sexual intercourse with another man. Spousal support was contingent on her fidelity during marriage, at the time of separation, and until the legal divorce—rather than on her unpaid domestic services during marriage, her caring responsibilities, or her financial need. If she left her husband, committed adultery, or remarried, she lost her right to his financial support (Baker, 1995: 293).

Under common law, former wives also tended to receive a smaller share of family property than husbands after divorce, which especially disadvantaged those wives who cared for their children at home rather than earning money for the household.

At the time of divorce, a portion of the family assets and/or spousal support payments could be awarded to 'blameless' ex-wives (i.e., women who had not committed adultery), depending on their husband's economic circumstances and judicial discretion. Yet, enforcement procedures often were ineffective and the former wife had to take her defaulting husband to court after each offence in an attempt to retrieve these payments. In Canada, the provinces were responsible for enforcing alimony, which meant that a former husband could avoid support payments by moving to another province (Baker, 2001b: 188). Spousal maintenance after divorce used to be paid to full-time homemakers and mothers, or simply to assuage a husband's guilt (Harrison, 1993). By the late 1970s, many lawyers and former partners viewed these laws as arbitrary: some husbands felt that they were paying ex-wives too much and many wives felt that their caring work and unpaid contributions to the home were undervalued.

Now, divorce terminates all marital rights and obligations in the common-law countries but *not* obligations to child support. Divorced spouses are expected to become economically self-sufficient shortly after divorce through their own earnings, and former wives are no longer awarded lifelong support although they may be granted temporary support based on financial need. While the former laws assumed that husbands were breadwinners and wives were homemakers and financial dependants, the amended laws suggest that both should be self-supporting after separation. The divorce laws still contain some judicial discretion with respect to spousal support, especially for older women unable to find work and long-term homemakers with few job skills, but young women are usually awarded only fixed-term support because they are seen as potential employees. In 2004, for example, spousal support was ordered in only 10 per cent of Canadian cases (VIF, 2004: 37) even though labour markets are still gendered and women's average earnings are considerably less than men's, especially when they also care for young children.

Separation is emotionally difficult for both men and women but research suggests that strategies to cope with divorce are somewhat gendered. Women are more likely than men to feel relieved and liberated following a divorce, to spend time with friends, to see a counsellor for therapy, and to show greater emotional strength (Sev'er, 1992; Walker, 2005). In contrast, men are more likely than women to find solace in drinking, to return to a former girlfriend, to have casual sex, or to join a dating agency. In addition, divorced men tend to enjoy a higher living standard, are less likely to live with their children, and tend to find a new partner faster than women.

Now, in common-law jurisdictions, after a specified period of living apart, a marriage can be dissolved through **no-fault divorce** even without one partner's consent and wives can no longer delay court proceedings in an attempt to negotiate a better financial settlement. Although this brings gender equality to the process, it may be less than equitable because women's earnings and assets tend to be lower than men's after separation (Funder, 1996; Baker, 2001b). Caring responsibilities clearly interfere with earning capacity, as we saw in Chapter 5. Lack of career planning, priority given to family needs, and discrimination in the workplace further diminish women's occupational mobility and earned incomes compared to men's.

Who should compensate for these gender differences? Should former husbands be asked to reimburse their ex-wives for raising their children, caring for the home, and therefore falling behind in their earnings? Or should the state attempt to create gender equity for girls, for women in the labour force, and especially for employed mothers with young children? The answers to these questions vary by lobby group and according to personal beliefs and circumstances, but can lead to considerable public debate.

Reforms in Child Custody and Residence

In the past two decades most industrialized countries have made numerous reforms to laws relating to divorce, child custody, child support, spousal support, and the division of family assets. Generally, laws and judicial practices have rejected any implications that children could be the property of either parent after marriage breakdown. For example, the 1985 Canadian divorce law clearly stated that either parent or both together could be granted 'custody' or legal decision-making rights after divorce and that this decision should be based on the 'best interests of the child' rather than any notion of parental rights. Yet, professionals and parents often disagree about what is the best living arrangement. Children are sometimes ambivalent when they are consulted, and young children generally prefer to live with both parents even when this is no longer possible. Despite legal changes, over three-quarters of children continue to live with their mothers after separation and divorce, although there is considerable variation by country (Millar and Rowlingson, 2001).

Child custody and residence arrangements after separation are currently in dispute in many jurisdictions. Although relatively few cases are contested, some lawyers and feminist activists argue that judges should base contested custody decisions on the 'primary caregiver presumption'. This means that they should assume that the parent who was responsible for the primary care during marriage should be the custodial or resident parent after separation unless there is a good reason to alter this arrangement (Boyd, 2003). If this principle were applied, it would be relatively easy to define and continuity would be provided for children. Also, following this principle would avoid the threat posed to women of unequal joint custody situations in which women perform most of the physical caring but men retain decision-making power (Smart and Sevenhuijsen, 1989). However, this principle could reinforce both the gendered division of labour in the home and women's primary role as mothers rather than workers (Pulkingham, 1994).

Child custody used to be awarded to only one parent (usually the mother). In the 1980s, the common-law countries introduced the concept of **joint custody**, which means shared *legal* responsibility rather than physical parenting. In most families, separating parents make their own arrangements for the care of their children; custody orders were made by the Canadian courts in only 30 per cent of divorces in 2002 (VIF, 2004: 37–8). However, when the courts do intervene, the trend towards joint custody in Canada is quite evident in official statistics. The percentage of children involved in awards of custody to both parents rose from 11.6 in 1986 to

Table 6.3   Court-Ordered Custody Arrangements in Canada, 1986, 1995, and 2002

Custody Arrangements	1986 %	1995 %	2002 %
Mother only	72.0	67.6	49.5
Joint custody			
(both mother and father)	11.6	21.4	41.8
Father only	15.3	10.9	8.5
Other	1.0	0.2	0.2

Source: Baker (1995: 300); VIF (2004: 38).

41.8 in 2002, as Table 6.3 indicates. Yet, research suggests that joint custody is most effective when it is voluntary rather than enforced by the court (Baker, 1995: 300).

A number of countries (including Australia) have amended legislation to remove the word 'custody' or any other notions of child ownership from the language of divorce and to replace them with the words 'parental responsibilities' (Funder, 1996). Divorcing parents are also expected to make a parenting plan for their children with the assistance of counselling, conciliation, and mediation. Both parents now retain parenting responsibilities, yet mothers tend to remain the 'resident parent' and the main provider of daily care after separation and divorce.

The Australian 'Caring for Children after Separation' Project found that 79 per cent of children live with their mothers after separation (Qu, 2004). The relatively few children living with their fathers tend to be older, but no gender differences were apparent in this study. Smyth and Weston (2004) noted that less than 6 per cent of parents share the regular care of their children after separation, but that this arrangement is more likely to be preferred by fathers than by mothers, by parents already sharing care, and by non-resident parents rather than by resident parents. The attitudes of resident mothers towards **shared parenting** tend to be negative; mothers' attitudes become more positive in low-conflict parental relationships and for older children. Australian fathers reported that they *want* to be more involved in their children's lives after separation, perhaps a reaction to 'the apparent shallowness of every-other-weekend contact schedules that have arisen from traditional sole (maternal) custody models of post-separation parenting' (ibid., 14).

In the same study, researchers found that about 51 per cent of non-resident parents (mainly fathers) maintain regular face-to-face contact with their children after separation but 30 per cent have little or no contact. Higher levels of contact between fathers and children were associated with lower levels of inter-parental conflict, lower levels of **re-partnering**, less physical distance between the parents' households, and higher levels of financial resources (Smyth, 2004). Where father–child contact was tenuous, the perceptions of mothers and fathers differed. Mothers perceived that fathers lacked interest in the children while fathers felt that their former partners were cutting them out of the children's lives. This study shows that experiences and attitudes in the post-divorce family often vary by gender.

Box 6.1 The Attitudes of Separated Mothers and Fathers to 50/50 Shared Care

It is perhaps from the vantage point of being the primary caregivers of young children, and as a consequence being especially sensitive to children's needs, that mothers are more likely than fathers to oppose the idea of 50/50 care. They may perceive shared care to be too disruptive to children. On this issue, it is noteworthy that mothers' views about 50/50 care seemed to be influenced by their own children's ages and stages, and the level of inter-parental conflict.

For most fathers, the disconnection from their children that relationship breakdown often brings may be a central factor explaining the appeal of 50/50. Indeed, fathers' attitudes appeared to be tied in with their dissatisfaction with contact and with the decision-making processes that occurred in relation to contact. The strong desire by fathers for 50/50 care may reflect what Walker (2003: 403) calls a 'radiating message'. In this context, the message would be something like 'I want to be more involved in my children's lives', and may well be a reaction to the apparent shallowness of every-other-weekend contact schedules that have arisen from traditional (maternal) sole custody models of post-separation parenting.

. . .

Of course, the apparent simplicity of such gendered attitudinal data in relation to 50/50 care belies the complexity of parents' and children's needs and interests. Children's voices are needed on this issue, and are likely to add to this complexity.

Source: Smyth and Weston (2004: 14–15).

Reforms in Child-Support Assessment and Enforcement

Before the 1990s, fathers were expected to support their children financially, and upon divorce the courts would order them to pay an amount that frequently was related to their ability to pay rather than to their children's needs. If a father failed to pay, the children's mother was expected to take him to court to retrieve the money. This meant she had to prove he was the father, to know where he lived, to take him to court in the jurisdiction where he lived, and to pay court expenses. These procedures were impractical and too expensive for most mothers (Baker, 2001b).

As divorce rates soared in the 1970s and 1980s, policy-makers and social service workers became concerned about the high poverty rates in lone-mother households where fathers were not paying child support. The concern particularly focused on the long-term consequences of poverty for children's development and life chances. Government-sponsored research in several common-law countries found that two-thirds to three-quarters of fathers failed to pay the full amount of court-awarded support within a few years of the divorce (Trapski et al., 1994; Funder, 1996; Richardson, 2001). Consequently, most lone mothers had to rely on paid work, on loans from friends or family, or on state income support. As an inducement to paying child support, the Canadian government used to offer non-custodial parents (mainly fathers) an income tax deduction on support paid, but (ironically) required custodial parents (mainly mothers) to pay income tax on that money (Baker, 1995: 330). This proved to be an ineffective inducement for most men and payment rates remained low (Richardson, 2001; Boyd, 2003).

Several jurisdictions introduced major reforms in the assessment and enforcement of child support in the 1980s, and others have followed. Child support agencies were established in some countries, such as Australia and the United Kingdom, to assess the amount to be paid by using a formula based on the number of children and the non-resident parent's income. The taxation office began collecting support money from non-resident parents (mostly fathers) and paying it to resident parents (mostly mothers) through welfare offices. These schemes involved both married and unmarried parents and generally increased the proportion of mother-led households receiving child support as well as the amounts paid (Harrison, 1993). Nevertheless, the state has been unable to collect the full amount from many separated fathers, especially those who are less affluent, unemployed, difficult to trace, never married, no longer in contact with their children, or who separated many years ago (Millar and Whiteford, 1993; Jones, 1996: 97; Smyth, 2004).

The Canadian provinces and territories design and administer their own child support schemes and all of them have tightened enforcement procedures since the 1980s. However, awards still are set by judges in court, based on national guidelines established in 1997 and amended in 2002. Some Canadian provinces focus their enforcement on families receiving income support, while others have used the **first default principle**, which means that the government scheme is activated only when parents make a complaint about unpaid support. Since 1987, the federal government has provided the provinces with enforcement tools, including sharing information to locate and intercept defaulters, suspending or denying federal licences or passports, and operating an automated telephone information system (Canada, Department of Justice, 2003).

Canadian research indicates that fathers were ordered to pay child support in 93 per cent of cases, with a median payment of $435 per month in 2004 (VIF, 2004: 37). However, some researchers suggest that national child support guidelines are inequitable because they are based on the non-resident parent's income but not his net assets. They also fail to consider the resident parent's socio-economic situation or the children's financial needs (Wu and Schimmele, 2005). While default rates decreased with the new enforcement systems, over half of cases were still in default, meaning that the total amount was not paid, it was not paid on time, or it was not paid at all (Richardson, 2001). Nevertheless, the percentage of fathers who clearly refuse to pay is small as most 'defaulters' report that they are temporarily unable to pay, are caught in administrative disputes, or are in the process of having the award adjusted in court (Lapointe and Richardson, 1994). The reasons given for lack of payment may be legitimate, but they could also represent a more socially acceptable way of avoiding payment.

In New Zealand, more non-resident fathers now pay child support than was the case before reforms, but many pay the minimum of $10 per week, which is merely a gesture in the direction of support and a fraction of the cost of raising children

(Baker, 2001b). Researchers in several countries have found that about one-third of non-resident fathers have little or no contact with their children after separation and that those with little contact are least likely to pay child support. Failure to pay is also associated with men's perceptions of **access** difficulties to their child (Smyth, 2002, 2004; Amato, 2004).

Australian research has shown that 41 per cent of non-resident fathers wanted to change the children's living arrangements five years after separation—two-thirds wanted the children to live with them and the remaining third wanted equal care (Smyth et al., 2001). Non-resident fathers also reported more contact with their children than the resident mothers reported that fathers have. Some non-resident fathers argued that the cost of contact should be given more weight in the process of child support assessment and that support payments should be reduced to compensate for the expenses paid when their child stays over. Although many people believe that child support legislation ought to foster and facilitate parent–child contact, legislators have argued that linking father–child contact to the amount of child support to be paid is not in the best interests of the child (Smyth, 2002).

New practices of awarding joint custody have given non-resident parents more access to their children after separation, but at the same time child support has been more stringently enforced. However, a number of controversial issues remain unresolved, including the impact of separation on children and how to deal with high rates of poverty in mother-led households.

CHILDREN, SEPARATION, AND DIVORCE

Poverty rates remain high among mother-led households despite the new procedures to enforce child support; despite the political rhetoric about reducing 'child poverty', these rates have actually increased in a number of countries since the 1990s (UNICEF, 2005). Obviously, poverty is influenced by many factors other than sporadic or low levels of paternal child support. Reasons include the inability of many mothers with young children to earn sufficient incomes because they receive low wages, work part-time, or care for their children at home on relatively ungenerous social benefits. Lone parents must also contend with soaring housing costs in some urban centres and unaffordable child-care and transportation expenses when they attempt to find paid work and become self-supporting. Yet conservative politicians and policy-makers often focus on effective ways to enforce paternal child support rather than address these other contributors to the poverty of lone-parent households.

Most researchers agree that living in a **lone-parent household** may be quite different from living with two parents in an 'intact' family, but they also conclude that most children do not seem to experience long-term psychological or behavioural problems after the initial upset of parental separation. Statistically, however, children living in lone-parent households are more likely to suffer from a variety of negative outcomes than children living in 'intact' families. These outcomes include lower educational attainment, behavioural problems, delinquency, leaving home earlier, teenage pregnancy or parenthood, higher divorce rates when they marry, and many others (Pryor and Rodgers, 2001). Studies on this topic typically investigate whether these negative outcomes arise from living without a male role model, experiencing parental conflict, or the drop in household income that so often accompanies parental separation.

The low-income characteristic of lone-mother households is a major factor influencing children's outcomes after separation. It is important to realize that many of these households have experienced economic disadvantage *before* separation as well as after. People from lower socio-economic groups tend to have higher rates of bereavement (i.e., more parents die in these families), separation, and divorce (ibid.). When children are raised in low-income households, regardless of the number of parents present, they are more likely to suffer from certain socio-economic disadvantages that follow them into adulthood. These include delayed school readiness, lower educational attainment, more trouble with school authorities and the law, more serious childhood illnesses, higher accident rates during childhood, premature death, high rates of depression, and high rates of smoking and alcohol abuse as young adults, to name only a few (NLSCY, 1996; Kiernan, 1997; Canadian Institute of Child Health, 2002).

When studies control for household income, the negative outcomes that are more apparent in lone-parent households decline but do not disappear (Elliott and Richards, 1991, Maclean and Kuh, 1991; Kiernan, 1997). For example, the Canadian National Longitudinal Survey on Children and Youth found that about 19 per cent of children from low-income families headed by a lone mother experience a 'conduct disorder' compared to 9 per cent of children from two-parent families. For those from higher-income families, this percentage drops to 13 per cent for lone-mother families and 8 per cent for two-parent families (Lipman et al., 1996). This suggests that other factors besides household income are influencing the outcomes for children living with lone parents.

The amount and quality of contact with the father are also important variables influencing the outcomes of children after parental separation or divorce. Children who live with their mother often experience diminished contact with their father and suffer distress from this loss, especially if the parents are not legally married (Furstenberg et al., 1987; Cockett and Tripp, 1994; Funder, 1996). The quality of time with the father and the absence of conflict in these meetings, however, are more important than the amount of time (Amato and Rezac, 1994; Pryor and Rodgers, 2001). Furthermore, whether or not the father continues to pay child support may influence both the children's adjustment and the socio-economic status of the child's household. Many children would resent the fact (some with maternal encouragement) that their father is not paying for their expenses and see this as an indication of his rejection of them, but without always considering the economic constraints under which he may be operating.

Never-married mothers who become pregnant before their education is completed are particularly vulnerable to low income and to behavioural problems by their children (Dooley, 1995). These mothers often re-partner within a few years of the child's birth but the socio-economic disadvantages of bearing a child at a young age may linger. The children are most likely to spend their early years in one or more stepfamilies, which are not always harmonious (Marcil-Gratton, 1998; Edin and Reed, 2005).

Numerous studies show that lone mothers report poorer health, more family problems, and lower incomes than partnered mothers. Dorsett and Marsh (1998) reported that British sole mothers show high rates of cigarette smoking, augmenting financial problems and poor health. Low income, poor health, and low morale all interfere with returning to paid work and improving their circumstances. Curtis (2001) found that Canadian sole mothers typically reveal poorer health than married mothers, but when they controlled for age, income, education, lifestyle factors, family size, and other recognized determinants of health, the differences diminished.

Sarfati and Scott (2001) found that New Zealand sole mothers were more likely to have lower family incomes, lower educational qualifications, to be Maori, and to live in more deprived areas. They also found poorer physical and mental health among lone mothers, but the physical health differences disappeared after controlling for socio-economic variables. My own research based on qualitative interviews with 120 lone mothers on welfare in New Zealand illustrates their concerns when they are expected to find paid work despite having sick children, poor health of their own, multiple family problems, and depression. Their stories, which coincide with research in other countries, confirm that many of the liberal welfare states expect low-income mothers to find paid work and become self-supporting but offer them little social support to maintain their jobs and enhance their family well-being (Baker, 2002b).

Whitehead et al. (2000) concluded that the Swedish social security system is more effective at keeping sole mothers healthier and out of poverty than the British system, yet Swedish sole mothers still report poorer mental and physical health than partnered mothers. Many lone mothers are prone to depression and anxiety about the future, and experience problems disciplining their children without assistance. All these factors help to account for higher rates of behavioural problems in the children of lone mothers, especially those who are younger and never married.

Despite these findings, researchers have found no *direct* relationship between the parental separation and children's adjustment, although many studies find differences between children from two-parent families and separated families (Amato and Keith, 1991; Burghes, 1994). Parental separation does add stress to children's lives through changes in relationships, living situations, and parental resources, but few studies conclude that psychological disturbance is severe or prolonged (Emery, 1994). It is difficult to determine, however, whether problems that surface later in adult life are attributable to parental divorce or other factors.

Woodward et al. (2000) analyzed longitudinal data from the Christchurch Health and Development Study in New Zealand. They found that exposure to parental separation was significantly associated with lower attachment to parents in adolescence and more negative perceptions of both maternal and paternal care and protection during childhood. The younger the child at the time of separation, the lower his or her subsequent parental attachment and the more likely the child was to perceive the parents as less caring but overprotective. Furthermore, other studies suggest that experiencing parental separation raises the chances of unstable relationships in adult life (Beaujot, 2000). This may result from poor relationship models in childhood, mistrust of the opposite sex learned from the custodial parent, or personal knowledge of divorce procedures and their aftermath.

Hughes (2005) used qualitative interviews with a small sample of Australian adults who had experienced parental separation as children to investigate some of the conclusions about the future of intimacy arising from the work of Giddens (1992) and Beck-Gernsheim (2002). These interviews suggested that experiencing parental separation may have a lasting impact by encouraging people to see intimate relationships as inherently fragile and to view the formation and termination of these relationships as part of their personal growth. Hughes's participants also saw the nuclear family as flawed and limited, especially in its potential to meet the needs of children. She concluded that if more people in the future live their lives outside the nuclear family in relatively 'loose formations', this will have 'monumental implications for public policy, and for the law in particular' (Hughes, 2005: 84).

REMARRIAGE AND STEPFAMILIES

More people are entering legal marriage for the second or third time, particularly in countries with relatively high divorce rates. In Canada, Australia, and New Zealand, over one-third of all marriages involved at least one partner who had been previously married (Baker, 2001b: 21). Remarriage rates increased in these countries from the 1960s to the early 1990s, but as cohabitation increased and first marriage rates declined, remarriage rates have also declined. Nevertheless, more people are creating stepfamilies or **blended families** through re-partnering.

Ferri and Smith (2003) have described stepfamilies as the fastest-growing family form in Britain in the last few decades. Because most children live with the mother after separation, the most typical stepfamily arrangement involves a mother and her new partner living with her children, who are still maintaining contact with their non-resident father. In Canada, stepfamilies with children accounted for 12 per cent of all families with children in 2001. Of these families, 10 per cent contained only the children of the male spouse while 50 per cent contained only children of the female spouse. An additional 32 per cent of 'blended families' include children that the remarried couple produced together, while 8 per cent contained no children (Statistics Canada, 2002b). About half of stepfamilies in Canada are legally married while half are cohabiting.

Despite the growth of stepfamilies, politicians, state officials, and social workers in many countries have expressed concern about the low remarriage rates among lone mothers. British research from the National Child Development Study found that 50 per cent of lone mothers re-partnered within three years if they had never been married, within about five years if divorced, and closer to eight years if they had been separated or widowed (McKay and Rowlingson, 1998). These figures are similar to but slightly longer than those reported from earlier studies from the United Kingdom (Ermisch, 1991) and longer than those found in American research. The duration of lone parenthood appears to be lengthening but is longer for mothers than fathers, for those living in social housing, and for men who are unemployed (McKay and Rowlingson, 1997).

Poor economic prospects, especially for young men, discourage marriage and remarriage among lone parents (ibid.). No financial advantage can be gained by a lone mother marrying an unemployed man, as her economic hardship could increase and she might disqualify herself from state income support. In addition, re-partnering does not necessarily lead to better child development, although it usually constitutes an economic gain for the lone mother and her children if the man is employed.

The National Child Development Study in the United Kingdom indicated that 16-year-old children in stepfamilies experienced more behavioural problems than those living in lone-parent households (Ferri, 1984). This is explained by the fact that stepfamilies typically involve more conflict than lone-parent families because they include more than two sets of adults (both resident and absent parents) as well as children from different parents and social backgrounds, who are all supposed to live together amicably (Pryor and Rodgers, 2001). In addition, stepfamilies often experience more financial problems, especially when fathers are supporting children in more than one household. These financial difficulties may lead to more general disputes about the fair allocation of resources, time, and attention.

Children in stepfamilies have been found to have higher rates of accidents, higher levels of bedwetting, more contact with the police, and lower self-esteem, and to leave school earlier without qualifications compared to children in lone-parent families (Ferri, 1984; Wadsworth et al., 1983; Elliott et al., 1993). Pryor and Rodgers (2001) argue that these experiences can be explained by the lower family aspirations and expectations that step-parents have for their stepchildren compared to their own biological children, as well as by family friction in these households. These researchers also note that young children fare better than older children in stepfamilies because adaptation is easier at an earlier age before allegiances are developed to the absent parent. Reviews of American research on stepfamilies report that the role of stepmother is more stressful than the role of stepfather, and find that mothers are described as being more negative towards step-parenting than are fathers (Cheal, 1996).

Stepfamily formation has been viewed as another stressful event to cope with for children who were not involved with their parents' decision to separate any more than they were party to their parent's decision to re-partner (Smith, 2004). While the new household members need to learn to be a functioning family unit, the relationship between the children and their non-resident father usually continues, even though it may change. Researchers agree that prolonged conflict between parents has a negative impact on the children, but they disagree about how feelings of closeness with biological fathers influence children's acceptance of stepfathers. Some studies suggest that children who develop strong bonds with their biological fathers may feel that forming a relationship with their stepfather would be disloyal to their biological father. However, most researchers have found little correlation (ibid.).

The Study of Stepchildren and Step-Parenting in the United Kingdom was a large cross-sectional study of stepfamilies living in and around London from one to four years between 1998 and 2002. Smith (2004) reported on children's views about contact with their non-resident fathers and the quality of relationships with their fathers and stepfathers using data from this study. Sixty-seven per cent of children reported contact with their non-resident parents within the past year. More frequent contact (at least monthly) was associated with children's perceptions of a 'good quality relationship' and with their father behaving in a 'normal way' rather than focusing mainly on treats and special activities.

Contrary to some American findings from the 1980s, the British study found no evidence that having a good relationship with the biological father precludes having a good relationship with the stepfather (Smyth, 2004). In fact, the authors concluded that children who have strong relationships with their mothers and non-resident fathers are more likely to develop good relationships with their stepfathers. More generally, Smith concluded that children who are well-adjusted and have a positive self-image are more likely to form positive relationships with those around them. New Zealand research reported by Jan Pryor (2004) also confirmed this finding.

CONCLUSION

Since the 1960s, the common-law countries have experienced similar socio-demo-graphic trends relating to relationship breakdown, including higher separation rates, more mother-led families, high rates of poverty in mother-led families, and well-publicized parental disputes over child support, custody, and access. In response to the political pressure arising from these trends, the common-law countries liber-alized their divorce laws and developed **gender-neutral** laws relating to divorce, support, and child custody. In deciding where the post-divorce child should live, these countries continue to emphasize the 'best interests of the child'. Co-operation between parents over access and care arrangements is encouraged, and the family courts include mediation and less adversarial practices than courts for dealing with non-family matters.

Despite these reforms, controversies continue. Mothers usually retain the daily care of their children after marriage breakdown but nearly half of mother-led households live on low incomes in Canada and some English-speaking countries (DECD, 2005b). Since the 1980s, non-resident fathers have gained more legal rights to make decisions about their children's welfare and more divorced fathers now maintain contact with their children. However, about a third of non-resident fathers lose contact. Child-support enforcement laws have been tightened, making more fathers pay, but the state has been unable to retrieve the full amount of financial sup-port from all fathers required to pay.

In the past few decades, numerous researchers from a variety of disciplines have investigated various aspects of marriage breakdown and its social and economic outcomes. High rates of separation reflect the rise of individualism, the greater **sec-ularization** of society, and the growing view that relationships should last only as long as they are mutually satisfying. However, high rates of re-partnering suggest that intimate cohabitation is still desired and valued. Furthermore, it is still the case that most people aspire to committed and permanent relationships and that most couples remain married for life.

If we add together legal marriages, remarriages, consensual heterosexual relationships, and same-sex cohabitation, we could argue that the percentage of people living in intimate partnerships remains as high as ever. However, fewer partners are willing to remain in unhappy relationships for an extended time. The desire for intimacy remains strong, but more social and economic forces work against the durability of relationships, including labour market changes, greater geographic mobility, and new ideas about creating personal biographies. Both the legitimation and the rising prevalence of separation and divorce continue to present challenges to former partners, families, communities, social service agencies, and the welfare state.

SUMMARY

In recent decades, more marriages and relationships are ending in separation. Laws have been reformed to acknowledge that marriages do not necessarily last for life and to help separating couples decide on care arrangements and the division of family assets. However, the law assumes more gender equity than exists in reality, especially in regard to the ability of mothers with young children to become self-supporting after divorce. This chapter argues that the increased impermanence of marriage has transformed family life for many.

Questions for Critical Thought

1. What impact does parental separation have on young people's attitudes and relationship experiences?
2. Do current laws and practices about divorce, child custody, and child support make accurate assumptions about the lives of men, women, and children?
3. Why are so many people concerned about experiences in the 'post-divorce family'?

Suggested Readings

Pryor, Jan, and Bryan Rodgers. 2001. *Children in Changing Families: Life after Parental Separation*. Oxford: Blackwell. This book, which covers international research on the impact of parental separation and stepfamily formation on children, offers insights into why some survive family change better than others.

Statistics Canada. 2002. *Changing Conjugal Life in Canada*. General Social Survey, Cycle 15, Catalogue no. 89–576–XIE, July. A recent account of the emergent types of cohabitation in Canada, including an overview of how separation and divorce have changed the nature of family life.

Wu, Zheng, and Christophe Schimmele. 2005. 'Divorce and Repartnering', in M. Baker, ed. *Families: Changing Trends in Canada*, 5th edn. Toronto: McGraw-Hill Ryerson, 202–28. This chapter provides a historical perspective on divorce in Canada and discusses divorce outcomes for various family members.

Suggested Websites

Australian Institute of Family Studies
www.aifs.gov.au
This organization has been carrying out research for several decades on a number of family issues, including separation and divorce.

Government of Ontario

www.gov.on.ca

The Ontario government provides a site to help people understand the legal issues and processes of separation and divorce in that province.

Divorce Magazine

www.DivorceMagazine.com

Divorce Magazine provides information and support for those going through the transition of separation and divorce, promoting a positive attitude towards divorce.

Chapter 7

Families and the Welfare State

Learning Objectives
- To understand how and why 'the state' regulates family life.
- To investigate in detail four different family policy areas.
- To understand how conceptualizations of family life influence policy options.

CHAPTER OUTLINE

The chapter begins by defining the 'welfare state' and noting cross-national differences in social programs for families with children. Four family policy areas are then discussed in detail to illustrate how and why the state regulates family life.

INTRODUCTION

In previous chapters, we saw that family life continues to be influenced by patterns of work, cultural practices, laws, and social programs, as well as personal choices. Even when people deliberately try to live outside traditions or laws, other people attempt to control their 'unsociable' behaviour and enforce family responsibilities. Social researchers have traced the development of family laws and policies over the years and attempted to uncover implicit understandings about the nature of family and the role of the state in family life. Although laws and policies vary in different jurisdictions and are reformed over the years, researchers have sought to explain why some countries have been willing to provide more generous support while others have left needy family members to cope on their own. Researchers have also attempted to explain why certain models of family are given more public support by specific political parties and interest groups.

Before the 1940s, state authorities, employers, and religious leaders generally respected family privacy unless families were unable to manage—meaning that children were flagrantly neglected or abused, discipline problems or violence came to the attention of authorities, or the family was visibly impoverished and the children malnourished. Nevertheless, the state has been involved in family life for over a hundred years, requiring the legalization of marriage and divorce, the registration of births and deaths, compulsory school attendance for children, and the enforcement of spousal and child support (Ursel, 1992; Gauthier, 1996). The state continues to expect parents to support, protect, and control their children and sees 'the family' as a major site of social control. At the same time, the state provides at least some measure of income security and social services for families in need.

Regardless of their political views, most people would agree that some aspects of family life should be subjected to public scrutiny and government regulation. There is widespread acceptance that parents must be required to support their children whether they are living with them or not. There is also considerable agreement that laws are needed to protect women, children, and the elderly from the abuse of other family members, and to prevent sexual activity and reproduction from occurring with offspring or between siblings. In addition, most citizens in Western industrialized countries would acknowledge that at least some parents need public assistance rearing and supporting their children, and would agree that a portion of the taxpayer's money should be used for this purpose. What remains controversial is how much public money should be used for what kinds of families and in what circumstances.

Policy-makers usually believe that they are improving family life when they reform social programs, but policy changes have not always been based on accurate knowledge about how people actually live or why they live this way. Instead, reforms are sometimes based on preconceived notions of the importance of marriage and reproduction to the nation, the 'natural' division of labour in families, parental and conjugal responsibilities, values and motives of low-income people, and ideas about the importance of paid work to moral development and the maintenance of social well-being. These preconceptions permeate our culture even though they are modified over time and vary among groups with different political and religious beliefs.

In previous chapters, I discussed a number of policy issues relating to cohabitation, paid employment, and the 'post-divorce family'. In this chapter, several additional areas of family policy will be introduced, including issues relating to medical advances in assisted conception, social programs for childbirth and child care, income support for families with children, and the protection of vulnerable family members. Before we do this, however, we need to clarify some definitions.

WHAT DO WE MEAN BY THE 'WELFARE STATE'?

When academics or politicians talk about the **state**, they usually are referring to legislative and executive bodies (such as parliament and government departments) as well as publicly funded agencies (such as the police and correctional services) mandated to enforce these policies. When studying family policies, the concept of **welfare state** refers to the social services and income support programs designed to improve the social and economic well-being of families and to regulate and control family and personal life. Researchers and theorists studying the development of welfare states have shown that nations differ in the ways they think about the nature of family life and social provision, the kinds of programs they actually create, and their preferences for funding and delivering social programs.

The welfare state was generally developed between the 1940s and 1970s, when social and family life differed substantially from the present, but new social programs continue to be established and existing ones are continually restructured. Table 7.1 shows the dates when various social programs were developed in Canada and when major modifications were made to these programs. Although most have been amended since they were established, some programs still imply that marital relationships and paid employment remain stable throughout life. Some public discourse about family also suggests that most people live in nuclear family units consisting of a breadwinner father who supports 'his dependants' in full-time paid work and a homemaker mother who cares for the children at home or works part-time. The couple is often assumed to be heterosexual, legally married for life, and living with their two or three children who are biologically related to both parents (Eichler, 1997). However, most people no longer live this way. If policy-makers acknowledged the degree of instability in some people's work patterns and relationships, the social programs they create or restructure might look quite different.

Table 7.1   The Establishment of Social Benefits in Canada

Family Allowance	This universal allowance was created in 1945 and paid to mothers for each child.
Old Age Pension	The OAS was originally established in 1926 as a pension for those with low incomes and was converted to a universal pension in 1951.
Mothers'/Widows' Pensions	These pensions were developed around 1920 but date varies by province.
Unemployment Insurance	UI was established as a federal social insurance program in 1941; maternity benefits were added in 1971 and parental benefits in 1984 and 1990. In 1996 the program was made more stringent and renamed Employment Insurance.
Hospital/Medical Insurance	Hospital insurance was established in 1958; medical insurance (i.e., universal publicly paid and privately delivered health care, or medicare) was established beginning in Saskatchewan in 1962, with other provinces participant by the late 1960s/early 1970s.
Canada/Quebec Pension Plan	C/QPP was established in 1966 (financed by contributions from employees and employers, and from government); this public pension program also pays survivor benefits and disability benefits to contributors.
Spouse's Allowance	This program (an income-tested pension for spouses—mainly women—aged 60–4 of old-age pensioners) was introduced in 1975.
Child Tax Benefit	The former Family Allowance and tax deductions/credits for children were rolled into this targeted tax benefit for lower- and middle-income families in 1993.
Parliamentary Resolution to end 'Child Poverty'	An all-party agreement was passed in 1989.
Canada Child Tax Benefit	The Child Tax Benefit and Working Income Supplement were rolled together to form this benefit in 1998.

Source: Adapted from Baker (2004b: 181).

Various countries have been compared and categorized according to the generosity of their social provision and the philosophy underlying it. A number of categorizations exist but Canada and the United States have usually been linked together with the English-speaking countries and labelled as 'liberal' or 'residual' welfare states, meaning that in these countries individuals and families are normally assumed to be responsible for their own economic and social well-being (Esping-Andersen, 1990, 1996; O'Connor et al., 1999). Parents are held responsible for the care and support of their children both when they live together and after separation (should it occur), and spouses are expected to support and assist each other during marriage. When state benefits are made available, they are relatively ungenerous, well below minimum wages and even below accepted poverty levels.

In contrast, the Nordic or **social democratic welfare states**, such as Sweden and Denmark, view children's well-being as a collective or social responsibility as well as a parental one, and place more importance than liberal welfare states on redistributing income, preventing poverty, and promoting gender equity. **Corporatist welfare states** such as France and Germany, so called because they involve business, labour, and the state working together as corporate entities to create **social insurance** programs, are financed through employer and employee contributions and are designed to replace lost wages due to unemployment, sickness, work-related injury, or retirement. These social insurance programs were developed by trade unions, employers' groups, and government to share the cost of income loss, and they continue to be managed by representatives from these three groups (Esping-Andersen, 1990).

Some theorists have argued that Australia and New Zealand should not be included with the liberal welfare states but should instead be classified as 'wage earners' welfare states' (Castles, 1985; Castles and Shirley, 1996). These countries used to be different because their trade unions and governments sought to ensure that (male) wages were high enough to support families at a comfortable level through centralized bargaining and restrictions on immigrant labour. State assistance was also provided for home ownership; but the basic income support programs targeted to low-income households were less important than these other factors were to family well-being. Increasingly, however, Australia and especially New Zealand resemble the other liberal welfare states (Kelsey, 1999).

Social support for families with children clearly varies cross-nationally (Hantrais, 2004; OECD, 2005b). However, important differences are also apparent among the various jurisdictions of the same country. Federal states like Canada and United States have decentralized many social programs, which are designed and administered at the provincial or state level. In Canada, for example, the federal government retains jurisdiction over some income support programs (such as Old Age Security, Canada Pension Plan, and Employment Insurance), federal tax concessions for families, maternity/parental benefits, and divorce law. The provinces have jurisdiction over marriage law, **maternity leave** provisions, social services such as child protection, and child-care services, health-care services, education, and social assistance. They also control the division of matrimonial property upon separation of spouses and laws pertaining to the implementation of child custody, access, child support, and spousal support (Guest, 1997; McGilly, 1998).

In addition, some Canadian provinces, such as Ontario, allow municipalities to create and administer child-care provisions and income support for some categories of welfare recipients. Divided jurisdiction within a federal state permits inconsistencies to develop among different regions and inhibits the creation of national programs in matters of provincial jurisdiction (Baker, 1995). This means that 'the welfare state' might not be internally consistent in its goals or in eligibility rules for benefits, even within the same country and the same kind of social policy. In addition, some jurisdictions might provide generous social provision for retired people but restrict services and public support for children or employed mothers.

GENDER, SOCIAL CLASS, AND WELFARE STATES

Research has also shown that state involvement in families varies by gender and social class as well as by country and jurisdiction. Feminist scholars, in particular, have argued that women's access to social provision has been shaped by their relationship to men and children, by different views about suitable roles for women and mothers, and by prevalent models of the typical family (Sainsbury, 1993; Leira, 2002). Men are assumed to be the main breadwinners and women the primary care providers within the liberal and corporatist welfare states, and parents are seen as fully responsible for their own children. In addition, men tend to receive more generous social benefits through paid work rather than parenthood, while women gain their entitlement mainly as mothers, especially when they have no male breadwinner, but also as wives. In contrast, the social democratic states tend to view marriage partners both as earners and as carers. They see the well-being of children as a joint responsibility between parents and the state, exemplified by the provision of affordable child care and generous social provision for leave for family responsibilities.

Historically, liberal welfare states have treated low-income wives and widows as more deserving of state income support than never-married or separated mothers. If women became lone mothers through premarital pregnancy, separation, or divorce, they used to be offered minimal benefits (Ursel, 1992). These benefits were sometimes delivered in discretionary ways by welfare officials rather than being seen as legal entitlements. The recipients were thought to require close scrutiny concerning their maternal and moral behaviour to ensure that they were truly eligible and not defrauding the taxpayers (Swift, 1995; Little, 1998). In contrast, wives and widows often became eligible for higher levels of income support through the husband's work-related social insurance entitlements as well as his private insurance policies. Now, the benefits available for lone mothers vary less by their route to lone parenthood, but married women and widows are still more likely to have access to private insurance or pension funds acquired through their male partners' earnings.

Men typically have received benefits from employers or from the state as workers and family providers rather than merely as husbands and fathers. Work-related benefits may be sponsored by employers but some are financed through social insurance programs, such as Canada's Worker's Compensation, Employment Insurance, and the Canada/Quebec Pension Plan. Receiving these benefits involves less investigation into recipients' personal lives and higher payments based on the contributions from employees and employers (Sainsbury, 1993, 1996).

As more women enter full-time paid work, they also become eligible for employment-related benefits, but because the benefits are wage-related, women's payments tend to be lower. Because women earn lower average wages, they also make lower contributions to pension plans and social insurance programs, and therefore receive lower average benefits than men. If they privately insure their earnings or their life, the final payment also reflects lower female earnings as well as their longer life expectancy.

State intervention has also varied by social class and ethnicity. Welfare workers have been permitted to investigate the family circumstances and living conditions of impoverished families even though such investigations would be considered an infringement of privacy for those with higher incomes. For example, a lone mother living on social assistance might be visited by social workers searching for evidence of another adult living in her home who might be considered a potential bread-winner (Little, 1998).

The state has been most interventionist with visible minorities and indigenous peoples. In the past, impoverished but much-loved children from indigenous families were considered to be 'at risk' of maltreatment, disease, and lack of education by well-intentioned missionaries and government officials in Canada, Australia, and New Zealand (Baker, 2001b). Consequently, these children used to be removed from their parental homes and placed in residential schools run by churches or the government, often against the wishes both of the children and of their parents. Since the 1960s, these practices have ceased because they are considered racist and psychologically damaging, although the 'Sixties Scoop' in Canada resulted in thousands of Aboriginal children from impoverished or dysfunctional families being placed in foster care and adopted into non-Aboriginal families (Dickason, 2006: 229). Today, income support programs and local schools have been developed, efforts are made to keep children from problem homes within their own communities, and local child welfare services are sometimes managed by the indigenous people themselves.

This discussion suggests that state involvement in family life changes over time because policy ideas and social programs originate from different governments with varying political agendas, and that ideas about human rights and the role of the state in family life evolve over the years. In addition, policy reform tends to be incremental and developed from previous programs, because it is easier in a democracy to make minor modifications to existing policy than to introduce major reforms.

In recent decades, young people have tended to postpone marriage as more formal schooling is required for employment and both men and women expect to establish their occupational life and save some money before settling down. Declining fertility rates have been influenced by the higher costs of raising children, the desire for different paths to personal fulfillment, and more effective contraception. More people are choosing to limit their family size, but new reproductive technologies also enable more individuals to reproduce. The capitalist state wants to motivate its citizens to reproduce—to maintain and increase material production and consumption and, thus, the tax base—but the state also seeks to ensure that fertility treatments are cost-effective and cause no harm. In the next section, we examine some policy issues associated with medically assisted conception, including government responses to regulation and funding.

FERTILITY SERVICES AND PUBLIC FUNDING

Fertility problems seem to be increasing in industrialized countries but they might simply be reported more often now that fertility clinics have become prevalent and encourage couples to seek medical assistance with conception. Those experiencing conception problems can use the Internet to find information about the location of clinics, the procedures offered, the probability of success, potential risks, and personal costs. In countries with private fertility clinics, patients with adequate resources can purchase the services they believe will help them, which could raise expectations about the effectiveness of medical intervention as well as the right to bear children.

Considerable research suggests that fertility treatments tend to be time-consuming, emotionally draining, and stressful for marital relationships (Doyal, 1995; Adair and Rogan, 1998; Malin et al., 2001; Baker, 2004c). For wives, treatments can involve injecting drugs that regulate ovulation but alter moods, maintaining sensitivity to the week of greatest fertility each month, and the painful extraction and implantation of eggs. For husbands, treatments may involve sex on demand, producing sperm specimens at inconvenient times, and dealing with their partner's mood changes. Both must maintain regular clinic visits and cope with the disappointment of negative pregnancy results. The effectiveness rates of most procedures have improved in recent years but the probability of pregnancy is much higher for younger women even though older women are more likely to become patients. Some couples try for years to conceive, only to find that the miscarriage rate is elevated with assisted conception, as are the rates of pre-term delivery, stillbirth, and neonatal death (Ford et al., 2003; OECD, 2005b).

The increasing demand for medically assisted conception requires state regulation of fertility research and clinic services, including licensing of clinics, monitoring the safety and effectiveness of procedures, and providing subsidies for specific services. Some governments require hospitals and medical practitioners to distinguish between medically necessary interventions and fertility treatments requested for social reasons. Consequently, people with no medically diagnosed reason for infertility or who are at no risk of passing on a genetic disease may be unable to receive publicly funded services in some jurisdictions, such as New Zealand (Baker, 2005b). Also, some jurisdictions preferentially offer treatment to married couples or to cohabiting heterosexual couples in long-term stable relationships.

My New Zealand research (Baker, 2005b) focused on the impact of fertility treatment on gender identity and touched on a number of policy issues. On two separate occasions I interviewed 12 men and 12 women. They all lived in the Auckland region; each individual or his/her partner was involved in medically assisted conception. Clinics in New Zealand are not permitted to provide state-subsidized treatment to individuals with no medical reason for infertility so lesbian women who are unwilling to have heterosexual intercourse are forced to pay the full fee for donor insemination. The one lesbian woman in my study, who was using inherited money to finance her treatments, talked about her decision to become a mother and to seek assistance from a fertility clinic:

> You know, it'd probably be a lot easier if I just went out and I had a fuck with some bloke. I mean that would be quite easy. I don't want to do that because it would feel like a violation of who I am and this, in a way, odd as it is, it's more normal [referring to donor insemination]. (Ibid.)

Assisted insemination with the husband's sperm can cost less than $1,000 NZ but at the time of my study **in vitro fertilization** (IVF) cost over $8,000 for one attempt, and only one attempt can be made per month (by 2006 the cost was over $12,000 NZ). Five of the 12 couples in my study were eligible for one publicly funded treatment, and only one woman from these couples became pregnant after one treatment, while the rest paid for additional treatments with their own money. Five of the couples paid from $10,000 to about $34,000, excluding expenses for alternative treatments or nutritional supplements to improve their general health and fertility. Some couples in my study went into debt to finance their treatments; men were more likely than their female partners to calculate and complain about the high costs.

One woman, who was pregnant from her third treatment, spoke about how she would have felt if the treatment hadn't worked:

> I would have been really disappointed if it hadn't worked, especially for the second time 'round, but I don't think I would have tried IVF for five years unsuccessfully. Realistically, I wouldn't have been able to try again for quite a few years because I would have had to pay off an $8,000 loan that it cost for the second treatment. . . . I think I would like to try again in another year's time [to have a second child]. Financially, we couldn't afford it, but I would still like to use the [frozen] embryo and hope that it works. It costs $350 a year to keep it frozen and we will pay for the first year and when it comes around to the next payment, I think we will then reconsider because of the cost. (Ibid.)

This comment suggests that it is not only the cost of one treatment that is the issue but the price of continuing treatments, as well as the storage of sperm, eggs, or embryos. Most participants in my study also paid for expensive drugs and nutritional supplements.

One couple already had a 13-month-old child conceived through in vitro fertilization but the wife insisted on trying for a second child even though she was told by staff at the private clinic that the probability of success for her at 44 years of age was less than 5 per cent. Her 46-year-old husband talked at length about the success rates (as three other men in the study did): 'it was a shock to find out that it didn't really increase our chances that much at all . . . I guess the shock was that we expected a massive increase in percentages' (ibid.).

Many critics have remained ambivalent about the promotion of certain reproductive technologies. They argue that the success rates are exaggerated by talk about pregnancy rates rather than live births and note that low-income women can be exploited if wealthier couples contract them to become surrogate mothers (Eichler, 1997). Birth mothers in surrogacy cases tend to have lower incomes because few women would agree to 'make a baby' for a woman they had never met unless there was some money exchanged. Although the law does not permit babies to be sold, some countries have permitted surrogate mothers to have their medical, legal, and other expenses paid by the commissioning parents. Nevertheless, medically assisted conception remains out of the financial reach of many couples because of the high financial cost and time-consuming interventions.

Patriarchal societies can and do use sex selection technologies to reinforce the cultural preference for sons rather than daughters, although this selection may involve a discrete violation of existing laws. To some extent, fertility treatments are still experimental, intrusive, and risky, although they have been 'normalized' by fertility specialists, the media, and some patients. However, the risk of multiple pregnancies and negative birth outcomes is higher with assisted conception than from normal conception (OECD, 2005b). These interventions also tend to medicalize the natural act of child-bearing and reinforce the pressure for all women to reproduce (Baker, 2004c). At the same time, these technologies offer new opportunities for lesbian women to become mothers without the risk of unscreened sperm, to enjoy safer hospital conditions, and to avoid heterosexual intercourse (Michaels, 1996; Letherby, 1999). Reproductive technologies offer the experience of motherhood to more women and give them greater choice over how and when they reproduce.

Wealthier patients can seek treatment in private clinics or travel to other jurisdictions with less stringent regulations, but low-income couples have fewer options. In addition to eligibility rules, most governments in OECD countries ban the sale of sperm and eggs, as well as payments for babies (for women who become surrogate mothers). They also regulate access to information about the identity of sperm donors and specify the rights of children conceived with the assistance of egg or sperm donors. Some of these issues have already been contested in the courts, but the speed of change in reproductive techniques has moved faster than the law.

This discussion suggests that assisted conception procedures can be fraught with legal and moral controversies. For example, should these treatments be permitted for reasons other than medical or genetic problems? Should same-sex couples be given access to these services because they do not choose to participate in heterosexual intercourse, with public tax revenue paying for these treatments? If the state pays, who should be covered, which treatments should be subsidized, and how many treatments should be permitted to each patient? Should donors and parents be asked to sign a pre-birth agreement? Should egg or sperm donors be granted any 'parental rights' if they so choose, after a child is born, which could give children three legal parents (Collins, 2005)? Should adult children born from donor insemination even have the right to know the identity of their donor? These are all issues that legal commissions and governments are currently struggling to resolve.

The next policy issue we consider relates to employed parents and leave entitlements for childbirth, adoption, and breast-feeding. Early programs were targeted at employed mothers but most programs now encourage fathers to take time off work when they have a new child in the household, in order to bond with and help care for their infant. We also want to consider social programs assisting employed mothers to care for their children while they earn household money to support them.

EMPLOYED MOTHERS, CHILDBIRTH, AND CHILD CARE

Increasingly, wives and mothers are working full-time and, depending on where they live, they may qualify for maternity or parental leave and benefits while their jobs are held open for them during childbirth or at the time of adoption. Leave provisions vary by country and jurisdictions within countries but international organizations such as the International Labour Organization (ILO) have urged member states to create at least minimum provisions. The latest ILO Maternity Protection Convention states that pregnant women should be entitled to at least 14 weeks of paid leave from work and that when they return they should be entitled to a daily reduction of working hours with full remuneration for breast-feeding (ILO, 2000). The World Health Organization encourages new mothers to breast-feed their babies because it is associated with numerous health benefits, including providing optimum nutrition for infants, reducing infectious diseases, and lowering infant mortality (WHO and UNICEF, 1990). For employed mothers, the duration of breast-feeding may be influenced by leave provisions and breast-feeding facilities. Table 7.2 shows leave provisions in selected OECD countries.

Paid leave at childbirth or adoption can be gender-specific or gender-neutral. Maternity benefits are gender-specific and tend to focus on maternal and child health and women's employment equity. Parental benefits are gender-neutral and have been used as an inducement to reproduce and for men to become more involved in infant care. Both have been seen also as citizenship rights for employees. Comparative research suggests that the model chosen depends mainly on political lobbying within the jurisdiction and the ideology of the party in power (Heitlinger, 1993; Gauthier, 1996; Hantrais, 2004). Political pressure may be national and come from women's groups or men's rights groups, or it can originate from supranational organizations, such as the ILO, that encourage member states to develop minimum standards (Hantrais, 2000). However, the type of leave and benefit provisions fit in with existing social programs, political priorities, and current views of citizenship rights.

Many countries also subsidize the cost of child care, usually for employed parents with low incomes and generally in not-for-profit centres or licensed homes (Jenson and Sineau, 2001b). These subsidies can be for all parents and relatively generous (as in Sweden, France, and the Canadian province of Quebec), or they may be targeted to low-income employed parents and be meagre, as in the United States and New Zealand. In countries such as New Zealand, two-parent families with average incomes are required to pay the full cost if they require non-family care. In contrast, the Canadian government provides tax breaks to cover the child-care expenses of employed parents, regardless of family income, while provincial governments subsidize child care for low-income families (with some federal grants). Obtaining subsidies or tax benefits usually requires official receipts from caregivers, which are sometimes difficult to obtain because many part-time carers do not report their earnings to avoid paying income tax.

Table 7.2   Maternity/Parental Leave Benefits in Selected OECD Countries

Country	Date of First Legislation	Length of Maternity/ Parental Leave	Percentage of Wages Paid in Covered Period	Provider of Coverage
Australia	1973 unpaid leave	1 year	No federal statutory requirement for paid leave but some unions pay	—
Canada	1971 maternity benefits 1990 parental benefits	15 weeks maternity + 35 weeks parental	55% to a ceiling	Social Insurance (Employment Insurance)
Denmark	1915 maternity benefits	18 weeks maternity and 10 additional weeks parental	100% to a ceiling	Social Security
France	1909 maternity leave 1913 maternity benefits	16–26 weeks	100%	Social Security
Germany	1883 parental leave 1927 maternity benefits	14 weeks	100%	Social Security to ceiling and employer pays difference
Japan	1926 maternity benefits	14 weeks	60%	Social Security or Health Insurance
New Zealand	2002 parental benefits	12–14 weeks parental	Flat rate	Social Security
Norway	1909 maternity benefits	18 weeks maternity + 26 weeks parental	48 weeks at 100% or 52 weeks at 80%	Social Security
Sweden	1937 maternity benefits 1974 parental benefits	480 days parental	390 days at 80% and 90 days at flat rate	Social Security
United Kingdom	1975 maternity benefits	14–18 weeks	90% for 6 weeks, flat rate thereafter	Social Security
United States	1993 parental leave	12 weeks	No federal statutory requirement for paid leave but some states/unions pay	—

Source: Baker (2006). Reprinted by permission of the publisher.

Even when governments subsidize child care, the level of subsidy can vary considerably from a fraction of the required fees to the entire cost. If governments see preschool care mainly as early childhood education, they may subsidize only a few hours a week. If they want to assist employed mothers, they may subsidize care that covers all their working hours. Subsidized spaces usually are regulated by government, but the regulations can be minimal, covering mainly physical facilities, or they can be extensive, covering physical facilities, the quality of the educational program, and the qualifications of providers.

Whatever arrangement is favoured by the state, the number of children requiring care usually outstrips the availability of spaces and highly recommended centres and not-for-profit daycare facilities often maintain long waiting lists, especially in the liberal welfare states. The shortage of regulated spaces means that most employed parents with preschool children in the liberal welfare states are forced to rely on unregulated sitters without being able to monitor the quality of these arrangements themselves (Jenson and Sineau, 2001b; Hantrais, 2004). Caring for children is a difficult job yet generally pays the minimum wage or less, which means that child-care centres often experience difficulty attracting and retaining trained staff.

Although most governments want to ensure that children are cared for by qualified providers in safe and stimulating environments, they are not always prepared to subsidize this kind of care. The provision of high-quality care is expensive, especially for infants, and costs rise when governments require professional qualifications for providers, educational programs and nourishing food for children, and safe and congenial facilities. If the full costs were passed on to parents in the form of fees, most would be unable to afford this kind of care. Consequently, both government and employers sometimes subsidize child care, but they also want to ensure that the costs are manageable. France, Sweden, and Belgium have chosen to provide high-quality, government-regulated child care, but few English-speaking countries offer the same level of services (Jenson and Sineau, 2001a). The liberal welfare states tend to focus on lower income taxes and rely on parents to pay most of the cost of child care. However, the cost of rearing children is rising for an increasing number of parents, who are unable to pay the bills from their own earnings.

INCOME SUPPORT FOR FAMILIES WITH CHILDREN

Many taxpayers in the liberal welfare states seem to feel that although they work hard to support their families, others are receiving a handout from government. Consequently, they question the need for state income support programs. Most OECD countries since the 1920s have provided some form of income support to families with children—early programs assisted disabled war veterans with dependants, widows, and deserted mothers with young children because these groups were considered to be the most deserving (Bock and Thane, 1991; Baker, 1995; Gauthier, 1996). A number of countries also offered income tax relief to male workers supporting children and a financially dependent wife. These policies were intended to create some measure of equity between taxpayers with dependants and those without, as well as to supplement family income at a time of growing labour unrest and demand for higher wages (Ursel, 1992).

During the Great Depression of the 1930s, many governments and employers' groups began to acknowledge that unemployment, accidents, and sickness could happen to the most diligent, were often beyond individual control, and required state support. In New Zealand, the first Labour government developed unemployment and sickness benefits in 1938, along with a state health-care program and extended public education. These programs were considered innovative among the English-speaking nations of the time (Cheyne et al., 2005). In Canada, Unemployment Insurance was first paid in 1941, after years of public debate and a constitutional change that was required to overcome jurisdictional problems because employment-related programs are under provincial jurisdiction (Cuneo, 1979).

By the 1940s, many governments also paid a universal child allowance for each child, regardless of the household income or employment status of the parents. Child allowances were paid monthly or bimonthly directly to the mother (or main care provider) in an attempt to ensure that the money was spent on children's needs (Baker, 1995). The idea behind universal child allowances was that bearing and raising children was not just something parents did for their own satisfaction but that reproduction within marriage was an expectation of citizenship, providing the nation with future workers, consumers, voters, and taxpayers.

In the prosperous years of the 1960s and early 1970s, income support programs were also developed for impoverished individuals and families, and family services and social housing were expanded. New social programs were created for mothers supporting children without a male breadwinner. In 1966, the Canadian federal government began to share the cost of social assistance with the provinces, which enabled them to expand services to families. In 1973, both Australia and New Zealand gave lone mothers with children the statutory right to state income support if they had low incomes, few assets, and needed to care for their children at home (Baker and Tippin, 1999).

Over the years, public discourse has changed about the purpose and value of state income support. Before universal family allowances in the 1940s, income support in the liberal welfare states was targeted to the poorest and most deserving families to prevent them from falling into destitution. During the 1960s and 1970s, programs were expanded to keep people out of poverty and to provide equality of opportunity. After the 1990s, however, many governments returned to the practice of targeting social assistance to moderate- or low-income families in order to provide a 'safety net' below which no family could fall (ibid.). Unlike other liberal states, the United States never developed a family allowance or child benefit, and in 1972 began to place employment expectations on lone mothers receiving social assistance (Aid to Families with Dependent Children). Legislation in 1981 and 1996 created punitive 'workfare' programs for lone mothers in the United States (Baker, 1995; Mink, 1998).

The United Kingdom retained its universal child benefit but the other liberal welfare states have targeted these payments to moderate- or low-income families. In Canada, the family allowance ceased to be paid to all families with children in 1993 (Baker, 1995: 130), but federal child benefits continue to be paid to moderate- and low-income families, with a stronger emphasis on supporting the 'working poor'. Since the 1970s, provincial income support programs have become less generous relative to living costs and average wages in a number of provinces, and poor families are relying once again on kin and charity (such as food banks) to supplement state services (NCW, 2003).

In recent years, international organizations such as the United Nations Children's Fund (UNICEF) have focused on 'child poverty' rates, which are calculated as the percentage of children (under 18 years) living in households with incomes less than 50 per cent of the national median income, after taxes and government transfers. Despite politicians' pronouncements about eliminating or reducing child poverty, these rates actually increased from the mid-1990s until 2000 in most OECD countries (UNICEF, 2005). In Canada, poverty rates changed very little during this period. The government reduced social expenditures from 1990 to 2000 but parental earnings increased and the government made minor increases in spending on families (OECD, 2005: 16, 24).

Poverty rates among children are highest when they live in one-parent households where the parent is not working for pay and the family depends on income support benefits. Comparative figures provide some indication of the relative levels of social benefits, which vary considerably by country. For example, in single-parent households with a 'non-working' parent, 93.8 per cent of children in United States and 89.7 per cent of children in Canada live in poverty (ibid., 57). However, the rate is only 22.2 per cent in Denmark and 24.7 per cent in Norway, as we saw in Chapter 5. The pattern is similar in two-parent households where neither parent is employed, although the poverty rates are lower. In the United States, 77.9 per cent of children with two non-working parents live in poverty compared to 75.3 per cent in Canada.

This suggests that income support programs in the liberal welfare states are far less generous than in social democratic countries, and that governments in North America offer considerably more income support to two-parent households than to those with one parent. Agencies attempting to reduce poverty tend to focus on children because they cannot be held responsible for their parents' unemployment, illness, or unwillingness to work. Yet, it is actually parental circumstances and earning capacity that cause children to live in poverty and reduce their life chances.

One reason why child poverty is rising is that income support programs are being restructured to shorten the length of time on state benefits and to tighten expectations that beneficiaries should retrain or more actively search for work. For lone mothers, this means that when the youngest child reaches a certain age, she will be expected to find part-time or full-time work unless there are extenuating circumstances. Yet the transition from 'welfare to work' is risky for families if they must forfeit income security and subsidies for child care and medical expenses when they move off social assistance. If former beneficiaries lose their jobs and experience delays re-enrolling for income support, they may be worse off than remaining on social benefits. For political reasons, however, governments want to ensure that the services accompanying state income support are not more generous than those available to low-wage workers (Baker, 2006).

Box 7.1 Child Poverty in Rich Nations

Rates of 'child poverty' are usually measured as the percentage of households with children who are living on low incomes (often defined as less than 50 per cent of national median incomes after government taxes and benefits, and adjusted for family size). These rates are influenced by a combination of socio-demographic trends, labour market conditions, and government policies, but the actual combination varies for each country.

The 2005 report by the United Nations Children's Fund compares the social and economic conditions in three groups of countries: those with rising rates of child poverty (such as Hungary and Italy), those with stable rates of child poverty (Canada and Finland), and those with falling rates (the United Kingdom and the United States) (UNICEF, 2005: 16–17). The UNICEF report shows that child poverty tends to increase when:

- more parents separate and the children live with their mother;
- unemployment rises;
- wages fall relative to living costs;
- governments cut social benefits and services or make them harder to obtain.

However, child poverty rates tend to fall as:

- older couples produce fewer children;
- workers gain more education and skills;
- more households acquire two earners;
- the economy is booming and wages rise relative to living costs.

This suggests that child poverty rates are not just influenced by child benefits but rates can fall if there is sustained economic growth bringing rising wages and employment opportunities.

Source: Summarized from UNICEF (2005).

PROTECTING VULNERABLE FAMILY MEMBERS

For over a century, the state has intervened in homes where parents could not properly care for their children or control their behaviour, but state assistance for women dealing with abusive partners is much more recent. In this section, I examine patterns in service provision for children who are abused or neglected by their parents, as well as for women abused by partners, and make some cross-national comparisons of trends in the delivery of these services.

Child Welfare Services

Children who were abused, neglected, or delinquent were sometimes removed from their family homes before the 1920s and placed in institutions that provided them with adequate care, a basic education, and employment training. Some children's institutions also found adoptive parents for orphans and younger children who could no longer live with their parents. However, over the years psychologists and social workers came to believe that institutional care set these children apart from others, both socially and emotionally, and failed to provide them with adequate love and stimulation. In addition, residential institutions were costly to run even with church or state support, and provided disciplinary challenges for care workers (Swift, 1995; Connolly, 2003; Krane, 2003).

After the 1960s, the state began to encourage more parents to care for their children at home with the assistance of income support and home visits by social service professionals, who provided family counselling and advice about budgeting and disciplining children. The state also regulated existing children's institutions and foster homes, and screened potential foster and adoptive parents. New procedures were developed to deal with family casework and higher educational standards were required for social service workers. State interventions were guided by new principles, such as the 'principle of least intrusion' and **family preservation** (Krane, 2003). Some jurisdictions, such as Quebec, provided their own child protection programs, while others, including Ontario, mandated private agencies to offer these services on behalf of the state.

By the 1970s, children were less often placed in orphanages and more often left with their own parents with social supports. Unrelated foster care (i.e., care by someone not a relative) was used for children whose parents were unable to look after them, and the state subsidized the basic expenses. However, foster parents continually argued that the amounts did not cover their costs. Foster care was seen as a temporary solution that permitted children to maintain contact with their birth parents and siblings, but to receive care in a home with two parents and more effective discipline. The state attempted to ensure that the family environment both for fostering and for adoption was suitable for the child's well-being and development, which usually meant that the families included two heterosexual parents living in a stable relationship with a middle-class income. Often, the father was the breadwinner and the mother was a full-time caregiver, and both were expected to be young and healthy (Speirs and Baker, 1994).

As more mothers entered the labour force and child-rearing costs increased, foster parents became more difficult to find. Social workers also became worried about the implications of placing children with strangers, especially those outside their own cultural group. Now, many states encourage extended family members to care for children when parents can no longer manage. The trend to kinship care is often justified by 'the best interests of the child' and more specifically by the concept of 'family preservation', or providing a sense of family support and continuity in the children's lives. However, kinship carers tend to receive fewer services and supports than non-related caregivers, which means that this practice could be seen as a form of neo-liberal restructuring designed to save public funds (Connolly, 2003).

Researchers have demonstrated that the standards of care are less rigorously applied in kin care compared to foster or residential care (Connolly, 2003; Hunt, 2003). Today care providers are approved who would be considered unacceptable foster parents due to their low income, older age, single-parent status, poor health, existing parenting problems, or substandard accommodation. Unrelated foster care usually moves the child into a home with a stable household income, but children cared for by relatives are more likely to continue to live in poverty. Considerable research indicates that remaining in impoverished households can be detrimental to children's health, psychological well-being, and life chances (Ross et al., 1996; Roberts, 1997).

Indigenous and minority group children have been over-represented among those coming to the attention of child welfare systems in countries such as Australia, Canada, and New Zealand (Baker, 2001b). The former practices of keeping indigenous children in state-regulated residential schools or of having them adopted by white families have fallen into disrepute. Many of these children suffered from cultural confusion and reported some form of abuse after living with white foster families and in residential schools. Kin care is now viewed as less contentious because it keeps children within their local community and cultural group. Consequently, considerable effort has gone into trying to apply foster care processes and standards to kinship care. Even though research comparing child well-being in kin care with foster care is underdeveloped and sometimes contradictory, governments continue to encourage these practices (Connolly, 2003).

Dealing with Child Abuse

Over the past three decades, children's rights have been expanded and neither parents nor teachers have the right to physically punish children under their care—in some countries (UNICEF, 2003). Child abuse registries are kept in some jurisdictions but child-protection workers and victimization studies indicate that these registries record only a fraction of cases. The number of reported cases has risen dramatically every year, but it is not known whether this indicates an increase in abuse cases or is a result of new reporting requirements.

Public attention began to focus on the sexual abuse of children in the 1980s, when government-sponsored reports found that the percentage of adults who had been victims as children was much higher than previously acknowledged. These studies also noted that sexual abuse tends to occur during the daytime, in the home of the victim or of a friend, and by a male relative or family friend (Baker, 2001b). While girls are more vulnerable than boys, many young boys also are sexually abused, usually by men. School and church leaders continue to search for new ways to identify potential abusers before an incident occurs and to deal effectively with perpetrators. However, allegations are difficult to verify because they are sometimes made decades after the incident and, generally, such abuse occurs without witnesses.

Measures to prevent and control child abuse, which includes sexual, physical, and verbal abuse as well as a lack of the necessities of life, include the appointment of children's ombudspersons, the establishment of children's helplines, the integration of home visiting services, and closer monitoring of children considered to be at risk. The UNICEF report on child maltreatment argued that effective strategies include home visits to all families with young children by a variety of qualified health, education, and social service staff rather than targeting children assumed to be 'at risk' (UNICEF, 2003). This report also argued that child abuse strategies must address the economic circumstances of parents because those living in impoverished and stressed conditions are statistically more likely to abuse their children (ibid., 21). Most adults who are abused as children do *not* become child abusers, although various factors accumulate to augment the risk. Parents who abuse alcohol and drugs, and who live in impoverished and violent homes, are more likely to maltreat their children. For children, maltreatment contributes to depression, anxiety, and hostility as well as certain types of behaviour such as physical inactivity, smoking, alcoholism, drug abuse, risky sexual practices, and suicide (ibid., 19). Lack of affordable housing encourages women and children to stay in abusive homes and creates overcrowded conditions that heighten family tensions and promote contagious and chronic diseases.

Children are also negatively affected by witnessing the abuse of their mother. Each year about 12 per cent of North American women experience intimate-partner violence and 10 million children witness this violence (Graham-Bermann and Edleson, 2001: 3). Many mothers who experience domestic violence say that they fear for their children's safety, but this fear is generally minimized by a complex and often hostile court system (Jaffe et al., 2003: 17). An international shift in awareness towards recognizing the effects of domestic violence on children has been precipitated by many international conferences (Jaffe et al., 2000: 2; Krug et al., 2002: 103). With this attention, many countries have amended child custody policies to take into account the parent's history of domestic violence. There is clear evidence of growing concern across industrialized countries about the cost of violent behaviour to individuals, families, employers, and taxpayers.

Male Violence against Female Partners

Male violence against female partners seems to be increasing; but it may just be reported more often. A Canadian telephone survey found that 29 per cent of women reported physical or sexual abuse by an intimate partner over their lifetime and one-third of these said that they feared for their lives at some point in the relationship (Jaffe et al., 2003: 5). Physical abuse is not usually an isolated event, as some women have been assaulted and have sought help many times from friends, neighbours, social workers, and the police (Johnson, 1990; Leibrich et al., 1995). Adults who abuse their spouses (and children) have a higher probability of coming from families where their parents engaged in similar behaviour, and women who were abused during 'courtship' have a much higher probability of being abused during marriage (O'Leary et al., 1989; Barnes et al., 1991). Furthermore, separated women are more likely than those who are married or divorced to be assaulted and killed by former partners (Wilson and Daly, 1994; Krug et al., 2002: 96; DeKeseredy, 2005). This suggests that remaining in a violent relationship is dangerous for women, but that taking action to escape the violence can also have lethal consequences.

Comparative research suggests that this kind of violence becomes more prevalent when a society condones violence, when violence has become a form of entertainment in films and sports events, and when a country is engaged in war (Krug et al., 2002). Women become more vulnerable to physical, sexual, and emotional abuse if they see their male partner as the 'head of the household' or if they are financially dependent on him and cannot support their children alone (Baker, 2001b: 110). Women are also more vulnerable to abuse if they are cohabiting, or separated from their partner and living in low-income housing developments with other single parents (DeKeseredy, 2005). Certain cultural groups, such as Canadian Aboriginal women, also report exceptionally high rates of wife abuse (McGillvray and Comaskey, 1998; Brownridge, 2003).

Domestic violence programs, operated by both government and private agencies, typically offer crisis intervention, first helping a woman to develop protection plans that could involve laying charges against her partner or former partner. The woman is also helped to find transitional housing for herself and her children, to engage a lawyer, and, if necessary, to apply for income support to cover living expenses. In both individual counselling and group therapy, battered wives are encouraged to view partner abuse as unacceptable regardless of the circumstances or their own behaviour, although most abused women find it difficult to erase lingering feelings that the abuse was somehow their own fault. Male abusers are more often charged with an offence and encouraged (or required) to accept counselling, which includes taking responsibility for their acts of violence rather than blaming their partners. They are also helped to control their emotions, develop better communication skills, learn non-violent behaviour from male role models, and redefine what it means to be a man.

Community agencies and school boards sometimes collaborate to develop violence-prevention strategies focusing on staff development and awareness, community involvement, and student programs (Wolfe and Jaffe, 2001: 290; Mullender et al., 2003: 147). One of the early American programs to promote violence awareness and safety skill development with school-age children was implemented by the Minnesota Coalition for Battered Women. The program targeted elementary and secondary students throughout the state to ensure that all children knew about alternatives to domestic violence (Wolfe and Jaffe, 2001: 290). Action against family violence also includes sensitization workshops for professionals, such as teachers and judges, to increase their knowledge of program options and the personal and social implications of this form of violence (DeKeseredy, 2005). In addition, support services for **at-risk families** have been provided when violence seems to be a possibility because of their stressful circumstances.

Despite these initiatives, Sev'er (2002) concluded that little has changed in the past two decades for urban Canadian women who do not turn to women's shelters. Many women remain in abusive relationships because they do not know where to turn for assistance, because they cannot find temporary and low-income housing, or because they cannot support their children on their own. Tolerance of abuse continues because some women feel that it may somehow be their own fault, while others fear reprisal from partners who threaten to kill them if they go to the police or tell anyone about the incident.

Over the past few decades, international concern and action have grown in regard to intimate partner violence against women, and various conferences have been held and resolutions and manifestos drafted in an effort to reduce its incidence.

The first convention to declare discrimination against women as an international issue was the 1979 United Nations Convention on the Elimination of all Forms of Discrimination against Women. In 1994, the UN designated domestic violence as a human rights issue (Rodney, 1995). Conventions, however, do not have the same binding force as domestic law, although they place an externally monitored international standard of accountability upon signatory countries. United Nations conventions are also designed to raise awareness and have widened the terms of reference associated with domestic violence.

Most governments continue to express concern about all forms of domestic violence and abuse but the absence of public money remains the major impediment to establishing effective programs and services. Private donations as well as public funds support transition houses for battered women, and these safe houses are often staffed by volunteers and operate on the verge of closing due to lack of ongoing funds. Follow-up therapy and counselling may also be necessary for the entire family but these services also cost money to establish and maintain. Despite acknowledging the serious nature of this kind of violence, states have not always delivered sufficient program funding to deal with the rising number of reported cases.

CONCLUSION

This chapter has examined four additional areas of social policy: medically assisted conception, childbirth leave and child-care subsidies for employed parents, family income support, and social protection for vulnerable family members. It has shown that levels of government support and delivery mechanisms vary by country and jurisdiction, with issues of income support quite controversial.

The increasing demand for fertility treatment requires state regulation of clinic services and government subsidies for certain procedures. This means that some potential patients are unable to obtain services or must pay the full cost themselves. This has led to continuing controversies concerning who has the right to reproduce, under what circumstances, and at what cost to the public purse.

Especially in the liberal welfare states, social conservatives have questioned whether we can afford various 'welfare' programs, especially for those outside the labour force or those who seem to be engaging in self-destructive or anti-social behaviour. However, most social researchers have concluded that the need for social welfare continues, especially for families with children living in countries experiencing rapid labour market changes. Furthermore, government efforts to promote greater reliance on market income have not reduced poverty rates but instead have increased the gap between rich and poor families and encouraged feelings of relative deprivation and injustice.

The private sector may contribute to economic growth and national productivity (as it is now measured), but can entrepreneurs be expected to contribute to social well-being? Will employers voluntarily provide family leave and child-care facilities unless they stand to profit by these measures? Governments can require employers to pay at least the minimum wage to all employees, to provide parental leave and benefits, and to offer some paid leave to employees for family responsibilities. In addition, governments can acknowledge that most workers also have family responsibilities by investing in public child-care services for employed parents or subsidizing employers to provide workplace daycare. But when these issues are left to employers or the private sector, families are likely to suffer.

Although some states provide social services and income support to all families with children, the liberal welfare states tend to focus public resources on families 'in need' or considered to be 'at risk'. This may mean that children are neglected, families have insufficient income for food or shelter, the home is violent, a lone parent is experiencing problems coping with children, and/or parents or children are involved with drugs or alcohol or are in trouble with the law. However, state support for the daytime care of children with employed mothers has become a more universal need as most mothers in many OECD countries are now employed.

In the 1930s, governments and employers began to accept the idea that unemployment and poverty are not always the fault of unwilling workers or of moral weakness. Social programs were expanded over the years with different goals, depending on political pressure and the ideology of the government in power. Now, neo-liberal interest groups are once again encouraging citizens and taxpayers to see social welfare as either too expensive or ineffective. Increasingly, public discourse about 'welfare dependency' and the high cost of the welfare state is exaggerated for political purposes. Although more people seem to want tax cuts, they often forget that this would likely lead to a reduction in a variety of social services for families with children.

SUMMARY

This chapter argues that different kinds of welfare states make varying assumptions about the nature of family life. In addition, they typically privilege parents living with young children compared to other adults and 'working families' compared to those relying on social benefits. Welfare states also tend to differentiate between the needs of mothers and fathers. Discussions of different kinds of family policy illustrate the changing nature of social programs, the continuing variations among countries, and how the state attempts to respond to different interest groups.

Questions for Critical Thought

1. How does the accepted 'model' of family influence the choice of social policies and programs?
2. Should governments direct social benefits and services at children, at parents, or at all citizens? What difference does the direction make?
3. Why are reported incidents of child abuse and neglect increasing despite efforts to reduce abuse?

Suggested Readings

Baker, Maureen. 2006. *Restructuring Family Policies: Convergences and Divergences.* Toronto: University of Toronto Press. This book examines the external and internal forces that influence the restructuring of family policies in OECD countries, including Canada.

———— and David Tippin. 1999. *Poverty, Social Assistance and the Employability of Mothers: Restructuring Welfare States.* Toronto: University of Toronto Press. Using a feminist and political economy perspective, the authors examine cross-national differences in restructuring social programs for low-income mothers in four liberal welfare states: Canada, Australia, New Zealand, and the United Kingdom.

Hantrais, Linda. 2004. *Family Policy Matters: Responding to Family Change in Europe.* Bristol: Policy Press. Hantrais compares recent family changes in Europe and examines the reactions of policy-makers and practitioners to these changes and the relevance of family policy to families themselves.

Krane, Julia. 2003. *What's Mother Got to Do with It?* Toronto: University of Toronto Press. Krane shows how state ideologies shift the responsibility of child sexual abuse away from the perpetrators by holding mothers responsible for protecting their children.

Suggested Websites

Campaign 2000

www.campaign2000.ca

This advocacy group, created in 1989 when Canada's federal Parliament pledged to eradicate child poverty by the year 2000, monitors child poverty in Canada and publishes an annual 'report card'.

Caledon Institute of Social Policy

www.caledoninst.org

The Caledon Institute is a centre-left think-tank based in Ottawa that produces discussion papers on a variety of social policy issues impacting on families.

Constraints on Personal Choices

CHAPTER OUTLINE

This chapter draws on past research and current statistics to predict family patterns in the near future. It also comments on changing trends in family studies and identifies current issues of investigation

INTRODUCTION

Two central questions underlie this book. The first asks which aspects of family and intimate relations are new and differ from previous patterns and which have remained relatively similar over recent decades. The second question asks which changes in the larger society have most constrained family life. Throughout the past seven chapters, I have shown that at least in the liberal welfare states, more young people now cohabit rather than marry in their first union and more couples delay legal marriage and reproduction. More dating, sex, and cohabitation occur between partners from different socio-cultural backgrounds, as well between couples of the same sex. Relationships last for shorter time periods, more children live in stepfamilies, and more people separate and find a new partner later in life.

These family trends, which are apparent in most OECD countries, are created by large numbers of people behaving in similar ways at the same time, which suggests that personal choices in a variety of countries are shaped by some of the same social changes and ideas. For example, new employment requirements, increased living costs, and new ideas about equity and human rights influence desires and decisions about choosing a partner, getting married, buying a house, having children, or leaving a relationship. At the same time, the types of work that people do, both paid and unpaid, continue to be modified by gendered and class-based ideas and practices, even though labour market practices are changing rapidly. Because personal life is influenced by so many social, psychological, cultural, and economic factors, efforts to shape family demography through policies such as 'wedfare' programs (designed to encourage lone mothers to marry so that they can be supported by a male breadwinner rather than state welfare payments) and 'baby bonuses' (benefits paid to parents at childbirth, to help with birth-related expenses) have not always had their desired effect.

In this book, I have argued that current labour market trends create an insecure environment for family formation, child-rearing, home ownership, and marital stability. Job requirements change as more governments sign free trade agreements and more companies export internationally, create branch plants in countries with cheaper production costs, and advertise globally for higher-level positions. The trend to hire a portion of lower-level staff on short-term contracts helps corporate managers maximize their profits and cushion their firms against international economic downturns because these workers can be laid off more easily when their labour is no longer required. In some jurisdictions, employers are also permitted to pay lower wages and benefits to temporary and part-time staff. Although some workers use casual jobs to manage studying or caring work, many find that current labour practices reduce income security and complicate personal planning.

Working in another country may bring new excitement and opportunities to individuals, but it alters their lifestyles and relationships, placing constraints on the activities of parents, partners, and children. Working from home or outside the main workplace permits employees to make more choices about how and when to work, but it may also influence domestic arrangements. Furthermore, the decision to pursue **telework** is often made by management rather than being the personal choice of individual employees. Generally, employees and the self-employed in the liberal welfare states are working longer hours, and higher percentages are working in the evenings and on weekends (Bittman, 2004; Crompton, 2004). Mobile telephones and laptop computers enable people to 'work anywhere', but this blurs the distinction between work time and family/leisure time, and may not improve the economic circumstances of the household.

The 24-hour economy requires special initiatives to maintain a work/life balance because working long hours is stressful, imposes on the personal time of couples, and requires the other partner to manage the child care or housework. Family practices such as eating the evening meal together are becoming less prevalent because more family members are employed and more are working non-standard hours. These changing work patterns gradually shape preferences about education and future occupational choices as students learn to anticipate the need for computer skills, post-secondary education, and national and international mobility in order to gain work experience and further their careers.

Changing work patterns modify our personal lives but so do media representations. Young persons are increasingly subjected to subtle forms of advertising that encourage them to look slim and fashionable in order to find friends or sexual partners, to indulge themselves with consumer goods, and to expect to create comfortable material lives. To afford this lifestyle, however, people require paid work, secure incomes, and few dependants. With readily available credit and insecure jobs, young people, especially, are encouraged to live beyond their means, accruing higher levels of personal debt that impact on the ability to build family assets throughout their lives. Increasingly, young couples respond to these pressures by delaying marriage, childbirth, and home ownership (Baker, 2006).

Many middle-class youth now live with their parents longer than was common a few decades ago and cohabiting couples tend to delay marriage, buying a home, and having a child while they establish careers and strengthen their financial security. Marriage and child-rearing still are viewed as long-term commitments. Fathers are expected to be the primary earners and mothers are still encouraged to make employment sacrifices to provide care. At the same time, relationships become more vulnerable to separation with more residential mobility, precarious income security, the need to accommodate two careers, high levels of personal debt, and larger mortgages. Personal life is altered in many ways by current labour market demands, new educational requirements, higher material aspirations, and rising levels of debt (ibid.).

Technological innovations also have influenced personal choices and family life. More effective birth control enables people to engage in sexual intercourse outside a secure relationship and to limit their family size within marriage, but new advances in assisted conception also permit a small percentage of low-fertility couples to reproduce (Ford et al., 2003). The ability to freeze sperm means that conception can happen after the 'father's' death. In addition, 'designer babies' are possible, post-menopausal women can have babies, and wealthy couples can commission low-income women to produce children for them (Eichler, 1997). Although these new reproductive practices are not yet common, the very possibilities alter our ways of thinking about sex, reproduction, and childbirth.

Innovations in transportation technology also influence family life. The invention of automobiles early in the twentieth century permitted more privacy for 'courting' couples, altering patterns of residence and intimacy. Now, many families own more than one car, which increases household costs but enables couples to work in different locations farther from home. International travel is also more feasible with lower airfares relative to wages. Affordable and faster international travel permits more people to take overseas holidays, to maintain contact with friends and family abroad, and to study or work in other countries. It also enables them to flee from family conflict or abusive partners and to find a safe haven in other jurisdictions. However, new computerized surveillance technologies and multilateral agreements between governments assist officials to apprehend parents who cross borders to shirk their family responsibilities (Baker, 2006).

More family members are now spread throughout the world and immigrants arrive from a larger range of countries with different family practices (OECD, 2005b). Although this increases diversity, research suggests that young migrants, especially, and the second generation modify their family demography to make it more consistent with patterns in their adopted country (Albanese, 2005). Nevertheless, more young people in Western countries have parents and grandparents living in arranged marriages, dressing in traditional clothes, and eating a wider variety of foods. Many migrants maintain regular contact with relatives back home through e-mail, electronic financial transfers, and regular air travel. Some parents even earn money in one place and raise children in another, and small percentages become 'transnational citizens' who are equally comfortable living in several countries.

Cellphones and electronic mail help family members and friends to maintain contact and permit parents to 'supervise' their children from a distance, even while working. Television and the Internet bring international news and controversies, sexual encounters, and advertising into our homes, introducing us to new forms of consumerism, raising our material aspirations, and spreading a more cosmopolitan outlook. The Internet also enables global marketing, the rapid spread of news, international lobbying, chat groups, and new dating practices, but also the dissemination of pornography and stalking. Technology increasingly permeates our sexual practices, child-rearing, the maintenance of relationships, the design of our homes, and patterns of work and leisure, introducing new ideas and irritations into our lives.

Increasingly, people around the world watch the same television programs and films, read the same books and material on the Internet, and view the same images and advertisements, although the 'globalization of culture' consists largely of Western ideas from United States, the United Kingdom, and Europe circulating to the rest of the world (Baker, 2006). Young people in remote or less developed areas can be enticed by these images and ideas, and may try to simulate the fashions and lifestyles of the West. Consequently, more people expect to choose where they live and with whom, what they buy, how they will earn a living, and how they spend their leisure time. Westernization tends to encourage contraceptive use, freer choice of marriage partners, nuclear family living, a greater acceptance of divorce, and more gender equality within marriage (Giddens, 1992).

New ideas about human rights, gender equity, family obligations, and entitlement to social benefits also shape expectations and family patterns in subtle ways (Baker, 2006). Policy reforms may initially force people to conform, but also to change their expectations over time and eventually alter their behaviour. Restructuring social programs may also help shape gender relations, the meaning of 'good parenting', and expectations about future social provision. Recently, governments in the liberal welfare states have encouraged both mothers and fathers to see paid employment as the normal activity for all adults, even though they have not always provided the necessary facilities or subsidies for child care.

Throughout this book I have argued that even though we can now exercise more choice in personal life, few of the new family patterns are entirely matters of individual choice. Our behaviour and even our personal ambitions tend instead to be influenced and modified by social and economic activities and events in the larger society, and these are often difficult for individuals to control. Constraints on relationships may relate to lack of money or power, new legal requirements, technological 'advances', pressures from family and friends, feelings of obligation or entitlement. Personal constraints can arise simply from the wishes or actions of a partner. For example, we might choose to live in an egalitarian relationship but if our partner refuses to share the household earnings or the domestic work, we cannot have what we want. We may choose to grow old with our partner, but if he or she leaves us, our own personal preferences may no longer be relevant.

It is difficult to anticipate how we would react to particular changes in our personal lives, such as an unexpected pregnancy or a separation, or how or where we will be living in 20 years. It is even more challenging for social scientists to predict future family patterns.

PREDICTING FUTURE FAMILY PATTERNS

Two important goals of science are to identify patterns and accurately predict future trends. Within the social sciences, predicting human behaviour seems complicated because so many factors are involved, such as new ideas, technological changes, economic and political transformations, labour market transitions, legal and policy changes, emotions, and personal choices. Researchers attempting to predict family trends have often relied on past and current demographic patterns as social indicators of the future, but human beings also can choose to resist prevailing family patterns and to contravene socially acceptable behaviour. Consequently, predictions have not always been accurate when researchers rely only on demographic trends. A successful prediction of personal and family life requires some knowledge of social psychology, political movements, policy reform, economic trends, technological innovations, and popular culture.

Despite the challenges of prediction in the social sciences, the rest of this chapter suggests the family patterns that are likely to continue into the future. These ideas, portrayed in Table 8.1, have been garnered from research on family demography, new forms of relationships, changing labour market trends, and the restructuring of public policy. However, the trends pertain only to people living in Western industrialized countries and especially the **liberal welfare states** of Canada, the United States, the United Kingdom, Australia, and New Zealand. In addition, these predictions stretch only a few decades into the future because it is so difficult to know how social, economic, and political life might change. Nevertheless, this exercise should enable us to draw some conclusions about the nature of family life and the power of certain constraints on our personal choices.

Will People Still Get Married?

Compared to the 1950s, more couples are now sexually active outside marriage, more cohabit without legal ceremony, and the average age of marriage has been rising. At the same time, live-in relationships have a shorter duration and more end in separation. In the next two decades, there is every indication that these trends will continue and even accelerate. More people will come to believe that their personal and intimate life is their own affair, with little relevance to religious leaders or civil authorities. Advanced birth control technology will continue to enable couples to enjoy sexual activity without pregnancy or marriage, and the social and legal differences between cohabitation and legal marriage will diminish even further. In addition, ideas about the right to privacy and personal happiness will continue to pervade much of Western culture, shaping patterns in sexuality and family formation.

As both men and women pursue busy careers and older people seek new partners, more individuals will rely on introductions by friends, dating agencies, self-advertising in newspapers or on the Internet, and clubs and organized activities in

Table 8.1　Future Trends in Family Life

Area of Family Life	Future Trend
Cohabitation	• Rates will rise among all age groups.
Age of Marriage	• Average age will rise as more first unions are consensual and more older couples remarry. • The age will remain higher for males than females, and lower for low-income groups.
Marriage Rate	• The rate will decline with more consensual unions. • It will remain higher for non-Christian religious groups and fundamentalist Christians.
Fertility Rate	• Fertility will decline for younger women and more educated women. • It will remain higher for low-income groups and certain cultural minorities.
Duration of Marriage	• Length of marriage will decline with the normalization and legitimation of divorce and more focus on self-development. • But older remarriages are often more stable.
Re-partnering and Remarriage Rate	• Remarriage will rise as more people divorce. • More cohabitation means less legal remarriage. • Non-legal re-partnering will be higher among low-income groups and divorced people.
Housework and Child Care	• More employed couples will hire home-cleaners and child-minders. • But women will continue to take responsibility for most indoor tasks, child care, and elder care. • Fathers will do more cooking, shopping, and child care but will retain responsibility for yard work and the family car.
Labour Force Participation	• More mothers will work full-time and increase their contributions to household finances. • More fathers will work overtime or at two jobs. • Parents will work longer hours, partly to support children's living expenses.

order to find partners. Many of these relationships will become sexual soon after the individuals meet and some will lead to cohabitation without much consideration about permanence. Young people pursuing higher education will continue to live with their parents until they are well into their twenties, but when they leave the family home many will need to share accommodation as housing costs rise, especially in the major cities. This means that more young people will live with various roommates and sexual partners but will not necessarily 'settle down' with one partner until they complete their education, develop some work stability, and acquire financial assets.

It also seems realistic to suggest that in a few decades fewer adults will be living with relatives such as parents and siblings, but more will be creating non-traditional households based on neither the nuclear nor the extended family models. Also, more adults will avoid legal marriage in the future as sexuality becomes even more sepa-rated from marriage and reproduction, and men and women can more easily live—both socially and financially—without a legal partner. However, the social pressure to marry and to reproduce will remain strong. Most people will either cohabit or marry at least once in their life, as shared living provides greater opportunities for love, regular sex, and companionship and reduces loneliness and accommodation expenses. Considering current rates of separation, however, more people will cohabit with several consecutive partners over their lifetime but spend time 'between relationships' with casual intimacies, roommates, living alone, or sharing a home with their children.

Judging from current trends in some European countries as well as in North America, a growing minority of intimate couples will 'live apart together' for specific periods of time while they study or work in separate locations. This will be especially prevalent among university-educated couples where overseas training and work are expected to bring higher occupational returns and where two high-level business or professional jobs are difficult to find in the same place. However, it will also remain a prevalent pattern for migrant couples, where one partner returns periodically to work or oversee family business in their country of origin. Commuting couples might live together on the weekend or even less frequently but will be free to devote considerable amounts of time and energy to paid work or other activities when they are apart. This 'choice' will be influenced by higher rates of unemployment or underemployment, more international migration, and the growing importance of financial security for both men and women in a globalizing economy.

Same-sex couples sharing a home will become more prevalent in the future, and more will live openly and choose to legalize their personal commitment. The legal-ization of same-sex relationships through 'civil union' legislation or the extension of marriage rights has already occurred in some jurisdictions and is under discussion in others. However, not all same-sex couples will choose to live in 'marriage-like relationships'. Gay men, especially, will opt for a series of sexual partners while living alone close to a community of like-minded friends, or will choose to cohabit for short periods without any expectation of a lifelong partnership.

If a higher percentage of the population lives outside nuclear families, lifestyle and housing preferences will change as more people choose low-maintenance apart-ments or flats rather than single-family dwellings with gardens. With fewer family responsibilities and less household maintenance work, these people will likely spend less time at home and more time eating out, enjoying time with friends, attending leisure events, and travelling. These individuals and couples will be more likely to work full-time and overtime, to earn higher incomes, to spend less on home owner-ship and child-related expenses, and therefore to have more discretionary income for entertainment, recreation, and travel.

Generally, relationships will become more consensual and less permanent, although most people will continue to marry and produce children. Anthony Giddens (1992) talked about the possibility of 'pure relationships' that would be unclouded by feelings of obligations, dependencies, and inequalities. Although this may be possible for some people, most couples will still depend on each other for financial support or domestic chores. Although more wives will earn household money, economic dependencies will continue as two incomes become essential to pay the household bills. In addition, economic inequalities and power differentials will continue between husband and wives, reflecting gender inequalities in paid and unpaid work, including the responsibility for the daily care of children. As more women become economically self-supporting, fewer children are born, and more fathers actively engage in child care, the probability of 'pure relationship' could increase. However, most couples will marry and produce at least one child, and more mothers than fathers will become economically dependent on their partners.

As women expect more control over their lives, they will be more likely to initiate sexual and cohabiting relationships. However, vestiges of the double standard of sexuality will linger, penalizing women—through social stigmatization and the possible negative impact on prospects for promotion—who appear to be too obvious in their sexual needs or who openly admit that they are seeking recreational sex. With more consensual unions and liberal divorce laws, relationships will also last for shorter periods of time but people will be seeking new partners throughout the lifespan. Current patterns suggest that men will continue to prefer women who are attractive, 'petite', and unencumbered with children at home, and the age gap will become larger as older men seek new younger partners. Most children will continue to live with their mothers after separation, but these mothers will be expected to combine paid work and caring obligations, managing on lower female earnings. Although more women are gaining higher education and are working full-time, neo-liberal **restructuring** in the labour force continues to reward those who are willing and able to work overtime. Many lone mothers will be unable to meet these expectations. As rates of legal marriage and fertility continue to fall, separation will become less complicated and more prevalent but it will still be emotionally and financially draining for all involved.

These predictions suggest that relationships in the future will be formed more easily and dissolved with less social disapproval and legal intervention. Fewer people will live in families but when they do, families will become smaller, with fewer children and fewer relatives sharing households. Although some new immigrants will initially live in extended family households, those who are wealthier, more educated, and fluent in the language of the host country will be more likely to live in nuclear families. Increasingly, the liberal welfare states are accepting educated immigrants with middle-class backgrounds. Certainly, the children of recent migrants, especially those born and educated in the host country, will be less likely to see extended family living as desirable when they reach adulthood. In the future, more people in the general population will live alone, which will counteract any trend for recent immigrants to share accommodation. The percentage of couples who remain childless will also increase as contraception becomes more effective and abortion is made easier, although a strong anti-abortion backlash is apparent in countries such as the United States, where abortion laws could be tightened. Young people will also raise their material aspirations and yearn for fewer family responsibilities, especially women who anticipate a life of full-time employment.

Box 8.1 The Deep-Seated Concern over 'The Family'

Family change is very complicated. It is not necessarily a cause for 'worry', although most academics and political commentators would, I think, be prepared to say that the pace of such change warrants careful attention. What to *do* in face of such change is more contentious still. For the most part, the nostalgia for the traditional family has not translated into firm policies designed to put the clock back, for example by returning working mothers to the home, or by making divorce much harder to obtain. Indeed, at least in the English-speaking countries, politicians on the right, who are most likely to wax eloquent on the subject of **family values**, are also usually the most loath to accept state intervention in the family.

Source: Lewis (2003: 12–13).

Social conservatives will continue to worry about low marriage rates and the impermanence of couple relationships, but policies to encourage legal marriage and permanent relationships will have limited success. State inducements to marry, such as tax benefits, seldom compensate for the perceived reasons to avoid legal marriage, such as concern about lifetime responsibilities, legal entanglements, restrictions on mobility, and gendered expectations of behaviour. Research shows that legal marriage is most likely to occur when men gain secure jobs with adequate incomes, and where couples and their children are severely disadvantaged if they cohabit but do not legally marry. As more women become self-supporting, the importance of finding a male breadwinner diminishes, although a steady male income provides a better standard of living even for high-earning women. However, living outside marriage will become easier as more services are developed for those without the time or skills to care for themselves, their homes, and their children. Furthermore, cohabitation has already begun to look more like legal marriage, both socially and legally, which reduces the need to marry. There is no reason that this trend will not continue in the future.

Will People Still Have Children?

In earlier chapters, I noted that fertility decline is influenced by economic and social changes in the larger society as well as personal preferences. Raising children has become more costly for all parents and combining paid work with child-rearing is increasingly difficult without heavy state subsidies for child care. In the past, people were taught that the purpose of marriage was reproduction but they also knew that children could contribute to their household resources and support them in old age, as well as bring them love, companionship, and personal satisfaction. In addition, women used to be encouraged to see child-rearing as a career but they are now pressured to become educated and help support the household, which means that it is more important to limit family size. Educated women are more knowledgeable about contraception and also are more likely than less educated women to believe that they have the right to use it. Forfeiting household income is also more consequential when educated women leave the labour force for child-bearing and child-rearing.

Fertility rates will continue to fall but cultural and class differences will remain visible in these rates. For example, young women from disadvantaged families and certain cultural groups will continue to experience higher rates of pregnancy and childbirth before completing their education, before marriage, and at younger ages within marriage. However, birth rates will continue to decline among younger age groups, although they will decline faster among 'white' or 'European' women and wealthier women. Certain religious groups (such as fundamentalist Christians and Muslims) and some 'visible minorities' (such as American blacks and New Zealand Maori, who are often fundamentalist Christians) will be less likely to use reliable contraception and will therefore produce more children.

In general, women will continue to delay child-bearing and more first births will occur when women are in their thirties. At this age, conception problems will increase and more women will turn to physicians and fertility clinics for advice about conception and fertility treatments. As women produce their first child at older ages, doctors will see more pregnant women as 'high-risk' patients requiring technological interventions in childbirth, such as induced births and Caesarean deliveries. However, the older average age of women at first birth also means that more women will have completed their education and established themselves in paid work before pregnancy. Therefore, more employees will require paid parental leave, infant child-care services, and flexible working arrangements.

Fewer babies will be born in the future but more of them will be born to unmarried as well as to older mothers. Most children will continue to be conceived within cohabitation or legal marriage but fewer of these relationships will last until the child reaches school age. This implies that more children will spend a portion of their childhood living with only one parent, and this parent is likely to be the mother. More children will also live in stepfamilies, probably with the mother and her new partner. Mothers will remain the resident parent after most cases of separation, although more fathers will have legal access to their children and will share joint custody or legal decision-making.

As more people cohabit rather than marry, relationships will become shorter and less stable. More men will produce children with more than one woman over their lifetime. Most of these children will continue to live with their mothers while their fathers move on to new partners, some of whom will be mothers living with children from their previous relationships. As more children live in stepfamilies, governments will experience more problems enforcing paternal child support, ensuring that fathers remain engaged with their biological children, and resolving disputes about child-rearing in the post-divorce family.

How Will Couples Combine Work and Family?

Recent labour market trends indicate that fewer workers in the future will retain one full-time job with the same employer throughout their working lives. Occupational transitions will become prevalent, with more adults returning to formal education and upgrading their skills, as well as moving from employment to self-employment, accepting contract jobs, and searching for better employment opportunities and conditions. At the same time, more family members will be employed. Already, more wives and teenage children are working for pay compared to those in the 1960s. In the future, fewer adults will be working the former business hours of 9 a.m. to 5 p.m., and more will be working in the evenings, on the weekends, and on statutory holidays. With so much time devoted to paid work, family schedules will be difficult to co-ordinate and family meals, discussions, negotiations, activities, and celebrations will become more complicated to manage. This could have negative implications for cohesion and communication within the household.

'Globalized' labour markets and freer trade arrangements will encourage more workers to follow employment opportunities to different regions of the country and even across international borders. The European Union now permits workers to move freely among some member countries. Workers can also move between Australia and New Zealand, and Canadians and Americans can cross borders for specific jobs but with more restrictions (Baker, 2006). Free trade agreements and common markets will continue to encourage employment mobility, but it is not always easy for workers to persuade their partners and children to follow, especially if the partner is already employed. There may also be settlement problems related to schooling, employment, and language in a new jurisdiction or country.

When families migrate for employment purposes, partners need to be recognized, which will still be difficult in some countries if they are the same sex or living in consensual unions. If partners or adult children expect to find employment, their credentials need to be recognized by potential employers and authorities in the new host country and all family members need to be able to speak the local language. More children will need to adapt to new schools and find new friends in a foreign country. Nuclear families crossing international borders often leave behind the support of extended family members, who might have offered financial and emotional support as well as child-care services. More geographical mobility in the future will bring new employment opportunities for parents and adventures for partners and children, but they will also heighten family conflict and lead to disruption and marital dissolution.

As employment becomes less secure for more people, many adults will continue working until older ages than a few decades ago. The trend towards early retirement, noticeable in the 1960s and 1970s, has already started reversing in some countries as both men and women work longer hours but do not necessarily increase their prosperity or family assets. Self-employment, short-term contracts, and temporary work may not provide access to the same retirement plans as permanent employees enjoy. Therefore, more workers in the future will be forced to remain in the labour force for financial reasons, perhaps taking gradual retirement at older ages in order to maintain their income security. This could restrict the opportunities of younger workers, especially in tightening labour markets.

Will Couples Stay Together?

Separation and divorce have become normalized and legitimized as they grow more prevalent, but the rising insecurity of intimate relationships will become more consequential in the future. First, the insecurity of legal marriage could discourage some young people from making public commitments because they will be afraid that their relationships might end in divorce, which could be legally complex, costly, and stigmatizing. Yet statistically, cohabiting relationships have higher rates of separation than legal marriages, suggesting that relationship instability will continue to increase at a societal level (Wu, 2000).

Second, relationship instability will discourage young girls from accepting the idea that they can rely on a male breadwinner and will encourage them to prepare for a lifetime of personal earning. More job-oriented education and career planning will reduce the gendered nature of paid work, raise the earnings of women relative to men, and increase wives' incomes relative to those of their husbands. However, the pattern for women to marry older men with higher incomes will continue. Furthermore, by becoming more financially independent, women will also increase their chances of relationship instability because women who are self-supporting tend to feel less obliged to stay in unhappy relationships. Not only do they have fewer economic reasons to stay, but their male partners may also feel less guilt about separating from women who could become self-supporting.

More children will experience the dissolution of parental relationships, and when their parents are between partners some children will begin to normalize living with one parent (usually the mother). If the mother re-partners, the children may initially feel some personal disruption but more children will view living in mother-led households or stepfamilies as normal. The boundaries of children's families will become more complex in stepfamilies, including both resident and non-resident parents and their new partners and parents, as well as step-siblings and grandparents from several relationships. Adapting to this complexity will undoubtedly challenge some children, but it will not necessarily lead to serious problems for them. Children will learn to become more flexible about their parents' intimate relationships, but parents and step-parents will also need to remain sensitive to children's perceptions and needs. No child or adolescent wants to feel displaced by her or his parent's new lover, and more parents will be required to work at creating social cohesion within their 'blended' families.

If more adults re-partner later in life, the average age in all marriages will rise, dynamics will change in many families, and images of middle age and aging will gradually be refashioned. For many older couples, their new intimate relationships will provide a new lease on life, altering daily routines and prevalent images of sexuality, maturity, and parental obligations. The fact that some of the same transitions experienced by parents could simultaneously be happening to their mature children might help to bridge the generation gap even though the years between generations will be growing longer.

Will Aging Be a Problem?

Many demographers and politicians see the 'aging population' as a social problem and assume that more seniors in the population will burden society with higher pension and health-care costs. However, older couples not only maintain high levels of independence but also provide services for friends and family, including lending money to their adult children and babysitting their grandchildren while the parents are working. In addition, many wives care for their husbands in their old age (Kendig, 1986; McDaniel, 1994). However, older unattached women are particularly vulnerable to poverty if they did not work for pay throughout their earlier years, if they suffer from health problems or disabilities, or if they did not own a home or inherit other assets.

Although life expectancy has been rising for centuries, some researchers now predict that it will begin to fall within the next two decades from high rates of obesity and its related diseases in developed countries such as Canada, the United States, and New Zealand (Walsh, 2005). Widespread obesity will raise the already high rates of diabetes, heart disease, and strokes, as well as increase fertility problems. Researchers and policy-makers are particularly concerned about high rates of childhood obesity, which will undoubtedly cause future health problems and shorten lives. In addition, high rates of pollution and continued tobacco use are expected to reduce life expectancy in the future (ibid.).

As fertility declines and mothers are older when they produce their first child, the spacing between generations will become larger in the future. This may mean that fewer children will know their grandparents, although with higher living standards and improvements in health care some of their grandparents will live longer. These demographic changes also suggest that many parents will reach the former retirement age before their children reach maturity and leave home, forcing some parents to work longer to help finance their children's living and educational expenses. This could delay the retirement of more parents, which might provide an opportunity for governments to increase the eligibility age for retirement benefits in order to save public money.

Although governments often reform social programs to make them more consistent with current lifestyles, they also use changing family demography to justify forms of restructuring that save public money or downsize the welfare state. Studying family trends is therefore essential for governments but it is also useful to business people who are trying to predict or manipulate market trends for consumer products. For academics, studying patterns in intimate experiences and family life reveals the impact of the transformations occurring in the wider society and sheds light on the diversity and adaptability of human life.

THE FUTURE OF FAMILY STUDIES

Researchers and theorists have been studying family life for over a hundred years but the academic field of family studies, and especially the sociology of the family, has changed considerably over the decades. The field is certain to develop further in the future. While early research made false assumptions about the extent of uniformity, consensus, and co-operation within families, current research highlights diversity and conflict in family experiences. This includes a focus on gendered differences in domestic labour, power differentials in marriage, new patterns of family formation (including same-sex unions and cohabitation), cultural variations in marriage systems and family dynamics, and the impact of marital separation on various family members. Current studies also address the impact of technology and the media on the creation of 'personal biographies', new sexual practices, and cosmetic work on the body.

While social class used to be a predominant variable in family research, gender, age, and **ethnicity** have become central to current analyses of personal life and family practices. However, more studies focus on young families rather than on families in mid-life. Women's family-related experiences have been researched more than men's but studies on masculinity and fathering are beginning to correct this imbalance. American and New Zealand research acknowledges the large differences in income, lifestyle, and family composition based on race and ethnicity. With higher rates of immigration and international travel, more researchers are focusing on cultural variations in marriage systems and family obligations, as well as the intergenerational differences between immigrants and their native-born children. The meaning of marriage and prevalent assumptions underlying family life are becoming especially relevant with immigration from Islamic and Hindu countries, as well as renewed interest in indigenous families. This indicates that the previous overemphasis on the Eurocentric, nuclear, and middle-class family is diminishing.

Despite this new focus, social class continues to be a central variable influencing aspirations, achievements, and lifestyle. Studies with social policy implications continue to see family income and wealth accumulation as crucial variables influencing all aspects of personal life. Many researchers continue to use the political economy approach to analyze the impact of global markets and social policy restructuring on family life. At the same time, new researchers tend to draw on theoretical perspectives, such as post-structuralism and postmodernism, that give primacy to the power of ideas and media representations, especially in feminist analyses and cultural studies. These approaches emphasize the importance of personal choice, identity, and consumerism, without always giving adequate consideration to the social and economic constraints on personal choices and identity creation.

In this book, I have used a theoretical perspective that I label the 'feminist political economy' approach because I focus on the impact of labour market and economic changes on gender relations. This approach reminds us that gendered patterns of work are promoted by current labour market practices but also that patterns of employment continue to shape the division of labour at home and the amount of time workers have to spend with their families. Working hours and conditions are modified by employers, unions, and governments, depending on their ideologies, political alliances, and power. However, the emphasis on the importance of paid work and the 'long-hours culture' is more prevalent in the liberal welfare states than in European countries. We need to know more about the impact of working long hours on relations between spouses and between workers and their children. Future research could also help to understand how the new consumerism that accompanies **neo-liberalism** influences young people's aspirations for intimate relationships and future lifestyles.

The study of family patterns and intimate relationships has a long academic history, forming a significant portion of research and theorizing in sociology, anthropology, social work, gender studies, social psychology, and cultural studies. In recent years, researchers have been analyzing the impact of globalization and new efforts to restructure welfare states on employment patterns, on the growing gap between the rich and the poor, and on rising levels of household debt. However, social scientists are only beginning to explore the consequences of these economic transformations, as well as the impact of consumerism and advertising, on intimacy and family life.

Throughout this book I have argued that labour market constraints, increased migration, new technologies, and global ideas about equity and human rights are shaping intimate relationships. Although we may have acquired more choice to create our own personal biographies, we continue to live with some of the same socio-economic constraints, as well as several new limitations on our relationships.

SUMMARY

Despite public concerns about the future of legal marriage and declining fertility rates, intimate relationships and child-bearing remain popular. However, more couples are marrying at later ages and fewer are producing large families because they believe that large families may jeopardize their opportunities and financial security. Current research in family studies focuses on cultural diversity, same-sex marriage, men's family experiences, and the growing impermanence of intimate relationships.

Questions for Critical Thought

1. Is there a future for legal marriage, considering that so many young couples now cohabit?
2. As more women remain in full-time employment, how will couples balance paid work, housework, and child-rearing?
3. How will declining fertility rates influence government programs and family life? If fewer couples reproduce, how will we finance future pensions and growing health needs in an aging population?

Suggested Readings

Beck-Gernsheim, Elisabeth. 2002. *Reinventing the Family: In Search of New Lifestyles.* Cambridge: Polity Press. This book discusses recent changes in family life, analyzes concerns about loss of stability, and argues that new forms of family life are expanding choices and opportunities.

Lewis, Jane. 2003. *Should We Worry About Family Change?* Toronto: University of Toronto Press. This book discusses the main policy debates about the family, outlining current socio-demographic changes and different views about how they should be interpreted.

Suggested Website

The Future Families Project
www.vifamily.ca
The *Future Families Project: A Survey of Canadian Hopes and Dreams* by Reginald Bibby (2004) is discussed on the website of the Vanier Institute of the Family.

Glossary

Access   The legal arrangement for contact between a non-custodial parent and his (her) offspring following separation or divorce.

Alimony   Spousal support awarded to divorced women before the enactment of no-fault divorce legislation.

Arranged marriage   A marriage in which the partner is selected by elder family members but the young people may have the right to veto the choice.

At-risk families   Families with a high probability of going hungry, having inadequate accommodation, or in which the likelihood of abusive behaviour is higher than normal.

Bilateral descent   Lineage traced through the families of both the bride and groom.

Blended families   Stepfamilies formed through post-marital cohabitation or remarriage that include stepsiblings, half-siblings, or both.

Census family   A term used by Statistics Canada to refer to a married or cohabiting couple living with or without never-married children, and a lone parent living with never-married children.

Child custody   The guardianship of a child and the authority to make decisions about the child's welfare and upbringing.

Child poverty   The percentage of children living with impoverished parents, a concept designed to enhance sympathy for the plight of blameless children.

Child support   The privately arranged or court-ordered financial support a non-custodial parent must pay to support his (her) offspring.

Civil code   Law, as in Quebec and many European countries, based largely on written statutes rather than previous court cases or custom (like common law).

Civil union   Marriage approved by the state but not necessarily by the church.

Cohabitation   An intimate union between a couple who share a household and live together in marriage-like circumstances; also called common-law marriage.

Common law   The body of general, largely unwritten legal conventions based on prior judicial rulings and traditional customs.

Common-law relationships   Cohabitation without legal marriage.

Complementary roles   Separate spheres for men and women in marriage.

Corporatist welfare states   States whose social security is based on social insurance programs funded by employers, employees, and government, with higher benefits for those with higher incomes.

Developmental theory   Learning theory that assumes that children pass through stages of cognitive, motor, and psychological development, and that particular tasks or concepts must be adequately learned before a child passes through the next stage of development.

Divorce rates   The annual number of divorces per 1,000 marriages (or per 1,000 population) within a specific jurisdiction, such as a country or province.

Double standard   The differential evaluation for men and women of identical situations and behaviours.

Endogamy   Marriage within one's group, which may be race, ethnicity, religion, caste, or socio-economic status.

Ethnicity   Process of shared awareness of ancestral differences and group belonging used as a basis for differential distribution of recognition, rewards, and relationships.

Exchange theory   Application of a market analogy to explain attraction and commitment, assuming that individuals maximize rewards and minimize costs in intimate relationships just as they are assumed to in classic liberal economic theory.

Exogamy   Marriage outside the group.

Extended family   Several generations, or siblings and their spouses and children, who share a household and resources.

Family economy   The waged and unwaged contributions of all family members to ensuring the survival of the household.

Family policy   The pursuit and attainment of collective goals and values in addressing problems of families in relation to the state.

Family preservation   A principle governing child welfare that relies on the extended family and social support to keep children living with family members rather than placing them in foster homes or institutions.

Family values   Beliefs and attitudes that emphasize the (patriarchal) nuclear family as the basic unit of society and the importance of raising children.

Family wage   A single wage, normally earned by a breadwinner father, sufficient to support the entire family, hence avoiding the need for the paid labour of the wife or children.

Feminist perspective   An analytical framework focused on women's viewpoint and experiences, as well as on how social structures and cultural understandings impact on women.

First default principle   The state begins to enforce child support only if the parent fails to make the necessary payments.

Gendered roles   The ways that males and females interact in a society, considering their different socialization and life experiences.

Gender-neutral   Something that could pertain equally to male or female.

Globalization   The world scale of economic and other activity made possible by the spread of information and telecommunications technology, as well as improved and relatively low-cost transportation.

Homogamy   The similarities in the age, social class, race, and ethnicity of couples.

Industrialization   The process by which manufacturing industries become dominant in a country's economy.

In vitro fertilization   The union of sperm and egg outside a human being, typically in a test tube.

Joint custody   The legal situation where both parents share authority over decisions regarding child welfare and upbringing after divorce.

Labour force   Those who are either engaged in formal paid employment or seeking paid employment.

Liberal welfare states   States in which social security is based largely on need and benefits are targeted to low-income and 'problem' families.

Lone-parent household   One parent sharing a residence with his or her never-married children.

Male breadwinner family   A two-parent family with the father as principal earner and the mother as care provider.

Marital breakdown   The legal grounds for divorce based on circumstances that impair marital functioning, such as spousal desertion or long-term separation.

Marriage market   A term that applies an economic analogy to describe the availability of potential marriage partners and how they are valued in a particular culture or period.

Maternity leave   The official time away from paid employment taken by a mother for childbirth or adoption.

Matriarchy   A system that gives women more authority than men.

Matrifocal family   A family focused around the mother.

Matrilineal descent   Tracing relatives through the mother's side of the family.

Matrilocal residence   The custom of the groom living with the bride's family or in her community.

Matrimonial fault   An act considered to violate the marriage contract and therefore to be a justification for divorce.

Monogamy   System of marriage in which each adult is allowed only one spouse at a time.

Monolithic bias   Assumption that all families are similar, with an overemphasis on uniformity of experience and structure at the expense of diversity.

Neo-liberalism   Political rationality that supports the restructuring of societies to better meet the demands of a global market economy, emphasizing competition, individual self-enhancement, and personal responsibility for problems.

Neo-local residence   The custom of bride and groom living in a separate location from both of their birth families.

No-fault divorce   The legal provision for marital dissolution through a non-acrimonious process, as opposed to fault-based divorce that involves proving a spouse guilty of a matrimonial offence or fault.

Nuclear family   A husband and wife and their children sharing the same household and co-operating economically.

Parental leave   Official time away from paid employment that may be taken by either the mother or father at childbirth or adoption.

Patriarchy   Social or family system giving men more authority than women.

Patrilineal descent   Lineage or family relationships traced through the male side of the family.

Patrilocal residence   The bride moves into or near her husband's family home.

Political economy perspective   Analytical approach emphasizing the links among economic changes, the work people do, policy decisions, and personal life.

Polyandry   A system of marriage in which women are allowed more than one husband at a time.

Polygamy   System of marriage in which adults are allowed more than one spouse at a time.

Polygyny   System of marriage in which men are allowed more than one wife at a time.

Post-structuralism   Theoretical perspective that explains social change through personal choices, the power of ideas, and public discourse rather than laws, rules, or expectations of behaviour.

Power of the purse   Theory that the person who earns most of the money controls the relationship or has greater decision-making power.

Psychoanalytic theory   An approach to socialization that stresses the importance of early childhood experiences and subconscious emotions in shaping personality.

Re-partnering   The transition into cohabitation or remarriage after divorce, but also union formation after a cohabiting couple separates.

Restructuring   Organizational changes in workplaces to increase efficiency and save costs, usually involving layoffs.

Roles   Patterns of behaviour governed by social expectations, rights, and duties, and associated with a specific position in a social situation (such as a husband in a family).

Role models   Persons whose behaviour is patterned by others.

Same-sex marriage   Gay and lesbian marriage.

Secularization   The process of becoming less constrained by religious writings or authorities, or involving the separation of church and state.

Serial monogamy   Marriage to one partner at a time but several over a lifetime.

Service sector   The part of the economy that provides services rather than goods.

Shared parenting   Both parents share the physical care and decision-making regarding the child during marriage or after divorce, regardless of who has legal custody.

Social class   A category of people who share a similar social and economic position, and are conscious of their similarities.

Social constructionism   A theoretical framework that argues that social reality and meaningful behaviour is created through social interaction and cultural understandings.

Social democratic welfare states   States that seek to prevent poverty and inequality by providing state services and income support for everyone, regardless of family income.

Social exchange theory   Use of economic analogies from cost-benefit analysis to explain marriage and family relations, which are assumed to involve a process of negotiation and the assessment of time/emotional investments.

Social institution   An established set of roles, norms, and relationships organized around some central activity or social need.

Social insurance   The pooling of the risk of unemployment, disability, or sickness among employers, employees/citizens, and the state, financed through contributions from all three groups.

Social learning theory   The view that development occurs when children process social and cultural information from their environment by observing others, interpreting what they see, and then acting.

Socialization   The complex learning process through which individuals develop their personality and acquire the knowledge, skills, and motivation necessary for participation in social life.

State   The government as well as the public agencies that support and enforce its policies.

Structural functionalism   An analytical approach focusing on how social structure influences individual behaviour and assuming that behaviour is governed by rules, laws, and expectations that maintain the structure of society.

Survey research   Questionnaire-based collection of a large sample of quantitative data.

Symbolic interaction perspective   An analytical approach that assumes that people create their own social reality by defining and interpreting the symbolic meanings of those responding to them.

Systems theory   An analytical perspective that sees the family as a system of interactions and relationships in which the behaviour of one member influences all others and behavioural patterns recur.

Telework   Work (often at home) through telecommunication or computer links to the main workplace.

Welfare state   The laws and social programs designed to protect citizens in times of unemployment, illness, old age, or insufficient income.

References

Abercrombie, Nicholas, Stephen Hill, and Bryan S. Turner. 1994. *The Penguin Dictionary of Sociology*, 3rd edn. London: Penguin Books.

Abu-Laban, Sharon M., and Susan A. McDaniel. 1998. 'Beauty, Status and Aging', in N. Mandell, ed., *Feminist Issues: Race, Class, and Sexuality*, 2nd edn. Scarborough, Ont.: Prentice-Hall Allyn and Bacon, 78–102.

Adair, V., and C. Rogan. 1998. 'Infertility and Parenting: The Story So Far', in V. Adair and R. Dixon, eds, *The Family in Aotearoa New Zealand*. Auckland: Addison-Wesley Longman.

Akyeampong, Ernest B. 1998. 'Work Absences: New Data, New Insights', *Perspectives on Labour and Income* 9, 1: 9–17.

Alford-Cooper, F. 1998. *For Keeps: Marriages That Last a Lifetime*. New York: M.E. Sharpe.

Amato, Paul. 2004. 'Parenting through Family Transitions', *Social Policy Journal of New Zealand* 23 (Dec.): 31–44.

—— and A. Booth. 1997. *A Generation at Risk: Growing Up in an Era of Family Upheaval*. Cambridge, Mass.: Harvard University Press.

—— and B. Keith. 1991. 'Parental Divorce and the Well-being of Children: A Meta-analysis', *Psychological Bulletin* 110, 1: 26–46.

—— and D. Previti. 2003. 'People's Reasons for Divorcing: Gender, Social Class, the Life Course and Adjustment', *Journal of Family Issues* 24: 602–26.

—— and S.J. Rezac. 1994. 'Contact with Nonresident Parents, Interparental Conflict, and Children's Behavior', *Journal of Family Issues* 15, 2: 191–207.

Ambert, Anne-Marie. 2005. 'Same-Sex Couples and Same-Sex-Parent Families: Relationships, Parenting and Issues of Marriage', Vanier Institute of the Family, at: <www.vifamily.ca>.

Arie, Sophie. 2003. 'EU Goes Dutch on Gay Rights', *The Guardian*, 26 Sept., at: <www.guardian.co.uk>.

Armstrong, P., C. Amaratunga, J. Bernier, K. Grant, A. Pederson, and K. Willson. 2002. *Exposing Privatization: Women and Health Care Reform in Canada*. Toronto: Garamond Press.

Asthana, Anushka. 2005. 'Too Posh to Push Births under Fire', *The Observer*, 4 Sept., at: <http://observer.guardian.co.uk>.

Baker, Maureen. 1982. 'Finding Partners in the Newspapers: Sex Differences in Personal Advertising', *Atlantis* 7, 2: 137–46.

——. 1993. *Families in Canadian Society*, 2nd edn. Toronto: McGraw-Hill Ryerson.

——. 1995. *Canadian Family Policies: Cross-National Comparisons*. Toronto: University of Toronto Press.

——. 2001a. 'Child Care Policy and Family Policy: Cross-National Examples of Integration and Inconsistency', in G. Cleveland and M. Krashinsky, eds, *Our Children's Future: Child Care Policy in Canada*. Toronto: University of Toronto Press, 275–95.

——. 2001b. *Families, Labour and Love: Family Diversity in a Changing World*. Sydney and Vancouver: Allen & Unwin and University of British Columbia Press.

——. 2002a. 'Child Poverty, Maternal Health and Social Benefits', *Current Sociology* 50, 6 (Nov.): 827–42.

——. 2002b. 'Poor Health, Lone Mothers and Welfare Reform: Competing Visions of Employability', *Women's Health and Urban Life* 1, 2 (Dec.): 4–25.

————. 2004a. 'Devaluing Mothering at Home: Welfare Restructuring and "Motherwork"', *Atlantis* 28, 2: 51–60.

————. 2004b. 'Families', in Lorne Tepperman and James Curtis, eds, *Sociology*. Toronto: Oxford University Press, 162–85.

————. 2004c. 'The Elusive Pregnancy: Choice and Empowerment in Medically Assisted Conception', *Women's Health and Urban Life* 3, 1 (May): 34–55.

————. 2005a. *Families: Changing Trends in Canada*, 5th edn. Toronto: McGraw-Hill Ryerson.

————. 2005b. 'Medically Assisted Conception: Revolutionizing Family or Perpetuating a Nuclear and Gendered Model?', *Journal of Comparative Family Studies* 36, 4: 521–44.

————. 2005c. 'Childbirth Practices, Medical Intervention and Women's Autonomy: Safer Childbirth or Bigger Profits?', *Women's Health and Urban Life* 4, 2 (Dec.): 27–44.

————. 2006. *Restructuring Family Policies: Convergences and Divergences*. Toronto: University of Toronto Press.

———— and David Tippin. 1999. *Poverty, Social Assistance and the Employability of Mothers: Restructuring Welfare States*. Toronto: University of Toronto Press.

———— and ————. 2002. 'When Flexibility Meets Rigidity: Sole Mothers' Experience in the Transition from Welfare to Work', *Journal of Sociology* 38, 4: 345–60.

———— and ————. 2004. 'More Than Just Another Obstacle: Health, Domestic Purposes Beneficiaries, and the Transition to Paid Work', *Social Policy Journal of New Zealand* 21 (Mar.): 98–120.

Bala, Nicholas, and Kenneth L. Clarke. 1981. *The Child and the Law*. Toronto: McGraw-Hill Ryerson.

Banting, Keith G., and Charles M. Beach, eds. 1995. *Labour Market Polarization and Social Policy Reform*. Kingston, Ont.: Queen's University, School of Policy Studies.

Barber, Jennifer S., and William G. Axinn. 1998. 'The Impact of Parental Pressure for Grandchildren on Young People's Entry into Cohabitation and Marriage', *Population Studies* 52, 2: 129–44.

Barker, John. 2003. 'Dowry', in Ponzetti (2003: 495–6).

Barnes, Gordon E., Leonard Greenwood, and Reena Sommers. 1991. 'Courtship Violence in a Canadian Sample of Male College Students', *Family Relations* 40 (Jan.): 37–44.

Baxter, Janine. 1994. *Work at Home: The Domestic Division of Labour*. Brisbane: University of Queensland Press.

————. 2002. 'Patterns of Change and Stability in the Gender Division of Household Labour in Australia, 1986–1997', *Journal of Sociology* 38, 4: 399–424.

———— and Michael Bittman. 1995. 'Measuring Time Spent on Housework: A Comparison of Two Approaches', *Australian Journal of Social Research* 1, 1: 21–46.

————, Belinda Hewitt, and Mark Western. 2005. 'Post-Familial Families and the Domestic Division of Labour', *Journal of Comparative Family Studies* 36, 4: 583–600.

Beaudry, Paul, and David Green. 1997. 'Cohort Patterns in Canadian Earnings', Working Paper #96. Toronto: Canadian Institute for Advanced Research.

Beaujot, Roderic. 2000. *Earning and Caring in Canadian Families*. Peterborough, Ont.: Broadview Press.

Beck-Gernsheim, Elisabeth. 2002. *Reinventing the Family: In Search of New Lifestyles*. Cambridge: Polity Press.

Beeby, Dean. 2006. 'Legalize Polygamy, Federal Study Urges', *GlobeandMail.Com*, 13 Jan.

Bélanger, Alain, Yves Carrière, and Stéphane Gilbert. 2001. *Report of the Demographic Situation in Canada 2000*. Statistics Canada, Catalogue 91–209–XPE. June. Ottawa: Ministry of Industry.

Bell, C., and V. Adair. 1985. *Women and Change*. Wellington, NZ: National Council of Women.

Benoit, Cecilia, Dena Carroll, and Alison Millar. 2002. 'But Is It Good for Non-Urban Women's Health? Regionalizing Maternity Care Services in British Columbia', *Canadian Review of Sociology and Anthropology* 39, 4: 373–96.

Berger, Peter, and Thomas Luckmann. 1967. *The Social Construction of Reality: A Treatise in the Sociology of Knowledge*. Garden City, NY: Doubleday.

Bernard, Jessie. 1972. *The Future of Marriage*. New York: World Publishing Company (revised in 1982).

Bibby, Reginald. 2004. *The Future Families Project: A Survey of Canadian Hopes and Dreams*. Available at: <www.vifamily.ca>.

———. 2004–5. 'Future Families: Surveying Our Hopes, Dreams, and Realities', *Transition* 34, 4: 3–14.

Bittman, Michael. 1991. *Juggling Time*. Canberra: Australian Bureau of Statistics.

———. 1998. 'The Land of the Lost Long Weekend? Trends in Free Time among Working Age Australians', Social Policy Research Centre Discussion Paper #83. Sydney: University of New South Wales.

———. 2004. 'Sunday Working and Family Time', paper presented to 'Work–Life Balance Across the Lifecourse' conference, University of Edinburgh, 2 July.

——— and Jocelyn Pixley. 1997. *The Double Life of the Family: Myth, Hope and Experience*. Sydney: Allen & Unwin.

——— and James Rice. 1999. 'Is the End of the Second Shift in Sight? The Role of Income, Bargaining Power, Domestic Technology, and Market Substitutes', paper presented at the Australian Sociological Association annual meeting. Melbourne, Monash University, 9 Dec.

Black, D., et al. 2000. 'Demographics of the Gay and Lesbian Population in the United States: Evidence from Available Systematic Data Sources', *Demography* 37: 139–54.

Bock, Gisela, and Pat Thane, eds. 1991. *Maternity and Gender Policies: Women and the Rise of European Welfare States 1880s–1950s*. London and New York: Routledge.

Bosch, Xavier. 1998. 'Spanish Doctors Criticised for High Tech Births', *British Medical Journal* 317, 7170 (21 Nov.): 1406.

Bowlby, J. 1953. 'Some Pathological Processes Set in Train by Early Mother-Child Separation', *Journal of Mental Science* 99: 265–72.

———. 1958. 'The Nature of the Child's Tie to His Mother', *International Journal of Psycho-Analysis* 39: 350–73.

———. 1969. *Attachment*. New York: Basic Books.

Boyd, Susan B. 2003. *Child Custody, Law, and Women's Work*. Toronto: Oxford University Press.

Bradbury, Bettina. 2005. 'Social, Economic, and Cultural Origins of Contemporary Families', in Baker (2005a): 71-98.

Bradbury, Bruce, and Kate Norris. 2005. 'Income and Separation', *Journal of Sociology* 41, 4 (Dec.): 425–46.

Broude, G. 1994. *Marriage, Family, and Relationships*. Denver: ABC-CLIO.

Brown, Judith. 1988. 'Iroquois Women: An Ethnohistoric Note', in B. Fox, ed., *Family Bonds and Gender Relations*. Toronto: Canadian Scholars' Press, 83–98.

Brownridge, D.A. 2003. 'Male Partner Violence against Aboriginal Women in Canada: An Empirical Analysis', *Journal of Interpersonal Violence* 18: 65–83.

Burghes, L. 1994. *Lone Parenthood and Family Disruption*. Occasional Paper #18. London: Family Policy Studies Centre.

Butler, Judith. 1997. *The Psychic Life of Power: Theories of Subjection*. Stanford, Calif.: Stanford University Press.

Callan, Victor J. 1982. 'How Do Australians Value Children? A Review and Research Update Using the Perceptions of Parents and Voluntarily Childless Adults', *Australian and New Zealand Journal of Sociology* 18, 3: 384–98.

Cameron, Jan. 1990. *Why Have Children? A New Zealand Case Study.* Christchurch: Canterbury University Press.

———. 1997. *Without Issue: New Zealanders Who Choose Not to Have Children.* Christchurch: Canterbury University Press.

Canada, Department of Justice. 2003. 'Child Support'. Available at: <http://canada.justice.gc.ca/en/ps/sup/index.html>.

Canadian Institute of Child Health. 2002. *The Health of Canada's Children*, 3rd edn. Ottawa: Canadian Institute of Child Health.

Castles, Francis G. 1985. *The Working Class and Welfare: Reflections on the Political Development of the Welfare State in Australia and New Zealand, 1890–1980.* Sydney: Allen & Unwin.

———. 2002. 'Three Facts about Fertility: Cross-National Lessons for the Current Debate', *Family Matters* 63 (Spring/Summer): 22–7.

——— and Ian F. Shirley. 1996. 'Labour and Social Policy: Gravediggers or Refurbishers of the Welfare State?', in F. Castles, R. Gerritsen, and J. Vowles, eds, *The Great Experiment: Labour Parties and Public Policy Transformation in Australia and New Zealand.* Auckland: Auckland University Press, 88–106.

Cheal, David. 1991. *Family and the State of Theory.* Toronto: University of Toronto Press.

———. 1996. 'Stories about Step-families', in *Growing Up In Canada: National Longitudinal Survey of Children and Youth.* Ottawa: Human Resources Development Canada and Statistics Canada, 93–101.

Che-Alford, Janet, and Brian Hamm. 1999. 'Under One Roof: Three Generations Living Together', *Canadian Social Trends* 53 (Summer): 6–9.

Cherlin, Andrew J. 1996. *Public and Private Families: An Introduction.* New York: McGraw-Hill.

Chesnais, J.C. 1992. *The Demographic Transition: Stages, Patterns, and Economic Implications.* Oxford: Clarendon Press.

Cheyne, Christine, Mike O'Brien, and Michael Belgrave. 2005. *Social Policy in Aotearoa New Zealand*, 3rd edn. Auckland: Oxford University Press.

Childcare Resource and Research Unit, University of Toronto (CRRU). 2003. 'Childcare in the News' (on-line), 11 Dec.

Chodorow, Nancy. 1978. *The Reproduction of Mothering: Psychoanalysis and the Sociology of Gender.* Berkeley, Calif.: University of California Press.

———. 1989. *Feminism and Psychoanalytic Theory.* New Haven: Yale University Press.

Christopher, K., P. England, S. McLanahan, K. Ross, and T.M. Smeeding. 2001. 'Gender Inequality in Affluent Nations: The Role of Single Motherhood and the State', in K. Vleminckx and T.M. Smeeding, eds, *Child Wellbeing, Child Poverty and Child Policy in Modern Nations.* Bristol: Policy Press, 199–220.

Clement, Wallace. 1975. *The Canadian Corporate Elite.* Toronto: McClelland & Stewart.

Clements, M., A. Cordova, H. Markman, and J. Laurenceau. 1997. 'The Erosion of Marital Satisfaction Over Time and How to Prevent It', in R.J. Stern and M. Hojjat, eds, *Satisfaction in Close Relationships.* New York: Guilford Press.

Cockett, M., and J.Tripp. 1994. *The Exeter Family Study.* Exeter, UK: University of Exeter.

Collins, Simon. 2005. 'Sperm Donors Could Become "Third Parents"', *New Zealand Herald*, 21 Apr., A3.

Coltrane, Scott. 1998. *Gender and Families.* Thousand Oaks, Calif.: Pine Forge Press.

Connidis, Ingrid. 1989. *Family Ties and Aging.* Toronto: Butterworths.

Connolly, Ellen. 2004. 'You've Come Almost No distance At All, Baby', *Sydney Morning Herald*, 15 Dec. (on-line).

Connolly, Marie. 2003. 'Kinship Care—A Selected Literature Review', unpublished paper prepared for the Department of Child Youth and Family Services, Wellington, NZ.

Cooley, Charles H. 1902. *Human Nature and Social Order*. New York: Charles Scribner's Sons.

Coveney, Peter. 1982. 'The Image of the Child,' in C. Jenks, ed., *The Sociology of Childhood*. London: Batsford, 42–7.

Cowan, Carolyn, et al. 1985. 'Transition to Parenthood: His, Hers, and Theirs', *Journal of Family Issues* 6: 451–81.

Crompton, Rosemary. 2004. 'Women's Employment and Work/Life Balance in Britain and Europe', plenary address at conference 'Work/Life Balance across the Life Course', University of Edinburgh, 1 July.

Cuneo, Carl. 1979. 'State, Class and Reserve Labour: The Case of the 1941 Unemployment Insurance Act', *Canadian Review of Sociology and Anthropology* 16, 2: 147–70.

Curtis, Lori J. 2001. 'Lone Motherhood and Health Status', *Canadian Public Policy* 27, 3: 335–56.

Dalley, Bronwyn. 1998. *Family Matters: Child Welfare in Twentieth Century New Zealand*. Auckland: Auckland University Press.

DeKeseredy, Walter. 2005. 'Patterns of Family Violence', in Baker (2005a: 229–57).

Dempsey, Ken. 1997. *Inequalities in Work and Marriage: Australia and Beyond*. Melbourne: Oxford University Press.

———— and David De Vaus. 2004. 'Who Cohabits in 2001? The Significance of Age, Gender and Religion', *Journal of Sociology* 40, 2: 157–78.

De Vaus, David. 2002. 'Marriage and Mental Health', *Family Matters* 62 (Winter): 26–32.

Devereux, Monique. 2004. 'Religious Leaders Say Wearing Veils Is a Personal Choice', *New Zealand Herald*, 2 Nov., at: <www.nzherald.co.nz>.

Dickason, Olive Patricia. 2006. *A Concise History of Canada's First Nations*. Toronto: Oxford University Press.

Dooley, Martin. 1995. 'Lone-Mother Families and Social Assistance Policy in Canada', in Dooley et al., eds, *Family Matters: New Policies for Divorce, Lone Mothers, and Child Poverty*. Toronto: C.D. Howe Institute, 35–104.

Dorsett, Richard, and Alan Marsh. 1998. *The Health Trap: Poverty, Smoking and Lone Parenthood*. London: Policy Studies Institute.

Douthitt, Robin A., and Joanne Fedyk. 1990. *The Cost of Raising Children in Canada*. Toronto: Butterworths.

Doyal, L. 1995. *What Makes Women Sick? Gender and the Political Economy of Health*. New Brunswick, NJ: Rutgers University Press.

Dranoff, Linda Silver. 1977. *Women in Canadian Life*. Toronto: Fitzhenry & Whiteside.

Drolet, Marie, and René Morissette. 1997. 'Working More? What Do Workers Prefer?', *Perspectives on Labour and Income* 9, 4: 32–8.

Dumas, Jean, and Yves Péron. 1992. *Marriage and Conjugal Life in Canada*. Ottawa: Statistics Canada (Catalogue no. 91–534E).

Dunne, G. 2000. 'Opting into Motherhood: Lesbians Blurring the Boundaries and Transforming the Meaning of Parenthood and Kinship', *Gender and Society* 14: 11–35.

Edin, Kathryn. 2003. 'Work Is Not Enough', Plenary Address to Australian Social Policy Conference, University of New South Wales, Sydney, 10 July.

———— and Maria J. Kefalas. 2005. *Promises I Can Keep: Why Poor Women Put Motherhood before Marriage*. Berkeley: University of California Press.

———— and Laura Lein. 1997. *Making Ends Meet: How Single Mothers Survive Welfare and Low-Wage Work*. New York: Russell Sage Foundation.

———— and Joanna M. Reed. 2005. 'Why Don't They Just Get Married? Barriers to Marriage among the Disadvantaged', *Marriage and Child Wellbeing* 15, 2: 117–36.

Edwards, Anne, and Susan Magarey, eds. 1995. *Women in a Restructuring Australia: Work and Welfare*. Sydney: Allen & Unwin.

Eichler, Margrit. 1988. *Families in Canada Today*, 2nd edn. Toronto: Gage.

———. 1997. *Family Shifts: Families, Policies, and Gender Equality*. Toronto: Oxford University Press.

———. 2005. 'Biases in Family Literature', Baker (2005a): 52–68.

Elliott, J., and M. Richards. 1991. 'Parental Divorce and the Life Chances of Children', *Family Law*: 481–4.

———, ———, and H. Warwick. 1993. *The Consequences of Divorce for the Health and Well-Being of Adults and Children*. Final Report for Health Promotion Trust #2. Cambridge, UK: Centre for Family Research.

Elizabeth, Vivienne. 2000. 'Cohabitation, Marriage, and the Unruly Consequences of "Difference"', *Gender and Society* 14, 1: 87–100.

———. 2001. 'Managing Money, Managing Coupledom: A Critical Investigation of Cohabitants' Money Management Practices', *Sociological Review* 49: 389–411.

Emery, R. 1994. 'Psychological Research on Children, Parents, and Divorce', in Emery, ed., *Renegotiating Family Relationships: Divorce, Child Custody, and Mediation*. New York: Guilford Press, 194–217.

Engels, Friedrich. 1972 [1884]. *The Origin of the Family, Private Property and the State*. New York: Pathfinder.

Erikson, E. 1963. *Childhood and Society*, 2nd edn. New York: Norton.

———. 1968. *Identity: Youth and Crisis*. New York: Norton.

Ermisch, John. 1991. *Lone Parenthood: An Economic Analysis*. Cambridge: Cambridge University Press.

———. 2003. *An Economic Analysis of the Family*. Oxford: Princeton University Press.

Esping-Andersen, Gøsta. 1990. *The Three Worlds of Welfare Capitalism*. Cambridge: Polity Press.

———, ed. 1996. *Welfare States in Transition: National Adaptations in Global Economies*. London: Sage.

Evenson, Ranae, and Robin W. Simon. 2005. 'Clarifying the Relationship between Parenthood and Depression', *Journal of Health and Social Behaviour* 46: 341–58.

Featherstone, M. 1991. 'The Body in Consumer Culture', in M. Featherstone and B.S. Turner, eds, *The Body: Social Process and Cultural Theory*. London: Sage.

Ferri, E. 1984. *Step Children: A National Study*. Windsor, UK: NFER-Nelson.

——— and K. Smith. 2003. 'Partnerships and Parenthood', in E. Ferri, J. Bynner, and M. Wadsmith, eds, *Changing Britain, Changing Lives*. London: Institute of Education.

Fleising, Usher. 2003. 'Bride-Price', in Ponzetti (2003): 175–6.

Fleming, Robin. 1997. *The Common Purse*. Auckland: Auckland University Press.

———, with Toni Atkinson. 1999. *Families of a Different Kind*. Waikanae, NZ: Families of Remarriage Project.

——— and S.K. Easting. 1994. *Couples, Households and Women: Report of the Pakeha Component of the Intrafamily Income Study*, Wellington Intrafamily Income Project. Palmerston North, NZ: Social Policy Research Centre, Massey University.

Fletcher, G. 1978. 'Division of Labour in the New Zealand Nuclear Family', *New Zealand Psychologist* 7, 2: 33–40.

Fletcher, R. 1973. *The Family and Marriage in Britain*. Harmondsworth: Penguin.

Ford, Jane, Natasha Nassar, Elizabeth Sullivan, Georgina Chambers, and Paul Lancaster. 2003. *Reproductive Health Indicators, Australia, 2002*. Sydney: Australian Institute of Health and Welfare.

Friedan, Betty. 1963. *The Feminine Mystique*. New York: Norton.

Funder, Kathleen. 1996. *Remaking Families: Adaptation of Parents and Children to Divorce.* Melbourne: Australian Institute of Family Studies.

——— and Margaret Harrison. 1993. 'Drawing a Longbow on Marriage and Divorce', in Funder, Harrison, and R. Weston, eds, *Settling Down: Pathways of Parents after Divorce.* Melbourne: Australian Institute of Family Studies, 13–32.

Furstenberg, F., F. Morgan, and P. Allison. 1987. 'Paternal Participation and Children's Well-Being after Marital Dissolution', *American Sociological Review* 52: 695–701.

Gauthier, Anne Hélène. 1996. *The State and the Family: A Comparative Analysis of Family Policies in Industrialized Countries.* Oxford: Clarendon Press.

Gazso-Windle, Amber, and Julie Ann McMullin. 2003. 'Doing Domestic Labour: Strategising in a Gendered Domain', *Canadian Journal of Sociology* 28, 3: 341–66.

Gershuny, Jonathan, and Oriel Sullivan. 2003. 'Time Use, Gender, and Public Policy Regimes', *Social Politics* 10, 2: 205–28.

Giddens, Anthony. 1992. *The Transformation of Intimacy: Sexuality, Love and Eroticism in Modern Societies.* Cambridge: Polity Press.

Gilding, Michael. 1997. *Australian Families: A Comparative Perspective.* Melbourne: Addison Wesley Longman.

———. 2002. 'Families of the New Millennium', *Family Matters* 62 (Winter): 4–10.

———. 2005. 'Families and Fortunes: Accumulation, Management Succession and Inheritance in Wealthy Families', *Journal of Sociology* 41, 1 (Mar.): 29–46.

Gillespie, R. 1999. 'Voluntary Childlessness in the United Kingdom', *Reproductive Health Matters* 7, 3: 43–53.

Glenn, Noval D., and Charles N. Weaver. 1988. 'The Changing Relationship of Marital Status to Reported Happiness', *Journal of Marriage and the Family* 50: 317–24.

Glick, Paul. 1984. 'Marriage, Divorce and Living Arrangements: Prospective Changes', *Journal of Family Issues* 5 (Mar.): 7–26.

Goffman, Erving. 1959. *The Presentation of Self in Everyday Life.* Garden City, NY: Doubleday Anchor.

Goldscheider, Frances, and Gayle Kaufman. 1996. 'Fertility and Commitment: Bringing Men Back In', *Population and Development Review* 22, suppl.: 87–92.

Goldthorpe, J.E. 1987. *Family Life in Western Societies.* Cambridge: Cambridge University Press.

Goode, W.J. 1964. *The Family.* Englewood Cliffs, NJ: Prentice-Hall.

Goodger, Kay, and Peter Larose. 1999. 'Changing Expectations: Sole Parents and Employment in New Zealand', *Social Policy Journal of New Zealand* 12: 53–70.

Goodnow, J.J. 1989. 'Work in Households: An Overview and Three Studies', in D. Ironmonger, ed., *Households Work.* Sydney: Allen & Unwin.

——— and D. Susan. 1989. 'Children's Household Work: Task Differences, Styles of Assignment, and Links to Family', *Relationships: Journal of Applied Developmental Psychology* 10: 209–26.

González-López, Maria José. 2002. 'A Portrait of Western Families: New Modes of Intimate Relationships and the Timing of Life Events', in A. Carling, S. Duncan, and R. Edwards, eds, *Analysing Families: Morality and Rationality in Policy and Practice.* London: Routledge, 21–48.

Graham-Bermann, Sandra, and Jeffrey Edleson. 2001. 'Introduction', in Graham-Bermann and Edleson, eds, *Domestic Violence in the Lives of Children: The Future of Research, Intervention and Social Policy.* Washington: American Psychological Association.

Greenwood, Gaye A. 1999. 'Dissolution of Marriage: Public Policy and "The Family-Apart"', Master's thesis, Auckland: School of Social Policy and Social Work, Massey University at Albany.

Guest, Dennis. 1997. *The Emergence of Social Security in Canada*, 3rd edn. Vancouver: University of British Columbia Press.

Hakim, Catherine. 2000. *Work-Lifestyle Choices in the 21st Century*. Oxford: Oxford University Press.

Hantrais, Linda. 2000. *Social Policy in the European Union*, 2nd edn. London: Macmillan.

———. 2004. *Family Policy Matters: Responding to Family Change in Europe*. Bristol: Policy Press.

Harrison, Margaret. 1993. 'The Law's Response to New Challenges', in K. Funder, M. Harrison, and R. Weston, eds, *Settling Down: Pathways of Parents after Divorce*. Melbourne: Australian Institute of Family Studies, 33–55.

Health Canada. 2000. *Canadian Perinatal Health Report 2000*. Ottawa: Minister of Health. Available at: <www.hc-sc.gc.ca>.

Heitlinger, Alena. 1993. *Women's Equality, Demography, and Public Policy: A Comparative Perspective*. London: Macmillan.

Hewitt, Belinda, Mark Western, and Janeen Baxter. 2005. 'Who Decides? The Social Characteristics of Who Initiates Marital Separation', paper presented at Australian Sociological Association annual meeting, University of Hobart, Tasmania, 5–8 Dec.

Hill, Reuben. 1971. 'Modern Systems Theory and the Family', *Social Science Information* 10: 7–26.

Hobcraft, John, and Kathleen Kiernan. 2001. 'Childhood Poverty, Early Motherhood and Adult Social Exclusion', *British Journal of Sociology* 52, 3: 495–517.

Hochschild, Arlie Russell. 1989. *The Second Shift: Working Parents and the Revolution at Home*. New York: Viking Penguin.

Hoffman, S.D., and E.M. Foster. 1997. 'Economic Correlates of Nonmarital Childbearing among Adult Women', *Family Planning Perspectives* 29, 3: 137–40.

Houston, Susan E., and Allison Prentice. 1988. *Schooling and Scholars in Nineteenth Century Ontario*. Toronto: University of Toronto Press.

Huber, Joan, and Glenna Spitze. 1980. 'Considering Divorce: An Explanation of Becker's Theory of Marital Instability', *American Journal of Sociology* 86, 1: 75–89.

Hughes, Karen. 2005. 'The Adult Children of Divorce: Pure Relationships and Family Values?', *Journal of Sociology* 41, 1 (Mar.): 69–86.

Humm, Maggie. 1995. *The Dictionary of Feminist Theory*, 2nd edn. London: Prentice-Hall/ Harvester Wheatsheaf.

Hunsley, Terrance. 1997. *Lone Parent Incomes and Social Policy Outcomes: Canada in International Perspective*. Kingston, Ont.: Queen's University, School of Policy Studies.

Hunt, J. 2003. *Family and Friends Carers*. Report prepared for the UK Department of Health. Available at: <www.doh.gov.uk/carers/familyandfriends.htm>.

Ihinger-Tallman, Marilyn, and David Levinson (revised by J.M. White). 2003. 'Definition of Marriage', in Ponzetti (2003): 1094–8.

International Labour Organization. 2000. 'International Labour Standards on Maternity Protection'. Available at: <www.ilo.org>.

Jackson, A., and P. Roberts. 2001. 'Physical Housing Conditions and the Well-Being of Children', background paper on housing for *The Progress of Canada's Children 2001*. Ottawa: Canadian Council on Social Development.

Jaffe, Peter, Nancy Lemon, and Samantha Poisson. 2003. *Child Custody and Domestic Violence: A Call for Safety and Accountability*. Thousand Oaks, Calif.: Sage.

———, Marlies Suderman, and Robert Geffner. 2000. 'Emerging Issues for Children Exposed to Domestic Violence', in Jaffe, Suderman, and Geffner, eds, *Children Exposed to Domestic Violence: Current Issues in Research, Intervention, Prevention, and Policy Development*. New York: Haworth Press.

Jagger, Elisabeth. 2005. 'Is Thirty the New Sixty? Dating, Age and Gender in Postmodern, Consumer Society', *Sociology* 39, 1: 89–106.

Jamieson, Lynn. 1998. *Intimacy: Personal Relationships in Modern Societies.* Cambridge: Polity Press.

Jamieson, L., M. Anderson, D. McCrone, F. Bechhofer, R. Stewart, and L. Yaojun. 2002. 'Cohabitation and Commitment: Partnership Plans of Young Men and Women', *Sociological Review* 50, 3: 356–77.

Jenson, Jane. 2004. 'Changing the Paradigm: Family Responsibility or Investing in Children', *Canadian Journal of Sociology* 29, 2: 169–92.

——— and Mariette Sineau. 2001a. 'The Care Dimensions in Welfare State Design', in Jenson and Sineau (2001b: 3–18).

———. 2001b. *Who Cares? Women's Work, Childcare, and Welfare State Design.* Toronto: University of Toronto Press.

Johnson, Holly. 1990. 'Wife Abuse', in C. McKie and K. Thomson, eds, *Canadian Social Trends.* Toronto: Thompson Educational Publishing, 173–6.

Jones, Michael. 1996. *The Australian Welfare State: Evaluating Social Policy.* Sydney: Allen & Unwin.

Kamerman, Sheila B., and Alfred J. Kahn, eds. 1997. *Family Change and Family Policies in Great Britain, Canada, New Zealand and the United States.* Oxford: Clarendon Press.

Karney, B., and T. Bradbury. 1995. 'The Longitudinal Course of Marital Quality and Stability: A Review of Theory, Method and Research', *Psychological Bulletin* 118: 3–34.

Kedgley, Sue. 1996. *Mum's the Word: The Untold Story of Motherhood in New Zealand.* Auckland: Random House.

Kelsey, Jane. 1999. *Reclaiming the Future: New Zealand and the Global Economy.* Wellington: Bridget Williams Books.

Kendig, H., ed. 1986. *Ageing and Families: A Social Networks Perspective.* Sydney: Allen & Unwin.

Kiernan, Kathleen. 1997. *The Legacy of Parental Divorce: Social, Economic, and Demographic Experiences in Adulthood.* London: Centre for Analysis of Social Exclusion.

Knaak, Stephanie. 2005. 'Breast-feeding, Bottle-feeding and Dr. Spock: The Shifting Context of Choice', *Canadian Review of Sociology and Anthropology* 42, 2 (May): 197–216.

Kobayashi, Karen M. 2007. '"Mid-Life Crises": Understanding the Changing Nature of Relationships in Middle-Age Canadian Families', in David Cheal, ed., *Canadian Families Today: New Perspectives.* Toronto: Oxford University Press.

Krane, Julia. 2003. *What's Mother Got to Do With It? Protecting Children from Sexual Abuse.* Toronto: University of Toronto Press.

Krug, E., L. Dahlberg, J. Mercy, A. Zwi, and R. Lozano, eds. 2002. *World Report on Violence and Health.* Geneva: WHO.

Kurdeck, L.A. 1998. 'Relationship Outcomes and Their Predictors: Longitudinal Evidence from Heterosexual Married, Gay Cohabiting and Lesbian Cohabiting Couples', *Journal of Marriage and the Family* 60: 553–68.

———. 2001. 'Differences between Heterosexual-Nonparent Couples and Gay, Lesbian and Heterosexual-Parent Couples', *Journal of Family Issues* 22: 728–55.

Land, Hilary. 1980. 'The Family Wage', *Feminist Review* 6: 55–7.

Lapointe, Rita Eva, and C. James Richardson. 1994. *Evaluation of the New Brunswick Family Support Orders Service.* Fredericton: New Brunswick Department of Justice.

Laslett, Peter. 1971. *The World We Have Lost.* London: University Paperbacks.

Laumann, E.O., G.H. Gagnon, R.T. Michael, and S. Michaels. 1994. *The Social Organization of Sexuality: Sexual Practices in the United States.* Chicago: University of Chicago Press.

Lawlor, Allison. 2003. 'Births on the Rise', *Globe and Mail*, 12 Aug. Available at: <www.globeandmail.com>.

Lawton, J. 1991. 'What is Sexually-Transmitted Debt?', in R. Meikle, ed., *Women and Credit: A Forum on Sexually-Transmitted Debt.* Melbourne: Ministry of Consumer Affairs.

Le Bourdais, Céline, and Evelyne Lapierre-Adamcyk. 2004. 'Changes in Conjugal Life in Canada: Is Cohabitation Progressively Replacing Marriage?', *Journal of Marriage and Family* 66 (Nov.): 929–42.

Leibrich, Julie, Judy Paulin, and Robin Ransom.1995. *Hitting Home: Men Speak about Abuse of Women Partners*. Wellington, NZ: Department of Justice.

Leira, Arnlaug. 2002. *Working Parents and the Welfare State: Family Change and Policy Reform in Scandinavia*. Cambridge: Cambridge University Press.

Leslie, Gerald, and Sheila K. Korman. 1989. *The Family in Social Context*, 7th edn. New York: Oxford University Press.

Letherby, G. 1999. 'Other than Mother and Mothers as Others: The Experience of Mother-hood and Non-motherhood in Relation to "Infertility" and "Involuntary Childlessness"', *Women's Studies International Forum* 22: 359–72.

Lewis, Jane. 1999. 'Marriage and Cohabitation and the Nature of Commitment', *Child and Family Law Quarterly* 11, 4: 355–63.

———. 2003. *Should We Worry about Family Change?* Toronto: University of Toronto Press.

Lipman, Ellen L., David R. Offord, and Martin D. Dooley. 1996. 'What Do We Know about Children from Single-Parent Families? Questions and Answers from the National Lon-gitudinal Survey on Children', in *Growing Up in Canada: National Longitudinal Survey on Children and Youth*. Ottawa: Human Resources Development Canada.

Little, Margaret. 1998. *No Car, No Radio, No Liquor Permit: The Moral Regulation of Single Mothers in Ontario, 1920–1997*. Toronto: Oxford University Press.

Lopata, Helena. 1971. *Occupation: Housewife*. New York: Oxford University Press.

Lundberg, Shelly, and Elaina Rose. 1998. 'The Determinants of Specialization within Marriage', discussion paper, Department of Economics, University of Washington.

Lupri, Eugen, and James Frideres. 1981. 'The Quality of Marriage and the Passage of Time: Mar-ital Satisfaction over the Family Life Cycle', *Canadian Journal of Sociology* 6, 3: 283–306.

Luxton, Meg. 1980. *More Than a Labour of Love*. Toronto: Women's Education Press.

———. 2005. 'Conceptualizing "Families": Theoretical Frameworks and Family Research', in Baker (2005a): 29–51.

McDaniel, Susan A. 1994. *Family and Friends* (Statistics Canada, Catalogue 11–612E, #9). Ottawa: Minister of Industry, Science and Technology.

——— and Lorne Tepperman. 2000, 2004. *Close Relations: An Introduction to the Sociology of the Families*, 1st and 2nd edn. Toronto: Pearson/Prentice-Hall.

McDonald, Peter. 2000. 'Gender Equity in Theories of Fertility Transition', *Population and Development Review* 26, 3: 427–39.

McFadden, Suzanne. 2005. 'Teen Money: Get Real', *Canvas, Weekend Herald* (New Zealand), 9 Apr., 10–12.

McGillvray, A., and B. Comaskey. 1998. '"Everybody Has Black Eyes . . . Nobody Don't Say Nothing": Intimate Violence, Aboriginal Women, and the Justice System Response', in K.D. Bonnycastle and G.S. Rigakos, eds, *Unsettling Truths: Battered Women, Policy, Politics and Contemporary Research in Canada*. Vancouver: Collective Press.

McGilly, Frank. 1998. *An Introduction to Canada's Public Social Services: Understanding Income and Health Programs*, 2nd edn. Toronto: Oxford University Press.

McKay, S., and K. Rowlingson. 1998. 'Choosing Lone Parenthood? The Dynamics of Family Change', in R. Ford and J. Millar, eds, *Private Lives and Public Responses: Lone Parenthood and Future Policy in the UK*. London: Policy Studies Institute, 42–57.

Mackey, R.A., and B.A. O'Brien. 1995. *Lasting Marriages: Men and Women Growing Together*. Westport, Conn.: Praeger.

McLaughlin, Diane K., and Daniel T. Lichter. 1997. 'Poverty and the Marital Behavior of Young Women', *Journal of Marriage and the Family* 59: 589.

Maclean, M., and D. Kuh. 1991. 'The Long Term Effects for Girls of Parental Divorce', in M. Maclean and D. Groves, eds, *Women's Issues in Social Policy*. London: Routledge, 161–78.

McMahon, A. 1999. *Taking Care of Men*. Cambridge: Cambridge University Press.

McNair, Ruth, Deborah Dempsey, Sarah Wise, and Amaryll Perlesz. 2002. 'Lesbian Parenting: Issues, Strengths and Challenges', *Family Matters* 63: 40–9.

Magarick, R.H., and R.A. Brown. 1981. 'Social and Emotional Aspects of Voluntary Childlessness in Vasectomized Childless Men', *Journal of Biosocial Science* 13: 157–67.

Malin, M., E. Hemminki, O. Raikkonen, S. Sihvo, and M. Perala. 2001. 'What Do Women Want? Women's Experiences of Infertility Treatment', *Social Science and Medicine* 53: 123–33.

Marcil-Gratton, Nicole. 1998. *Growing Up with Mom and Dad? The Intricate Family Life Courses of Canadian Children*. Ottawa: Ministry of Industry.

Marshall, Katherine. 1993. 'Employed Parents and the Division of Labour', *Perspectives on Labour and Income* 5, 3: 23–30.

———. 1994. 'Balancing Work and Family Responsibilities', *Perspectives on Labour and Income* 6, 1: 26–30.

———. 1998. 'Stay-at-Home Dads', *Perspectives on Labour and Income* 10, 1: 9–15.

May, Elaine Campbell. 1995. *Barren in the Promised Land: Childless Americans and the Pursuit of Happiness*. New York: Basic Books.

Mead, George H. 1934. *Mind, Self and Society*. Chicago: Chicago University Press.

Mead, Margaret. 1935. *Sex and Temperament in Three Primitive Societies*. New York: Dell.

Meezan, William, and Jonathan Rauch. 2005. 'Gay Marriage, Same-Sex Parenting, and America's Children', *Marriage and Family Well-being* 15, 2: 97–114.

Michaels, M.W. 1996. 'Other Mothers: Toward an Ethic of Postmaternal Practice', *Hypatia* 11, 2: 49–70.

Millar, Jane, and Karen Rowlingson, eds. 2001. *Lone Parents, Employment and Social Policy: Cross-National Comparisons*. Bristol: Policy Press.

——— and Peter Whiteford. 1993. 'Child Support in Lone-Parent Families: Policies in Australia and the UK', *Policy and Politics* 21, 1: 59–72.

Millett, Kate. 1970. *Sexual Politics*. New York: Doubleday.

Mink, Gwendolyn. 1998. *Welfare's End*. Ithaca, NY: Cornell University Press.

———. 2002. 'Violating Women: Rights Abuses in the American Welfare Police State', in Sylvia Bashevkin, ed., *Women's Work Is Never Done*. New York: Routledge, 141–64.

Mitchell, Juliet. 1974. *Psychoanalysis and Feminism*. Harmondsworth: Penguin.

——— and Jack Goody. 1997. 'Feminism, Fatherhood and the Family in Britain', in Ann Oakley and Juliet Mitchell, eds, *Who's Afraid of Feminism? Seeing through the Backlash*. London: Hamish Hamilton.

Moore, Oliver. 2003. 'Bush Wants to "Codify" Heterosexual Unions', *Globe and Mail*, 31 July. At: <www.theglobeandmail.com>.

Mongeau, P.A., and C.M. Carey. 1996. 'Who's Wooing Whom: An Experimental Investigation of Date Initiation and Expectancy Violation', *Western Journal of Communication* 60, 3: 195–213.

Montgomerie, Deborah. 1999. 'Sweethearts, Soldiers, Happy Families: Gender and the Second World War', in Caroline Daley, ed., *The Gendered Kiwi*. Auckland: Auckland University Press, 163–90.

Morell, Carolyn M. 1994. *Unwomanly Conduct: The Challenges of Intentional Childlessness*. New York: Routledge.

Mullender, Audrey, G. Hague, U. Imam, L. Kelly, E. Malos, and L. Regan. 2003. 'Could Have Helped but Didn't: The Formal and Informal Support Systems Experienced by Children Living with Domestic Violence', in C. Hallett and A. Prout, eds, *Hearing the Voices of Children: Social Policy for a New Century*. London and New York: Routledge Falmer.

Murdock, George. 1949. *Social Structure*. New York: Macmillan.

Myles, John. 1996. 'When Markets Fail: Social Welfare in Canada and the United States', in Esping-Andersen (1996: 116–40).

Nanda, Serena. 1991. *Cultural Anthropology*. Belmont, Calif.: Wadsworth.

National Council of Welfare (NCW). 2003. *Welfare Incomes 2002*. Ottawa: Minister of Public Works and Government Services Canada.

National Longitudinal Survey of Children and Youth (NLSCY). 1996. *Growing Up in Canada*. Ottawa: Human Resources Development Canada and Statistics Canada.

Nelson, E.D., and Barrie W. Robinson. 1999. *Gender in Canada*. Scarborough, Ont.: Prentice-Hall Allyn and Bacon Canada.

Nelson, F. 1996. *Lesbian Motherhood*. Toronto: University of Toronto Press.

———. 2001. 'Lesbian Families', in Bonnie J. Fox, ed., *Family Patterns, Gender Relations*, 2nd edn. Toronto: Oxford University Press.

Nett, Emily. 1981. 'Canadian Families in Social-Historical Perspective', *Canadian Journal of Sociology* 6, 3: 239–60.

———. 1993. *Canadian Families Past and Present*, 2nd edn. Toronto: Butterworths.

Oakley, Ann. 1974. *The Sociology of Housework*. Oxford: Martin Robertson.

O'Connor, Julia S., Ann Shola Orloff, and Sheila Shaver. 1999. *States, Markets, Families: Gender Liberalism and Social Policy in Australia, Canada, Great Britain and the United States*. Cambridge: Cambridge University Press.

O'Leary, K.D., et al. 1989. 'Prevalence and Stability of Physical Aggression between Spouses: A Longitudinal Analysis', *Journal of Consulting and Clinical Psychology* 57: 263–8.

Organization for Economic Co-operation and Development (OECD). 2001. *Society at a Glance: OECD Social Indicators 2001*. Paris: OECD.

———. 2002. *OECD Employment Outlook July 2002*. Paris: OECD.

———. 2005a. *OECD Employment Outlook 2005*. Paris: OECD.

———. 2005b. *Society at a Glance: OECD Social Indicators*. Paris: OECD.

Pahl, Jan. 1995. 'His Money, Her Money: Recent Research on Financial Organisation in Marriage', *Journal of Economic Psychology* 16: 361–76.

———. 2001. 'Couples and Their Money: Theory and Practice in Personal Finances', in R. Sykes, C. Bochel, and N. Ellison, eds, *Social Policy Review 13*. Bristol: Policy Press, 17–37.

———. 2005. 'Individualisation in Couple Finances: Who Pays for the Children?', *Social Policy and Society* 4, 4: 381–91.

Parker, Robyn. 2002. 'Why Marriages Last. A Discussion of the Literature', Research Paper #28. Melbourne: Australian Institute of Family Studies.

Parsons, Talcott, and Robert F. Bales. 1955. *Family Socialization and Interaction Process*. New York: Free Press.

Patterson, C.J. 2000. 'Family Relationships of Lesbians and Gay Men', *Journal of Marriage and the Family* 62: 1052–69.

——— and R.W. Chan. 1997. 'Gay Fathers', in M.E. Lamb, ed., *The Role of the Father in Child Development*, 3rd edn. New York: Wiley and Sons, 245–60.

Phillips, J. 1988. *The Mother Experience: New Zealand Women Talk about Motherhood*. Auckland: Penguin Books.

Phipps, Shelley and Peter S. Burton. 1992. 'What's Mine Is Yours? The Influence of Male and Female Incomes on Patterns of Household Expenditure', Discussion Paper #92–12. Halifax: Dalhousie University, Department of Economics.

Pierson, Ruth, Marjorie G. Cohen, Paula Bourne, and Philinda Masters, eds. 1993. *Canadian Women's Issues*, vol. 1. Toronto: James Lorimer.

Ponzetti, James J., ed. 2003. *International Encyclopedia of Marriage and Family*, 2nd edn. New York: Thomson Gale.

Potuchek, J.L. 1997. *Who Supports the Family: Gender and Breadwinning in Dual-Earner Marriages*. Stanford, Calif.: Stanford University Press.

Pryor, Jan. 2004. 'The Child-Stepparent Relationship: Its Fragility and Importance', paper presented at Australian Institute of Family Studies conference, 9–11 Feb., Melbourne.

———. 2005. 'What Is Commitment? How Married and Cohabiting Parents Talk about Their Relationship', *Family Matters* 71 (Winter): 28–35.

——— and Bryan Rodgers. 2001. *Children in Changing Families: Life after Parental Separation*. Oxford: Blackwell Publishers.

Pulkingham, Jane. 1994. 'Private Troubles, Private Solutions: Poverty among Divorced Women and the Politics of Support Enforcement and Child Custody Determination', *Canadian Journal of Law and Society* 9, 2: 73–97.

Qu, Lixia. 2004. 'Children's Living Arrangements after Parental Separation', *Family Matters* 67 (Autumn): 4–7.

Queen, Stuart, Robert W. Habenstein, and J.S. Quadagno. 1985. *The Family in Various Cultures*, 5th edn. New York: Harper and Row.

Ram, Bali. 1990. *New Trends in the Family: Demographic Facts and Figures*. Prepared for Statistics Canada (Catalogue 91–535E). Ottawa: Minister of Supply and Services Canada, Mar.

Ramu, G.N., and Nicholas Tavuchis. 1986. 'The Valuation of Children and Parenthood among the Voluntarily Childless and Parental Couples in Canada', *Journal of Comparative Family Studies* 17, 1: 99–115.

Ranson. Gillian. 2005. 'Paid and Unpaid Work: How Do Families Divide Their Labour?', in Baker (2005a): 99–120.

Richardson, C. James. 2001. 'Divorce and Remarriage', in M. Baker, ed., *Families: Changing Trends in Canada*, 4th edn. Toronto: McGraw-Hill Ryerson, 206–37.

Roberts, Helen. 1997. 'Children, Inequalities and Health', *British Medical Journal* 314, 7087 (12 Apr.): 11–22.

Rodney, Patricia. 1995. 'Domestic Violence in Vulnerable Populations: International Models Relevant to American Healthcare and Safety for Women'. At: <www.i3m.org/main/pcpc/ppoint/ws6-rodney.pdf>.

Ross, David, K. Scott, and M. Kelly. 1996. *Child Poverty: What Are the Consequences?* Ottawa: Canadian Council on Social Development.

Sainsbury, Diane. 1993. 'Dual Welfare and Sex Segregation of Access to Social Benefits: Income Maintenance Policies in the UK, the US, the Netherlands and Sweden', *Journal of Social Policy* 22, 1: 69–98.

———. 1996. *Gender, Equality and Welfare States*. Cambridge: Cambridge University Press.

Sarantakos, Sotirios. 1996. *Modern Families: An Australian Text*. Melbourne: Macmillan Education Australia.

———. 1998. 'Sex and Power in Same-sex Couples', *Australian Journal of Social Issues* 33, 1: 17–36.

Sarfati, Diana, and Kate Scott. 2001. 'The Health of Lone Mothers in New Zealand', *New Zealand Medical Journal* 114, 1133: 257–60.

Saxton, L. 1993. *The Individual, Marriage, and the Family*. Belmont, Calif.: Wadsworth.

Scanzoni, John. 1982. *Sexual Bargaining: Power Politics in American Marriage*, 2nd edn. Chicago: University of Chicago Press.

Scanzoni, Letha Dawson, and John Scanzoni. 1988. *Women, Men and Change*, 3rd edn. New York: McGraw-Hill.

Sev'er, Aysan. 1990. 'Mate Selection Patterns of Men and Women in Personal Advertisements', *Atlantis: A Women's Studies Journal* 15, 2: 70–6.

———. 1992. *Women and Divorce in Canada: A Sociological Analysis*. Toronto: Canadian Scholars' Press.

———. 2002. *Fleeing the House of Horrors: Women Who Have Left Abusive Partners*. Toronto: University of Toronto Press.

Sharlin, S.A., F.W. Kaslow, and H. Hammerschmidt. 2000. *Together through Thick and Thin: A Multinational Picture of Long-Term Marriages*. New York: Haworth Clinical Practice Press.

Shorter, Edward. 1975. *The Making of the Modern Family*. New York: Basic Books.

Skolnick, A. 1987. *The Intimate Environment*, 4th edn. Toronto: Little, Brown.

Singh, S. 1997. *Marriage Money: The Social Shaping of Money in Marriage and Banking*. Sydney: Allen & Unwin.

Smart, Carol, and Bren Neale. 1999. *Family Fragments?* Cambridge: Polity Press.

———, and Selma Sevenjuijsen. 1989. *Child Custody and the Politics of Gender*. London: Routledge.

Smith, Marjorie. 2004. 'Relationships of Children in Stepfamilies with their Non-Resident Fathers', *Family Matters* 67 (Autumn): 28–35.

Smith, Raymond T. 1996. *The Matrifocal Family: Power, Pluralism and Politics*. New York: Routledge.

Smyth, Bruce. 2002. 'Research into Parent–Child Contact after Separation', *Family Matters* 62 (Winter): 33–7.

———, ed. 2004. *Parent–Child Contact and Post-Separation Parenting Arrangements*. Research Report #9. Melbourne: Australian Institute of Family Studies.

———, G. Sheehan, and B. Fehlberg. 2001. 'Patterns of Parenting after Divorce: A Benchmark Study', *Australian Journal of Family Law* 15, 2: 114–28.

——— and Ruth Weston. 2004. 'The Attitudes of Separated Mothers and Fathers to 50/50 Shared Care', *Family Matters* 67 (Autumn): 8–15.

Speirs, Carol, and Maureen Baker. 1994. 'Eligibility to Adopt: Models of "Suitable" Families in Legislation and Practice', *Canadian Social Work Review* 11, 1: 89–102.

Statistics Canada. 2002a. '2001 Census: Marital Status, Common-law Status, Families and Households', *The Daily*, 22 Oct.

———. 2002b. 'Changing Conjugal Life in Canada', *The Daily*, 11 July.

———. 2003. 'Marriages', *The Daily*, 2 June.

Strong-Boag, Veronica. 1982. 'Intruders in the Nursery: Childcare Professionals Reshape the Years One to Five, 1920–1940', in Joy Parr, ed., *Childhood and Family in Canadian History*. Toronto: McClelland & Stewart, 160–78.

Swift, Karen. 1995. *Manufacturing 'Bad Mothers'? A Critical Perspective on Child Neglect*. Toronto: University of Toronto Press.

Synnott, Anthony. 1983. 'Little Angels, Little Devils: A Sociology of Children', *Canadian Review of Sociology and Anthropology* 20, 1: 79–95.

Taylor-Gooby, Peter, ed. 2004. *New Risks, New Welfare: The Transformation of the European Welfare State*. Oxford: Oxford University Press.

Tew, Marjorie. 1998. *Safer Childbirth? A Critical History of Maternity Care*, 3rd edn. London and New York: Free Association Books.

Thomas, Derrick. 2001. 'Evolving Family Living Arrangements of Canada's Immigrants', *Canadian Social Trends* (Summer): 16–22.

Thorne, Barry. 1982. 'Feminist Rethinking of the Family: An Overview', in Barry Thorne, with Marilyn Yalom, eds, *Rethinking the Family: Some Feminist Questions*. New York: Longman, 1–24.

Torjman, Sherri, and Ken Battle. 1999. *Good Work: Getting It and Keeping It*. Ottawa: Caledon Institute of Social Policy.

Trapski, Judge, et al. 1994. *The Child Support Review*. Wellington: New Zealand Parliament.

Turner, B.S. 1995. 'Aging and Identity', in M. Featherstone and A. Wernick, eds, *Images of Aging*. London: Routledge, 245–60.

United Nations (UN). 2000. *The World's Women: Trends and Statistics.* New York: UN.

United Nations Children's Fund (UNICEF). 2000. *A League Table of Child Poverty in Rich Nations.* Florence: Innocenti Research Centre.

———. 2003. *A League Table of Child Maltreatment Deaths in Rich Nations.* Florence: Innocenti Research Centre.

———. 2005. *Child Poverty in Rich Nations 2005.* Report Card #6. Florence: Innocenti Research Centre.

United States Department of Health and Human Services. 2002. 'Births: Final Data for 2001', *National Vital Statistics Reports* 51, 2: 1–103.

Ursel, Jane. 1992. *Private Lives, Public Policy: 100 Years of State Intervention in the Family.* Toronto: Women's Press.

Van den Berg, Axel, and Joseph Smucker, eds. 1997. *The Sociology of Labour Markets: Efficiency, Equity, Security.* Toronto: Prentice-Hall Allyn and Bacon Canada.

Vanier Institute of the Family (VIF). 1994. *Profiling Canada's Families.* Ottawa: VIF.

———. 2000. *Profiling Canada's Families II.* Ottawa: VIF.

———. 2004. *Profiling Canada's Families III.* Ottawa: VIF.

Van Laningham, J., D.R. Johnson, and P. Amato. 2001. 'Marital Happiness, Marital Duration and the U-shaped Curve: Evidence from a 5-Wave Panel Study', *Social Forces* 78, 4: 1313–41.

Veblen, T. 1953 [1899]. *The Theory of the Leisure Class.* New York: Mentor.

Veevers, Jean E. 1980. *Childless by Choice.* Toronto: Butterworths.

Vogler, C., and J. Pahl. 1994. 'Money, Power and Inequality within Marriage', *Sociological Review* 42: 263–88.

Vosko, Leah F. 2000. *Temporary Work: The Gendered Rise of a Precarious Employment Relationship.* Toronto: University of Toronto Press.

Wadsworth, J., I. Burnell, B. Taylor, and N. Butler. 1983. 'Family Type and Accidents in Preschool Children', *Journal of Epidemiology and Community Health* 37: 100–4.

Waite, Linda. 2005. 'Marriage, Family and Health', keynote address to the Australian Institute of Family Studies Conference, 9–11 Feb., Melbourne.

Walker, Seb. 2005. 'Divorce Makes Women Happier Than Men', *The Guardian*, 5 July. At: <www.guardian.co.uk>.

Walker, R., D. Turnbull, and C. Wilkinson. 2002. 'Strategies to Address Global Caesarean Section Rates: A Review of the Evidence', *Birth* 29 (1 Mar.).

Wall, Glenda. 2004. 'Is Your Child's Brain Potential Maximized? Mothering in an Age of New Brain Research', *Atlantis* 28, 2: 41–50.

———. 2005. 'Childhood and Child Rearing', in Baker (2005a: 163–80).

Wallace, P. 1999. *The Psychology of the Internet.* Cambridge: Cambridge University Press.

Wallerstein, J., and S. Blakeslee. 1996. *The Good Marriage.* New York: Warner Books.

Walsh, Rebecca. 2005. 'Obesity To Shorten Many Lives', *New Zealand Herald*, 19 Mar., 1.

Ward, Peter. 1990. *Courtship, Love, and Marriage in Nineteenth-Century English Canada.* Montreal and Kingston: McGill-Queen's University Press.

Weeks, Jeffrey. 2002. 'Elective Families: Lesbian and Gay Life Experiments', in A. Carling, S. Duncan, and R. Edwards, eds, *Analysing Families.* London: Routledge, 218–28.

Weir, L. 1996. 'Recent Developments in the Governance of Pregnancy', *Economy and Society* 25, 3: 372–92.

Weston, Ruth, and Robyn Parker. 2002. 'Why Is the Fertility Rate Falling? A Discussion of the Literature', *Family Matters* 63 (Spring/Summer): 6–13.

Whitehead, Margaret, Bo Burström, and Finn Diderichsen. 2000. 'Social Policies and the Pathways to Inequalities in Health: A Comparative Analysis of Lone Mothers in Britain and Sweden', *Social Science and Medicine* 50, 2: 255–70.

Willen, Helena, and Henry Montgomery. 1996. 'The Impact of Wish for Children and Having Children: Attainment and Importance of Life Values', *Journal of Comparative Family Studies* 27: 499–518.

Wilson, M., and M. Daly. 1994. *Spousal Homicide*. Ottawa: Canadian Centre for Justice Statistics.

Winch, Robert. 1955. 'The Theory of Complementary Needs in Mate Selection: A Test of One Kind of Complementariness', *American Sociological Review* 20 (Oct.): 552–5.

Wolfe, David, and Peter Jaffe. 2001. 'Prevention of Domestic Violence: Emerging Initiatives', in S. Graham-Bermann and J. Edleson, eds, *Domestic Violence in the Lives of Children: The Future of Research, Intervention and Social Policy*. Washington: American Psychological Association.

Woodward, Lianne, David M. Fergusson, and Jay Belsky. 2000. 'Timing of Parental Separation and Attachment to Parents in Adolescence: Results of a Prospective Study from Birth to Age 16', *Journal of Marriage and the Family* 62: 162–74.

World Health Organization (WHO). 1998. *The World Health Report 1998: Life in the Twenty-First Century: A Vision for All*. Geneva: WHO.

———— and UNICEF. 1990. *Innocenti Declaration on the Protection, Promotion and Support of Breastfeeding*. Available at: <www.unicef.org>.

Wu, Zheng. 1996. 'Childbearing in Cohabitation Relationships', *Journal of Marriage and the Family* 58: 281–92.

————. 2000. *Cohabitation: An Alternative Form of Family Living*. Toronto: Oxford University Press.

———— and Christoph Schimmele. 2005. 'Divorce and Repartnering', in Baker (2005a: 202–28).

Zelizer, V. 1994. *The Social Meaning of Money*. New York: Basic Books.

Index

DATE DUE